Lecture Notes in Computer Science 12718

More information about this subseries at http://www.springer.com/series/7411

Miguel Matos · Fabíola Greve (Eds.)

Distributed Applications and Interoperable Systems

21st IFIP WG 6.1 International Conference, DAIS 2021
Held as Part of the 16th International Federated Conference
on Distributed Computing Techniques, DisCoTec 2021
Valletta, Malta, June 14–18, 2021
Proceedings

Springer

Editors
Miguel Matos 🅳
University of Lisbon
Lisbon, Portugal

Fabíola Greve 🅳
Federal University of Bahia
Salvador, Brazil

ISSN 0302-9743 ISSN 1611-3349 (electronic)
Lecture Notes in Computer Science
ISBN 978-3-030-78197-2 ISBN 978-3-030-78198-9 (eBook)
https://doi.org/10.1007/978-3-030-78198-9

LNCS Sublibrary: SL5 – Computer Communication Networks and Telecommunications

This Springer imprint is published by the registered company Springer Nature Switzerland AG
The registered company address is: Gewerbestrasse 11, 6330 Cham, Switzerland

Foreword

The 16th International Federated Conference on Distributed Computing Techniques (DisCoTec 2021) took place during June 14–18, 2021. It was organised by the Department of Computer Science at the University of Malta, but was held online due to the abnormal circumstances worldwide affecting physical travel. The DisCoTec series is one of the major events sponsored by the International Federation for Information Processing (IFIP), the European Association for Programming Languages and Systems (EAPLS), and the Microservices Community. It comprises three conferences:

- *COORDINATION*, the IFIP WG 6.1 23rd International Conference on Coordination Models and Languages;
- *DAIS*, the IFIP WG 6.1 21st International Conference on Distributed Applications and Interoperable Systems;
- *FORTE*, the IFIP WG 6.1 41st International Conference on Formal Techniques for Distributed Objects, Components, and Systems.

Together, these conferences cover a broad spectrum of distributed computing subjects, ranging from theoretical foundations and formal description techniques, to systems research issues. As is customary, the event also included several plenary sessions in addition to the individual sessions of each conference, which gathered attendants from the three conferences. These included joint invited speaker sessions and a joint session for the best papers from the respective three conferences. Associated with the federated event, four satellite events took place:

- *DisCoTec Tools*, a tutorial session promoting mature tools in the field of distributed computing;
- *ICE*, the 14th International Workshop on Interaction and Concurrency Experience;
- *FOCODILE*, the 2nd International Workshop on Foundations of Consensus and Distributed Ledgers;
- *REMV*, the 1st Robotics, Electronics, and Machine Vision Workshop.

I would like to thank the Program Committee chairs of the different events for their help and cooperation during the preparation of the conference, and the Steering Committee and Advisory Boards of DisCoTec and its conferences for their guidance and support. The organization of DisCoTec 2021 was only possible thanks to the dedicated work of the Organizing Committee, including Caroline Caruana and Jasmine Xuereb (publicity chairs), Duncan Paul Attard and Christian Bartolo Burlo (workshop chairs), Lucienne Bugeja (logistics and finances), and all the students and colleagues who volunteered their time to help. I would also like to thank the invited speakers for their excellent talks. Finally, I would like to thank IFIP WG 6.1, EAPLS, and the Microservices Community for sponsoring this event, Springer's Lecture Notes in

Computer Science team for their support and sponsorship, EasyChair for providing the reviewing framework, and the University of Malta for providing the support and infrastructure to host the event.

June 2021   Adrian Francalanza

Preface

This volume contains the papers presented at the 21st IFIP International Conference on Distributed Applications and Interoperable Systems (DAIS 2021), sponsored by the International Federation for Information Processing (IFIP) and organized by the IFIP WG 6.1. The DAIS conference series addresses all practical and conceptual aspects of distributed applications, including their design, modeling, implementation, and operation, the supporting middleware, appropriate software engineering methodologies and tools, and experimental studies and applications. DAIS 2021 was meant to be held during June 14–18, 2021, in Valletta, Malta, as part of DisCoTec 2021, the 12th International Federated Conference on Distributed Computing Techniques, but due to the COVID-19 pandemic it was held completely online.

We offered three distinct paper tracks: full research papers, full practical experience reports, and work-in-progress papers. We received 19 initial abstract submissions, 18 of which were for research papers and 1 for a practical experience report. All submissions were reviewed by three to four Program Committee (PC) members. The review process included a post-review discussion phase, during which the merits of all papers were discussed by the PC. The committee decided to accept six full research papers, two full practical experience reports, and two work-in-progress papers.

The accepted papers cover a broad range of topics in distributed algorithms, scalability and availability, network virtualization, stream processing, privacy, and trusted hardware.

The virtual conference, especially during these last months full of unpredictable events, was made possible by the hard work and cooperation of many people working in several different committees and organizations, all of which are listed in these proceedings. In particular, we are grateful to the PC members for their commitment and thorough reviews, and for their active participation in the discussion phase, and to all the external reviewers for their help in evaluating submissions. Finally, we also thank the DisCoTec general chair, Adrian Francalanza, and the DAIS Steering Committee chair, Luís Veiga, for their constant availability, support, and guidance.

June 2021

Miguel Matos
Fabíola Greve

Organization

General Chair

Adrian Francalanza   University of Malta, Malta

Program Committee Chairs

Miguel Matos   University of Lisbon and INESC-ID, Portugal
Fabíola Greve   Universidade Federal da Bahia, Brazil

Steering Committee

Lydia Y. Chen   TU Delft, Netherlands
Frank Eliassen   University of Oslo, Norway
Rüdiger Kapitza   Technical University of Braunschweig, Germany
Rui Oliveira   University of Minho and INESC TEC, Portugal
Hans P. Reiser   University of Passau, Germany
Laura Ricci   University of Pisa, Italy
Silvia Bonomi   Università degli Studi di Roma "La Sapienza", Italy
Etienne Riviére   Ecole Polytechnique de Louvain, Belgium
Jose Pereira   University of Minho and INESC TEC, Portugal
Luís Veiga (Chair)   INESC-ID and Universidade de Lisboa, Portugal

Program Committee

Eduardo Alchieri   Universidade de Brasília, Brazil
Pierre-Louis Aublin   Keio University, Japan
Silvia Bonomi   Università degli Studi di Roma "La Sapienza", Italy
Davide Frey   Inria, France
Paula Herber   University of Münster, Germany
Mark Jelasity   University of Szeged, Hungary
Vana Kalogeraki   Athens University of Economics and Business, Greece
Evangelia Kalyvianaki   University of Cambridge, UK
Fábio Kon   University of São Paulo, Brazil
João Leitão   Universidade Nova de Lisboa, Portugal
Kostas Magoutis   University of Ioannina, Greece
Claudio Antares Mezzina   University of Urbino, Italy
Hein Meling   University of Stavanger, Norway
Alberto Montresor   University of Trento, Italy
Daniel O'Keeffe   Royal Holloway, University of London, UK
Emanuel Onica   Alexandru Ioan Cuza University of Iasi, Romania
Marta Patino   Universidad Politecnica de Madrid, Spain

José Orlando Pereira   Universidade do Minho and INESC TEC, Portugal
Hans P. Reiser   University of Passau, Germany
Romain Rouvoy   University of Lille, France
Valerio Schiavoni   University of Neuchâtel, Switzerland
Pierre Sutra   Telecom SudParis, France
Spyros Voulgaris   Athens University of Economics and Business, Greece

Additional Reviewers

Christian Berger
Philipp Eichhammer
Johannes Köstler
Vitor Menino

iExec: Building a Decentralized, Trusted and Privacy-Preserving Computing Infrastructure (Invited Speaker)

Gilles Fedak

CEO & co-founder of iExec, France

Abstract. iExec is a French startup company based in Lyon which built the first decentralized marketplace in which entities (e.g. traditional cloud providers, research centers and even individuals) can contribute and monetize Cloud Computing resources (CPU, GPU), Decentralized Applications (Dapps) and data-sets (Data Renting) in a secure and confidential way, ensuring the confidentiality and ownership of data. During this talk, I will present how iExec combines Ethereum Smart Contracts, a unique Proof-of-Contribution (PoCo) protocol and Trusted Execution Environments (TEE) to ensure trust between providers and consumers of resources. The project, however, is still facing several scientific and technological barriers related to scalability, interoperability and to supporting more classes of applications. I will discuss several research topics (e.g. ZK-proofs and rollups) and two H2020 projects in which iExec is involved: OntoChain, which aims at building a trusted and transparent knowledge management ecosystem and Datacloud, which goal is to build a platform for big data analytics in the edge-to-cloud continuum.

Contents

Invited Paper

Cloud and Fog Computing

A Methodology for Tenant Migration in Legacy Shared-Table Multi-tenant Applications

Guillaume Rosinosky[1]([✉]), Samir Youcef[2], François Charoy[2],
and Etienne Rivière[1]

[1] ICTeam, UCLouvain, Louvain-la-Neuve, Belgium
`guillaume.rosinosky@uclouvain.be`
[2] LORIA - Inria, Nancy, France

Abstract. Multi-tenancy enables cost-effective SaaS through resource consolidation. Multiple customers, or tenants, are served by a single application instance, and isolation is enforced at the application level. Service load for different tenants can vary over time, requiring applications to scale in and out. A large class of SaaS providers operates legacy applications structured around a relational (SQL) database. These applications achieve tenant isolation through dedicated fields in their relational schema and are not designed to support scaling operations. We present a novel solution for scaling in or out such applications through the migration of a tenant's data to new application and database instances. Our solution requires no change to the application and incurs no service downtime for non-migrated tenants. It leverages external tables and foreign data wrappers, as supported by major relational databases. We evaluate the approach using two multi-tenant applications: Iomad, an extension of the Moodle Learning Management System, and Camunda, a business process management platform. Our results show the usability of the method, minimally impacting performance for other tenants during migration and leading to increased service capacity after migration.

Keywords: Scalability · Multi-tenancy · Databases · Cloud computing

1 Introduction

Software-as-a-Service (SaaS) is the cloud service model with the highest market size [8]. It allows client organizations, or *tenants*, to benefit from turn-key applications. Multi-tenancy is the sharing application instances across multiple tenants [9]. It enables SaaS providers to benefit from economies of scale, consolidating service load for different tenants, and reducing total cost of ownership. Multi-tenancy can be implemented by sharing computing resources (virtual machines (VM) or containers), by sharing application servers, storing data for multiple tenants in the same database or using a combination of these approaches.

© IFIP International Federation for Information Processing 2021
Published by Springer Nature Switzerland AG 2021
M. Matos and F. Greve (Eds.): DAIS 2021, LNCS 12718, pp. 3–20, 2021.
https://doi.org/10.1007/978-3-030-78198-9_1

For instance, Rightnow, a customer relationship SaaS provider, reported millions of dollars of savings thanks to multi-tenancy [18].

Despite the current trend towards building new applications using microservices [5] and using cloud-native scalable databases [21,24], a large class of SaaS operators still operate applications based on tried-and-tested monolithic applications using a relational (SQL) database to store customer data. In such legacy applications, multi-tenancy is typically implemented at the database level, either using distinct dedicated databases, dedicated tables or shared tables [28]. We focus in this paper on shared-table multi-tenancy: Database tables are shared between tenants, and a tenant identifier enables queries to distinguish the tenants' rows (i.e., a shared-table schema [2]). SaaS provider Salesforce has been, for instance, using such a shared-table architecture for over ten years [29]. Other examples of applications using shared-table multi-tenancy include learning management such as Iomad (an evolution of Moodle), content management (e.g., Cortex-CMS), business process modelling (e.g., Activiti, Bonita, Camunda), or cloud billing (e.g., CloudKitty).

The application load for multi-tenant applications hosted in the cloud is dynamic. In order to enforce the essential pay-as-you-go model of cloud computing, applications must support elastic scaling operations, whereby new resources are added and removed as the operation workload changes. Typically, scaling out requires starting new application instances and migrating data for certain tenants to this instance. In legacy shared-table multi-tenant applications, this requirement is impaired by two factors. First, there is limited support for scalability operations in traditional relational database engines [14][1]. Second, legacy applications are generally designed on the basis that a single, centralized, and unified view of the entire database is available, which includes in particular information (tables) shared across tenants. Migrating data for a tenant to the new database instance associated with the new application server invalidates this assumption, requiring non-trivial adaptations in the legacy code.

Contributions. We present a non-intrusive and efficient methodology for stop-and-copy tenant migration in legacy multi-tenant applications using the shared-table approach. Our method enables such legacy applications to scale in and out based on tenants' requirements (e.g., the volume of requests or data). It is adapted to the constraints of SaaS providers: (1) it does not require changes to the code of legacy applications, and maintain guarantees on unified views of the database and of common data; (2) it enables migrations of a tenant with no interruption of service for *other* tenants and only minimal and temporary impact for the migrated one; (3) it effectively enables the provider to scale up the number of requests that can be supported after migration and can, reversely, be used for tenant consolidation and resource savings.

---

[1] Database sharding, e.g., using PL/Proxy [22] allows splitting the content of tables over multiple database nodes, but it is not elastic: changing the sharding plan requires to restart the database. Database specific extensions such as the Citus extension for Postgresql or Vitess for Mysql permit automatic scaling. However, they imply switching to specific engines, with their limitations and limited support.

Our method leverages external tables and foreign data wrappers (FDW), ISO standard features supported by major relational database engines. These features enable a *unified view* of the database, and *unmodified* queries while allowing data to be stored onto different instances of the database engine hosted by different VMs or containers. We present a SQL-based systematic process for the migration of tenants' data between these instances. We implemented our approach for two representative multi-tenant applications: (1) Iomad, a learning management system evolved from the popular Moodle system; (2) Camunda, a business process management system. These two case studies confirm the ability of our method to enable migrations with no change to the application. Our performance evaluation of the applications in a Kubernetes cluster using PostgreSQL shows the effectiveness of our approach. Tenants migrations happen with negligible impact on query performance for other tenants and enable increased service throughput after migration.

The remainder of the paper is structured as follows. Section 2 presents our migration method. Section 3 presents our two case studies, evaluated in Sect. 4. We discuss related work in Sect. 5 and conclude in Sect. 6.

2   A Method for Tenant Migration

We describe in this section our methodology and migration method for multi-tenant software under the shared-table model. We list our design goals (Sect. 2.1), present the architecture (Sect. 2.2), detail the classification of database tables (Sect. 2.3), and describe the tenant migration process (Sect. 2.4).

2.1   Design Goals

In a multi-tenant application, tenants' resource requirements vary depending on clients activity. These variations are hard to predict and can bring under-utilization or over-utilization of resources, resulting in additional costs for the provider or severed QoS for the customer. A possibility to address this problem is to migrate the corresponding data and software to another server. However, tenant migration in shared-table multi-tenant applications is a complicated process, due to the meddling of tenant data in different rows of common database tables. Besides, some data can be shared between tenants: For instance, global parameters such as the list of tenants cannot be separated between different tenants. This makes the task of consistently backup or export data challenging to do without changes to the application code.

We propose a method for migrating tenants in legacy applications using a relational database and the shared-table model. Its goals are as follows:

– **Non-intrusion:** It should not require changes to the source code of the application, as these are typically expensive to implement and maintain over time. Instead, it may only apply simple transformations of the database schema.

- **Parsimony:** Only the data relevant for a migrated tenant should be transferred between origin and target database instances, to limit the impact of migrations on resource consumption for the provider.
- **Transparency:** Migration operations should have minimal impact on the application clients, and particularly those of the non-migrated tenants. Application or database restart is not desired to implement migration, and the slowdown imposed by a migration operation must be limited.
- **Reliability:** Changes to the database schema, as required by the architecture to enable migrations, should not impact data and queries consistency.

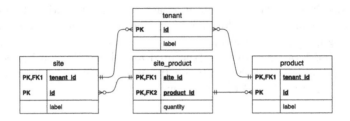

Fig. 1. Multi-tenant stock management application: Entity-Relation schema.

We also make the following assumption of tenant isolation, that is, tenants' queries should be specific for their tenant, i.e. they should not target other tenants [9].

In the remainder of this section, we illustrate our discussion using an example of a multi-tenant stock management application, whose schema is given by Fig. 1. This example application allows different tenants (listed in table **tenant**) to trace the availability (association table **site_product**) of products (table **product**) on different sites (table **site**). Tenants can only access their sites and products (e.g., as the primary key for **product** is <tenant_id,id> there is no sharing of product identifiers between tenants).

2.2 Overview

The foundation of our method is to split the tables of the application schema between a single *reference database* and multiple *tenant databases*. Each tenant database hosts data for multiple tenants, but data for a given tenant is not split across tenant databases. All tenant databases link with the unique reference database by using *foreign tables*. The reference database contains data common to the whole installation. The application servers connect to the corresponding tenant databases and do not need to be aware of the existence of the reference database accessed through foreign tables. Figure 2 presents an example of deployment with two tenants databases.

Foreign tables are supported by major relational databases [30], and are enabled by Foreign Data Wrappers (FDW), an ISO standard feature for relational databases since SQL/MED (ISO/IEC 9075-9:2003 [11])[2]. Foreign Data Wrappers allow accessing foreign data through *virtual tables*. Foreign data can be tables in a remote database instance, or other data sources accessed through a specific wrapper. Virtual tables behave like regular tables for queries and provide ACID guarantees for foreign data stored in the remote database. It is important to note, however, that foreign tables do not allow the automatic enforcement of integrity constraints (e.g., foreign keys) between local tables and foreign tables: Such constraints can only be declared between local tables[3]. The transparency of queries using foreign tables directly enables our property of *non-intrusion*: queries in the application do not have to be modified, and we only need to operate changes to the database schema, as we present next.

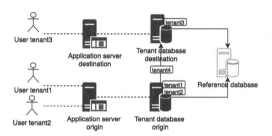

Fig. 2. Application of the method to two tenant databases and migration of tenant 4.

2.3 Mapping Tables to Tenant or Reference DB

Our method requires classifying which of the tables should be hosted in tenant databases and which should be kept in the reference database, and accessed, therefore, as foreign tables from the former. This classification is application-dependent and cannot be easily automated. We discuss, therefore, guidelines to allow SaaS operators to make informed decisions, as we detail with our two use cases in Sect. 3.

We propose to classify tables using the following categories. (1) **Active tables** contain tenant-specific data about currently running processes, tasks, events, users, roles, etc. (2) **Temporary tables** contain system-related data

---

[2] Foreign Data Wrappers availability is vendor-dependent. Postgres, MySQL, and MariaDB support the ISO standard. Db2, SQL Server and Oracle do not support it, but offer similar features (with respectively *distributed databases*, *linked servers*, and *database link*). Support of distributed transactions is also vendor-dependent: they are not supported in MySQL, are only partially supported in PostgreSQL and the Open Source engine FederatedX of MariaDB, and fully supported in commercial engines such as Oracle, SQL Server, DB2, and the Spider engine of MariaDB.

[3] This inconvenience can be addressed by using database triggers emulating the integrity constraints.

linked to the tenant application server, for instance, cache tables. (3) **System tables** contain system-related data concerning the global installation (e.g., the list of tenants). (4) **Archive tables** contain tenant-specific data about past processes, tasks, events, ... Active tables (containing tenant-specific data) can be further split into two categories: (1.1) tables containing a tenant identifier as a field, and (1.2) tables that do not contain such a field.

The SaaS operator must decide on the classification of tables between the reference database and tenant databases. The choice can consider the following principles: (1) **Distributed queries cost:** Distributed queries (i.e., involving tables in the tenant database and the reference database) are more expensive in term of response time than queries for a single database engine instance. (2) **Data volume:** The deployment must seek a balance between the volume of data kept in the reference database and the volume of data hosted by tenant databases. Large volumes of data in the reference database may lead to scalability issues due to its uniqueness, whereas an arbitrary number of tenant databases can be used. On the other hand, large volumes of data in tenant databases increase the migration duration.

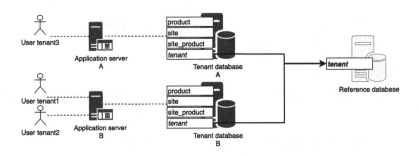

Fig. 3. Multi-tenant stock management application: table placement.

The choice of classification impacts the performance and behaviour of the application. As a general principle, the following is generally a good starting basis: active tables and temporary tables are assigned to the tenant database, and system and archive tables are assigned to the reference database.

We apply this approach to the stock management example of Fig. 1. First, table `tenant` is a *system table*: it contains the list of tenants and is global to the system as a whole. Second, `site` and `product` are tenant-specific tables: they should be located on tenant databases. Finally, `site_product` is a tenant-specific table that does not feature a tenant identifier. It can be located either on the reference or tenant database. As frequent queries return the list of products per site or the list of sites holding products, the operator considers that it is preferable to host `site_product` alongside the `site` and `product` tables in the tenant database. Another reason for her choice could be the need to declare integrity constraints between these two tables.

We present our method applied to the tables of Fig. 2 in Fig. 3. In this case, we keep the tables `site_product`, `site` and `product` on the tenant database. The `tenant` table is located on the reference database, and a permanent foreign table in the tenant database will target it. In the end, an application connecting to the tenant database will be able to access all four tables and issue DQL (Data Query Language), and DML (Data Manipulation Language) queries as if they were accessing a unique database. For tables using sequentially-generated identifiers, collisions could happen in the case of consolidation of tenants in the same database. For reference tables, sequences should be managed at the reference database level. For tenant tables, this issue is manageable with a shift on the sequence for each tenant database in each table to avoid collisions (for instance, keys from 10,000,000 to 19,999,999 from a first tenant, keys from 20,000,000 to 29,999,999 from a second tenant, etc.).

Our methodology supports production features such as database backups, security, or the evolution of schemas. Database backup tools can be configured to use foreign tables. Tables and schemas security access can be tuned in the corresponding tenant databases. Database schemas updates needed by the software evolutions should be done on the tenant and reference databases: Schema upgrade scripts should be split as well and be applied on all databases, and foreign tables should also be updated.

2.4   Migration of a Tenant

The use of our proposed evolution of the application schema enables migrations using a series of SQL statements (i.e., in concordance with our objective of non-intrusion, we do not require specific features from the database system itself). Table data stored in the tenant database and specific to the migrated tenant should be inserted in the corresponding table at the destination (which can be, in the case of a horizontal scale-out operation, a freshly-started database instance, or an existing instance in the case of a consolidation). Current transactions on tenants should have been all committed or rollbacked before a migration to avoid data loss. Multi-tenant applications generally feature the possibility to pause or set to "maintenance mode" a specific tenant, and we assume the availability of such a function. When migration occurs, client queries directed at the origin application server should be put on hold during migration and redirected on the destination application server after the migration. Figure 2 illustrates the migration of tenant 4.

The migration process requires the following steps to migrate tenant t from one stack a featuring database D_a and application A_a to stack b formed of database D_b and application A_b:

1. stop the tenant on application A_a and disconnect users;
2. disable foreign key checks for the database connection;
3. for each table in the tenant database, instantiate a temporary foreign table using a foreign data wrapper in database D_a, targeting the corresponding table in database D_b; then, in database D_a, insert data corresponding to tenant t in the foreign tables, thereby inserting it in database D_b;

4. enable foreign key checks for the database connection;
5. if there were no errors, delete temporary foreign tables used for the transfer from database D_a and tenant t data from this database;
6. re-activate the tenant on application A_b. Queries from users of tenant t should now target application A_b;
7. in the advent of an error, remove modifications on A_b and D_b, and reactivate the tenant on application A_a.

The step 3. where we insert tenant-specific data using the temporary foreign table uses regular SQL statements, i.e., INSERT, SELECT, and DELETE. These queries are prepared alongside the schema classification by the SaaS operator deploying the application. In the advent of a fault during the migration, the tenant data remains available at its original location until the migration ends. The system can then be rollbacked to the previous state (i.e. before migration) for the migrated tenant if such a fault is detected.

In our example stock management application, the case of tables site and product is straightforward: We insert into the temporary foreign tables lines with the corresponding tenant identifier. For the site_product table, however, we need to use a JOIN with either of the site or product tables using the tenant identifier. This is necessary to recover the related tenant data, as there is no tenant identifier used in this table. If the temporary foreign tables are named f_site, f_product, and f_site_product, respectively, the transfer uses the following three queries to migrate tenant of identifier 1 (we omit the corresponding deletion queries that follow on tables site, product, and site_product):

```
INSERT INTO f_site SELECT * FROM site WHERE tenant_id = 1
INSERT INTO f_product SELECT * FROM product WHERE tenant_id = 1
INSERT INTO f_site_product SELECT * FROM site_product sp \
    JOIN site s ON sp.tenantid = s.tenantid WHERE s.tenantid = 1
```

After performing table classification and preparing parameterized table subqueries, we can automatize the operations of schema creation and migration. We developed a configurable tool for this purpose, used in our experiments (Sect. 4).

Only active data is migrated, thus reducing the duration of migrations compared to a regular backup/restore operation. However, tenants with a high quantity of active data will take longer to be migrated. This duration needs to be taken into account depending on QoS needs for migrations. In this matter, wisely choosing which tables should be placed on the tenant and reference databases is an important step, as we discuss in the next section with two real-world applications.

3   Case Studies

In this section, we detail our experience in enabling tenant migrations for two shared-table multi-tenant applications: Iomad, a learning management system and Camunda, a business process management engine.

3.1   Iomad

Iomad (https://www.iomad.org) is an open-source *fork* of Moodle, the popular Learning Management System. Iomad adds features to Moodle, enabling its use in a SaaS context, including multi-tenancy, better reporting, and e-commerce features. As Moodle, Iomad is developed in PhP and uses a traditional database management system to persist its data, such as Mysql, Postgresql, or SQL server. Multi-tenancy in Iomad is implemented using a limited shared-table approach by the addition of tenant-specific tables to the original Moodle schema, without tenant identifiers in tenant-related tables.

The schema of Iomad contains 457 tables. We proceeded as follows for the classification. We first identified the `company` table, containing the tenants. Tenants are linked to users and courses by association tables. Only a handful of tables use tenant identifiers as a foreign key, as should have been expected under the shared-table model. However, we could trace back a large fraction of the association between the core tenant-specific tables and corresponding data in the other tables by following foreign keys dependencies. We selected first these tables (tenant and the associations to user and course) as **system tables** for storage in the reference database.

We then identify **active tables** and **temporary tables**, using two approaches to perform the classification: **(1)** we selected tables having fields corresponding to users or courses (for instance: `user`, `userid`, `course`, `courseid`, etc.) for tenant databases; **(2)** we considered tables involved in the GDPR-compliance [19] feature of Iomad, in order to select tables containing user-specific data, and assigned these tables to the tenant database.

We leveraged the Moodle's entity-relationship schema extracted by Green [7] to classify the tables. In total, 314 tables are assigned to tenant databases. All others (i.e., 143 tables) are assigned to the reference database as **system tables**.

We note the following two limitations, due to the implementation of multi-tenancy in Iomad:

- In Iomad, users and courses can be associated with multiple tenants. With our classification and split, we lose this possibility. Users and courses should be created independently for each tenant. The independence of tenants is a necessary feature for multi-tenant software [9]. This is what we believe to be the normal mode of operation for shared-table multi-tenant applications, and the impact should be limited in practice;
- Identifiers are serial-based, and the tenant identifier is not part of the primary key of each table. When scaling in and consolidating tenants from two to a single database, there is a risk of collision between tenant identifiers. This risk could be mitigated by using appropriate serial ranges, or UUID primary keys, but we did not implement these changes as they would have no impact on performance.

3.2 Camunda

Business Process Modeling (BPM) allows companies to represent, execute, and analyze business processes. A BPM schema is a graph representing a sequence of business tasks. These tasks can be automated (e.g., a call to a web service) or manual (e.g., a form that a human operator should fill). Business processes embed variables that can be modified by these different tasks.

Numerous commercial BPM tools exist, such as IBM Business Process Manager, Oracle Business Process Management. Open-source alternatives include Bonita BPM, Activiti, and Camunda, one of the targets of our experiments. We focus here on the usage of the BPM engine that executes the tasks of business processes. Camunda, being a multi-tenant BPM solution, is a perfect target for our method.

The database schema of Camunda 7.8.0 contains 46 tables. In Camunda, tenants are listed in table `act_id_tenant`, that we classify as a **system table**. Most of the other tables include a tenant identifier as part of their primary key, as a field `tenant_id`. We selected for tenant databases as **active tables** all tables containing such a `tenant_id` field, with two exceptions for tables `act_ge_bytearray` and `act_re_deployment`. These two tables are, indeed, necessary for the application bootstrap and should be classified as **system tables**. As a result, we keep them in the reference database for common access by all tenant databases and all application servers. In total, we select 35 tables for storage in the tenant databases and 11 tables for storage in the reference database. We note that the risk of tenant id collision upon a consolidation we mentioned for Iomad is not present here: Tenant identifiers are part of the primary keys of each tenant table; tenants are well isolated.

4 Evaluation

While our use cases show that legacy multi-tenant applications can have their schema adapted to support tenant migration under our proposed architecture, we are interested in the experimental evaluation reported in this section in evaluating its cost and performance. We extend a migration benchmark that we introduced in our previous work [16] to answer the following research questions:

1. What is the overhead of porting a legacy application's data schema to comply with our architecture?
2. What is the duration of a tenant migration, and how does it impact performance for clients of that tenant?
3. What effect do migrations of a tenant have on the performance experienced for other tenants?
4. Is tenant migration successful in enabling scale-out, i.e., a higher service capacity after migrating a tenant?

As our main performance metric for questions 1, 3 & 4, we consider the response time as experienced by the client application (*i.e.*, in response to HTTP queries accessing various features of the application). We further consider migration time from the SaaS operator's perspective when answering question 2.

We use JMeter as a load injection tool. For Iomad, we extended Moodle's load tests, which include HTTP user queries for login, course display, forum display, response and attachment sending, and logout operations. The Iomad database is pre-filled with users and tenants data prior to load injection. For Camunda, we developed a JMeter scenario emulating a user creating and executing a process containing a BPM human task (i.e., a task that must be filled and validated by an operator). The scenario claims the task for the user and emulates its processing. As for Iomad, we pre-fill the database with the process definition and the tenant-specific data prior to load injection.

4.1   Experimental Setup

We run all tests in a Kubernetes cluster hosted on the Azure IaaS cloud. We use eight 4-core Azure D3 v2 instances for hosting application containers, and one 2-core B2ms instance for the Kubernetes master. Our deployment includes (1) the host reference database; (2) two application *instances*, origin and destination, each composed of two nodes: a web server and a tenant database; (3) two load injectors; (4) an experiment orchestrator. We developed a script allowing to instantiate the different databases and application instances, orchestrate experiments, and trigger migrations. This script is generic and applies to both applications. We target reproducible research: All our deployments are described using Helm charts and Argo workflows. The source code and experimental data are open-source and available online[4].

We use a distributed architecture with an origin and destination *instances* and a reference database. We make experiments following the scenarios detailed in Table 1, with variations on the numbers of fixed tenants on the origin *instance* (origin tenants), and tenants originally on origin *instance*, and then migrated on destination *instance* (migrated tenants). Similar runs are launched for Iomad and Camunda. Based on our observation of the two applications in our test infrastructure, we select the HTTP input query throughput. The max throughput for Iomad is the one where the application servers' CPU usage reaches 100%. For Camunda, it is the saturation point for our two injector nodes. We report, for each scenario and RPS value in the considered ranges, aggregate distributions over five individual runs.

For scenarios involving a tenant live migration (1M-fdw and 101M-fdw) we consider one or two tenants originally with the origin instance. One tenant is migrated from the origin to the destination during the experiment. In the 1M-fdw, we only apply queries to the migrated tenant to evaluate the impact of migration on the migrated tenant performance, for multiple durations of injection (this permitting to observe different tenant sizes), while in configuration 101M-fdw we apply workload to both tenants, and migrate after 300 s of injection. It allows

---

[4] https://github.com/CloudLargeScale-UCLouvain/legacy-sql-migration.

Table 1. List of experiments. `Orig.T` specifies the number of tenants that start, and stay, in the origin instance. `Migr.T` is the number of tenants that start in the origin instance and later migrate to the destination instance. `Dur.O` is the time during which a workload of `RPS` requests per second per tenant is injected on all tenants staying on origin instance. It lasts during the entire run. `Dur.M` is the time during which a workload of `RPS` requests per second per tenant is injected on the migrated tenant (symbol → denotes the injection of this load before, and after, the migration). `RQ` is the corresponding research question.

Name	Distributed ?	Application	Orig.T	Migr.T	Dur.O	Dur.M	RPS	RQ
10-nofdw	No	Iomad	1	0	300	–	10–30	1
10-nofdw	No	Camunda	1	0	300	–	50–150	1
20-nofdw	No	Iomad	2	0	300	–	10–30	1
20-nofdw	No	Camunda	2	0	300	–	50–150	1
10-fdw	Yes	Iomad	1	0	300	–	10–30	1
10-fdw	Yes	Camunda	1	0	300	–	50–150	1
20-fdw	Yes	Iomad	2	0	300	–	10–30	1
20-fdw	Yes	Camunda	2	0	300	–	50–150	1
1M-fdw	Yes	Iomad	0	1	–	60–300→0	30	2
1M-fdw	Yes	Camunda	0	1	–	60–300→0	200	2
101M-fdw	Yes	Iomad	1	1	660	300→300	10–30	3,4
101M-fdw	Yes	Camunda	1	1	660	300→300	50–150	3,4

evaluating the impact of the migration operation on the performance of the non-migrated tenant.

4.2   Results

Figure 4 presents an evaluation of the overhead of using the distributed architecture, enabling live migrations through the use of foreign tables (denoted as "split"), versus the same application using a regular one database deployment (denoted as "single"). With a single database, Iomad response times increase drastically beginning with 40 RPS, with a 90th percentile reaching over 3 s for 50 and 60 RPS, where the system becomes saturated. Camunda median response times slightly increase while staying below 50 ms. The performance of Iomad with a split database is moderately degraded compared to a single deployment, with an additional 20 to 30 ms median response time over the 120 to 150 ms of the single-database configuration. For Camunda, response times are doubled, yet remain low and consistent. These increases are as expected: They are the results of some of the relational queries needing to access data through foreign tables and two database instances. They represent a baseline cost for being able to enable live migrations, that will be compensated by the scalability they allow in large deployments.

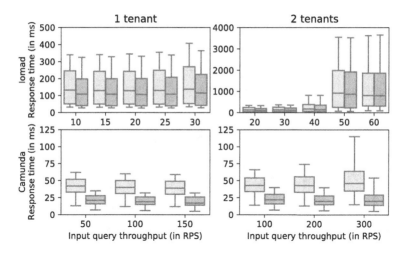

Fig. 4. Comparison of the split architecture performance with the original architecture (experiments 10-* (1 tenant) and 20-* (2 tenants)). Light grey is the *split* installation, dark grey the *single* installation. The X axis represents the cumulated throughput from all tenants, the Y axis the distribution of the latencies, with the 10th and 90th percentiles represented by the whiskers.

Our evaluation of the scalability improvement enabled by live migrations is in figure Fig. 5. We present the latency of operations for the tenant staying at the origin (origin tenant) and for the migrated tenant. As expected, performance after the migration is comparable to the performance would both tenants be deployed on separate instances directly. It results in increased service throughput for Iomad: after migration, the application supports 60 RPS with acceptable latencies, in contrast with the maximum of 40 RPS with a single-database configuration. Gains for Camunda are more modest than Iomad's, yet we can observe diminished response times and better throughput scaling. We explain the fact that the latencies for the origin tenant are slightly higher than for the migrated tenant by the additional accumulated data during the migration, only applying to the origin tenant.

We evaluate the live migration duration in Fig. 6 using configuration 1M. The migration time for Iomad is around 11 s and slightly increases for longer injection times prior to migration (accumulating more data through more requests). With Camunda, migration duration increases linearly with the duration of the injection before this migration. This is a direct effect of the additional volume of data to be migrated, resulting from the additional queries (a total of 60'000 queries in 300 s in the case of Camunda, 9'000 for Iomad).

Migrating a tenant involves copying data from the origin database to the destination database. It can provoke negative effects on the response time of other hosted tenants. We evaluate in Fig. 7 the impact of a tenant migration on the performance of the other tenants staying at the origin. Our evaluation considers the latencies for both applications, 20 s before the migration, and during

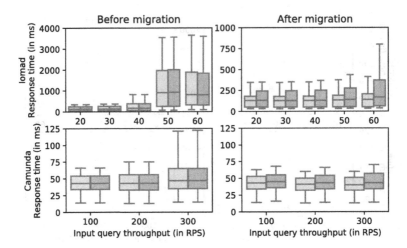

Fig. 5. Performance gain with migration (experiments 101M-*). The migrated tenant is shown in light grey, the origin tenant in dark grey.

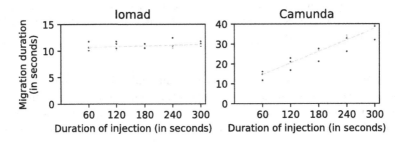

Fig. 6. Duration of injection vs. duration of migration (experiments 1M-*) represented by the dots. The corresponding linear regression is presented by the dashed line.

the migration operation. The latency is only marginally impacted for Iomad, especially in high throughputs, and not perceptible for Camunda. The probable cause of the small effects on Camunda compared to Iomad is that the instalment does not approach saturation.

Discussion. Our split-database architecture successfully enables live migration in multi-tenant shared-table applications. Migration operations enable scaling out and supporting higher service throughput, while only minimally impacting the performance for non-migrated tenants, satisfying our objective of *transparency*. Migration time is, unsurprisingly, impacted by the volume of data. As the transfer happens through a series of sequential SQL requests, migration latency (and, therefore, the unavailability period for the migrated tenant) can be high for large tenants. This is a compromise due to our property of *non-intrusion*, that highlights the importance of properly classifying tables for the tenant database, i.e., respecting the *parsimony* property. Using parallel transfers

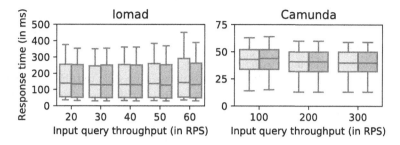

Fig. 7. Effects of migration on colocated tenants (experiments 101M-*, 20 s before migration, and during migration). Performances during migration are in light grey, before migration in dark grey.

(e.g., using several threads to transfer data from origin tables to the destination tables) could speed up the process, but we leave this optimization to future work.

5 Related Work

We review related work on migration in databases, database sharding, and related approaches to multi-tenancy.

Work towards migrations in multi-tenant databases mainly focused on shared-process database [3,6,10], in engines such as H-Store or Elastras. In the industry, Azure proposes a scalable version of Postgresql named *Hyperscale* and based on the Open Source *Citus* Postgresql extension [4]. This approach, like ours, is based on distribution keys and works well with multi-tenant applications. However, join operations on distributed tables are not allowed, thus making adaptations of the source code necessary for most applications. Oracle proposes multi-tenant live migration features [15]. Their solution is based on Real Application Cluster, Oracle's distributed database product, and enables service relocation. However, it provides only *full* database migration (shared disk architecture) [12] and cannot be applied to shared-row multi-tenancy scenarios. Google provides distributed and highly consistent databases F1 and Spanner [21]. Spanner allows redistribution of data across shards. These database systems are only available on Google Cloud, and lack some RDBMS features such as sequences, or DML queries on non-key fields. Vitess is an evolution of MySQL that provides automatic sharding [26]. It does not, however, comply totally to the MySQL feature matrix and applications require code adaptation. Compared to our approach, these works need the usage of specific database engines, and adaptations in the code base. Our migration methodology runs natively on legacy database engines.

Microsoft Azure offers several tools for shared-table multi-tenant applications. The Azure SQL database, based on SQL Server, includes an Elastic Database client library [13]. A tool called *SplitMerge* enables live shard migration based on an identifier or range of values in specific fields. Tables for a sharded tenant can be moved depending on a classification over three table types: shard tables, reference tables and other tables. During a migration, shard tables are copied based on the key of the tenant, reference tables are fully copied (leading to errors if these tables are already initialized), and other tables are ignored. This approach, while interesting, require software adaptation and the use of the specific Elastic database client. It also needs a specific database for tenant management. Our architecture does not require modifications to applications' codebase, as common tables between tenants stay available with the usage of foreign tables. Ghostferry [20] is a live migration tool based on Github's `gh-ost` tool for MySQL. Ghostferry allows copying a list of tables from an origin to a target database and offers filtering capabilities. It is based on the replication feature of MySQL databases and uses the binary log of the database for the migration operation. There are some limitations, such as the need of integer primary keys, the need for row-based replication on the source server, and it is specific to MySQL. Ghostferry does not address the system tables problem in multi-tenant applications as we do in our architecture. Jetpants by Tumblr [25] is an automation toolkit to automatize sharding operations. However, it does not permit to keep the codebase of a legacy application untouched. We note that both Ghostferry and Jetpants could be coupled with our architecture to implement the actual migration operation.

We finally review approaches that are orthogonal or complementary to our work. Slacker [1] is a middleware for automating migration upon SLA violations. Slacker can leverage automated backup or other live migrations methods. Numerous authors proposed models for multi-tenant resource allocation and tenant placement [17,23,27]. The goal of these works is to minimize operational costs and limit the number of quality of service violations. They do not consider, however, the means used for the live migration operations, or the constraints the support for live migration poses on the architecture.

6   Conclusion

We presented a novel migration method for shared-table multi-tenant applications. Our approach is adapted to the needs of SaaS providers wishing to offer scalable installments of legacy applications based on relational databases. Our proposal does not require changes to the application source code but only to its data schema. We proposed guidelines for classifying which tables should be included in the migratable part of this schema, and we presented the application of these guidelines to two real-world multi-tenant applications. Our experimental evaluation in the cloud shows a real gain in capacity for these applications and low overhead. In our future work, we wish to explore the automation of the classification of tenant tables, e.g., using learning techniques and data from actual deployments, and the improvement of the performance of the migration itself through its parallelization.

Acknowledgments. This work was partially funded by the Belgian FNRS project DAPOCA (33694591).

References

1. Barker, S., Chi, Y., Moon, H.J., Hacigümüş, H., Shenoy, P.: Cut me some slack: latency-aware live migration for databases. In: 15th International Conference on Extending Database Technology, EDBT. ACM (2012)
2. Chong, F., Carraro, G., Wolter, R.: Multi-tenant data architecture, pp. 14–30. MSDN Library, Microsoft Corporation (2006)
3. Das, S., Agrawal, D., El Abbadi, A.: ElasTraS: an elastic, scalable, and self-managing transactional database for the cloud. ACM Trans. Database Syst. **38**(1), 1–45 (2013)
4. Data, C.: citus: Scalable PostgreSQL for multi-tenant and real-time analytics workloads (2020). https://github.com/citusdata/citus
5. Di Francesco, P., Lago, P., Malavolta, I.: Migrating towards microservice architectures: an industrial survey. In: International Conference on Software Architecture, ICSA. IEEE (2018)
6. Elmore, A.J., Arora, V., Taft, R., Pavlo, A., Agrawal, D., El Abbadi, A.: Squall: fine-grained live reconfiguration for partitioned main memory databases. In: ACM SIGMOD International Conference on Management of Data (2015)
7. Green, M.: Moodle Database schema (2020). https://www.examulator.com/er/
8. IDC: Worldwide Semiannual Public Cloud Services Tracker. https://www.idc.com/tracker/showproductinfo.jsp?prodid=881
9. Kalra, S., Prabhakar, T.: Multi-tenant quality attributes to manage tenants in SaaS applications. In: 2020 IEEE International Conference on Software Architecture Companion (ICSA-C), pp. 83–88. IEEE (2020)
10. Lin, Y.S., Pi, S.K., Liao, M.K., Tsai, C., Elmore, A., Wu, S.H.: MgCrab: transaction crabbing for live migration in deterministic database systems. Proc. VLDB Endow. **12**(5), 597–610 (2019)
11. Melton, J., Michels, J.E., Josifovski, V., Kulkarni, K., Schwarz, P.: SQL/MED: a status report. SIGMOD Rec. **31**(3), 81–89 (2002)
12. Michael, N., Shen, Y.: Downtime-free live migration in a multitenant database. In: Nambiar, R., Poess, M. (eds.) TPCTC 2014. LNCS, vol. 8904, pp. 130–155. Springer, Cham (2015). https://doi.org/10.1007/978-3-319-15350-6_9
13. Microsoft: Scaling out - Azure SQL Database (2019). https://docs.microsoft.com/en-us/azure/sql-database/sql-database-elastic-scale-introduction
14. Moniruzzaman, A.B.M.: NewSQL: towards next-generation scalable RDBMS for online transaction processing (OLTP) for big data management. Int. J. Database Theory Appl. **7**(6), 121–130 (2014)
15. Oracle: Database Live-Migration with Oracle Multitenant and the Oracle Universal Connection Pool (UCP) on Oracle Real Application Clusters (RAC) (2015). http://www.oracle.com/technetwork/database/multitenant/learn-more/pdblivemigration-2301324.pdf
16. Rosinosky, G., Labba, C., Ferme, V., Youcef, S., Charoy, F., Pautasso, C.: Evaluating multi-tenant live migrations effects on performance. In: Panetto, H., Debruyne, C., Proper, H.A., Ardagna, C.A., Roman, D., Meersman, R. (eds.) OTM 2018. LNCS, vol. 11229, pp. 61–77. Springer, Cham (2018). https://doi.org/10.1007/978-3-030-02610-3_4
17. Rosinosky, G., Youcef, S., Charoy, F.: A genetic algorithm for cost-aware business processes execution in the cloud. In: Pahl, C., Vukovic, M., Yin, J., Yu, Q. (eds.) ICSOC 2018. LNCS, vol. 11236, pp. 198–212. Springer, Cham (2018). https://doi.org/10.1007/978-3-030-03596-9_13

18. Schaffner, J., Jacobs, D., Kraska, T., Plattner, H.: The multi-tenant data placement problem. In: 4th International Conference on Advances in Databases, Knowledge, and Data Applications, DBKDA (2012)

19. Shah, A., Banakar, V., Shastri, S., Wasserman, M., Chidambaram, V.: Analyzing the impact of GDPR on storage systems. In: 11th USENIX Workshop on Hot Topics in Storage and File Systems. HotStorage (2019)

20. Shopify: ghostferry: The swiss army knife of live data migrations (2018). https://github.com/Shopify/ghostferry

21. Shute, J., et al.: F1: a distributed SQL database that scales. Proc. VLDB Endow. **6**(11) (2013)

22. Suursoho, S., Kreen, M.: PL/Proxy: Function-based sharding for PostgreSQL. https://plproxy.github.io

23. Taft, R., Lang, W., Duggan, J., Elmore, A.J., Stonebraker, M., DeWitt, D.: STeP: scalable tenant placement for managing database-as-a-service deployments. In: 7th ACM Symposium on Cloud Computing, SoCC (2016)

24. Taft, R., et al.: CockroachDB: the resilient geo-distributed SQL database. In: ACM SIGMOD International Conference on Management of Data (2020)

25. Tumblr: jetpants: MySQL toolkit for managing billions of rows and hundreds of database machines (2020). https://github.com/tumblr/jetpants

26. Vitess: A database clustering system for horizontal scaling of MySQL (2020). https://vitess.io/

27. Wang, F., Li, J., Zhang, J., Huang, Q.: Research on the multi-tenant placement genetic algorithm based on eucalyptus platform. In: 12th International Conference on Computational Intelligence and Security, CIS. IEEE (2016)

28. Wang, Z.H., Guo, C.J., Gao, B., Sun, W., Zhang, Z., An, W.H.: A study and performance evaluation of the multi-tenant data tier design patterns for service oriented computing. In: International Conference on e-Business Engineering. IEEE (2008)

29. Weissman, C.D., Bobrowski, S.: The design of the force.com multitenant internet application development platform. In: ACM SIGMOD International Conference on Management of Data (2009)

30. Yu, X., Gadepally, V., Zdonik, S., Kraska, T., Stonebraker, M.: FastDAWG: improving data migration in the BigDAWG polystore system. In: Gadepally, V., Mattson, T., Stonebraker, M., Wang, F., Luo, G., Teodoro, G. (eds.) DMAH/Poly -2018. LNCS, vol. 11470, pp. 3–15. Springer, Cham (2019). https://doi.org/10.1007/978-3-030-14177-6_1

Network Federation for Inter-cloud Operations

Johannes Köstler$^{(\boxtimes)}$ ⓘ, Sven Gebauer ⓘ, and Hans P. Reiser ⓘ

University of Passau, Passau, Germany
{jk,hr}@sec.uni-passau.de, gebauers@fim.uni-passau.de

Abstract. This paper introduces the NetFed network federation approach, which enables inter-cloud operations on the basis of shared overlay
networks. This allows to match the particular application needs to the
most suitable infrastructure provider. The agent-based federation approach utilizes WireGuard and GRE to deliver a flexible and transparent
layer 2 or layer 3 overlay network, while maintaining data integrity and
confidentiality. The evaluation shows that our prototype can be deployed
to arbitrary cloud platforms and benefits from a low traffic and processing overhead.

Keywords: Network federation · Network virtualization · Virtual
private network · Cloud orchestration · Inter-cloud operation

1 Introduction

Cloud federation is the practice of interconnecting two or more private or public
cloud infrastructures. This practice allows clients to optimize the use of cloud
infrastructures by using resources of the best cloud service provider in terms
of costs, flexibility, availability, legal constraints, and particular technological
needs. By using multiple different cloud platforms, a customer can avoid potential vendor lock-in, and the combination of public cloud and private in-house
infrastructure can offer advantages in terms of security and privacy.

One of the major challenges with cloud federation is the federation of networks: The transparent distribution across multiple cloud platforms, in particular in the IaaS service model, requires a distributed virtual network that behaves
much like a virtual network within a single cloud platform. Most cloud platforms
offer some ways of connecting external machines to their networks through virtual private networks (VPNs), but protocols and configurations differ significantly between various cloud platforms. These differences make a combination
of several cloud networks non-trivial. Especially under the aspects of flexibility
and vendor lock-in, the question arises whether and how it is possible for a cloud
user to federate multiple cloud networks in a generic way that allows for addition
and removal of network segments.

© IFIP International Federation for Information Processing 2021
Published by Springer Nature Switzerland AG 2021
M. Matos and F. Greve (Eds.): DAIS 2021, LNCS 12718, pp. 21–37, 2021.
https://doi.org/10.1007/978-3-030-78198-9_2

In this paper, we explore existing approaches to cloud federation and present a novel solution based on WireGuard tunneling and distributed agents for automated configuration. Our research focuses on a number of goals: (i) Optimizing performance, i.e., minimizing latency, maximizing throughput, and avoiding potential central bottlenecks in the over-all architecture; (ii) federation at the data link layer, in order to enable the use of broadcast, unknown-unicast, and multicast traffic (BUM traffic) as well as the use of IPv4 and IPv6 traffic; (iii) easy-to-use and transparent deployment on any private and public cloud infrastructure; (iv) security, in particular prevention of unauthorized access from outside, as well as confidentiality and integrity for any network traffic forwarded between cloud endpoints; (v) support for efficient multiple, isolated virtual networks via a single inter-cloud tunnel.

The remainder of this paper is structured as follows. The next section discusses existing approaches and related work in the field of network federation. In Sect. 3 we systematically explore and compare existing technology for network tunnel protocols that potentially can be used for network federation, and justify why WireGuard is the best choice for our purposes. Section 4 presents our NetFed architecture that enables automated federation of isolated network segments based on federation agents. Section 5 presents evaluation results, before the paper closes with a short conclusion.

2   Related Work

Federating isolated networks for resource aggregation on the basis of VPNs is a common concept. Wood et al. [24] define the hybrid cloud use case as virtual private cloud (VPC), in which VPN technology connects computing resources from cloud sites to the enterprise site. The cloud provider deploys custom edge routers that can be configured by a network manager to serve as VPN tunnel endpoint in the cloud network. The authors also propose a reference architecture called CloudNet that uses multiprotocol label switching (MPLS) and virtual local area networks (VLANs) to provide isolated tunnels for each cloud customer. With the emergence of software defined networks (SDNs) [12], the provision and control of such cloud gateways was centralized and simplified with OpenFlow [20]. Nowadays, all major cloud providers offer some sort of VPC service for site-to-site and client-based point-to-site connections. These VPCs can provide benefits with respect to scalability and interoperability for confined use cases [19], but are restricted to a single cloud provider and do not necessarily provide the full networking functionality. For instance, Amazon Web Services (AWS) only transports traffic based on a proprietary routing mechanism and all address ranges used in a virtual network must be known to the AWS platform, what prevents BUM packets from being forwarded [21]. Google Cloud Platform (GCP), on the other hand, does currently only support IPv4 unicast traffic [5].

Vendor-specific solutions ultimately bear the risk of vendor lock-in. Tai et al. [23] propose cloud federation as a way to avoid this risk and underline the advantages arising from multi-cloud deployments. Many cloud federation architectures leverage SDNs to combine isolated clouds in virtual overlay networks

[3,10,13,16,17]. Mechtri et al. [13] deploy Cloud Networking Gateways (CNG) as OpenFlow switches in each cloud, which are controlled by a central CNG manager. Gateways provide different tunnel protocols like IPsec, OpenVPN, Generic Routing Extension (GRE) or OpenFlow as drivers. Gaul et al. [3] deploy the OpenVirteX (OVX) [1] network virtualization platform over multiple clouds. Each cloud provider runs the network hypervisor on its gateways, so that the SDN controllers of the tenants can provision multiple virtual SDNs over all participating clouds. OVX maps multiple virtual resources to physical resources and uses MAC and IP rewriting in the flows communicated to the underlying networking infrastructure. Levin et al. [10] also provide multi-cloud interoperability through inter-cloud networking based on federation agents. These agents are in fact OpenDaylight [14] controllers that run OpenDOVE (Distributed Overlay Virtual Network) to provide overlay networks and communicate with each other to established Virtual Extensible LAN (VXLAN) tunnels across multiple clouds. The agents are controlled by a central federation manager, which manages the cross-cloud networks of the cloud tenants. The BEACON framework proposes a similar architecture with an envisioned extension of OpenDOVE [16].

Another group of more use-case-driven approaches renounce the complexity of SDNs [4,9,11,15,25]. WAVNet [25] builds a virtual cloud by directly connecting common desktop computers on a layer 2 overlay. The peers are connected by tap devices tunneled over the Internet. Rendezvous servers are used to make peers known to each other and UDP hole punching accesses computers behind network address translation (NAT) services. Moreno-Vozmediano et al. [15] present a framework that connects devices of fog and cloud environments via tunnel agents controlled by a central management instance. The agents establish layer 2 or layer 3 tunnels using GRE and IPsec. Compared to connections without overlay, their prototype achieves 50% of the original throughput with a secure layer 2 overlay and almost 70% with a secure layer 3 overlay. The approach proposed by Kimmerlin et al. [9] has a similar structure, but instead of a central manager the overlay can be shaped by all participating agents. The agents provide layer 2 tunnels using VXLAN, GRE, or Geneve over IPsec. The resulting throughput stagnates at around 60–70% of the reference throughput depending on the used IPsec ciphers. Mansouri et al. [11] propose a network federation based on the WireGuard VPN and Terraform in a database evaluation use case. WireGuard agent VMs are provisioned using Terraform and establish layer 3 tunnels between arbitrary clouds. The solution does not support layer 2 networking and unfortunately there are no evaluations on the sole tunnel performance. Goethals et al. [4] provide cross-domain federation in orchestration environments by deploying OpenVPN containers in different networks. The deployment is integrated into the Docker orchestrator. However, the use of OpenVPN limits their throughput to barely 10% of the available bandwidth.

Summing up, it can be concluded that there exist very different solutions with distinctive characteristics. SDN-based solutions offer the greatest flexibility and can provide far more extensive functionality. However, they require heavyweighted controller and their large protocol stack adds additional complexity.

There are various agent-based solutions that impress with their simplicity, but not all support all networking functionality and their performances differ to a large extent.

3   Tunnel Protocols

For selecting the optimal tunnel protocol for our overlay networks, we compare a variety of modern and freely available VPN protocols. Proprietary protocols like Microsoft's Secure Socket Tunneling Protocol (SSTP) or rather dated protocols like Point-to-Point Tunneling Protocol (PPTP) are not considered. Besides the possibility to transport IP packets and Ethernet frames over the Internet, our main protocol requirements are low connection overhead and high throughput as well as encryption and authentication support for security purposes. We set up VPN tunnels with all these technologies to measure their performance, assess their security features, and gain insights about their usage. The results of this evaluation are shown in Table 1 and discussed in the following.

3.1   Forwarding

The private networks of the VPN protocols are provided at different network layers. OpenVPN and tinc support both the creation of virtual tap or tun devices in order to act as virtual Ethernet switches or virtual routers. SoftEther provides the same functionality, but follows its own terminology (virtual hub/L3 switch). ZeroTier offers emulated Ethernet networks only, whereas WireGuard and IPsec operate only on layer 3. In that case, an additional transport protocol is required to run Ethernet over the IP tunnel. Traditionally IPsec is often combined with L2TP, but we found GRE to be more light-weight and fully stateless. L2TP adds additional overhead through its session concept. OpenVPN and SoftEther follow a star topology with a central server, whereas the other support a full mesh topology. Link deactivation examines whether the internal routing can be controlled to favor certain links. This is only possible with IPsec and WireGuard, as the routing has to be implemented manually. A key requirement for the utilized VPN protocol is the ability to forward BUM traffic. IPsec and WireGuard on layer 3 have no built-in broadcast support. Thus, such traffic requires a layer 2 tunnel for transport and virtual switches for propagation. In OpenVPN and SoftEther, the central server sends broadcast traffic to all connected clients. tinc maintains its own spanning tree routing structure that is used to send messages to all connected clients during broadcasts, and ZeroTier uses sender-side replication and internal multicast groups. All solutions that support broadcast traffic have also some kind of loop prevention.

3.2   Performance

In order to assess the performance of the VPN candidates, we measured throughput and latency between each VPN client and server with the standard network

Table 1. VPN protocol comparison

	IPsec	OpenVPN	SoftEther	tinc	WireGuard	ZeroTier
Forwarding						
Operation Mode	L3	L2/L3	L2/3	L2/L3	L3	L2
Mesh topology	✓	✗	✗	✓	✓	✓
Link deactivation	✓	✗	✗	✗	✓	✗
Broadcast replication	None	Central	Central	Tree	None	Sender
Performance						
Multi-core utilization	✗[a]	✗	✗[a]	✗	✓	✓[a]
Cloud deployment[b] (Download: 948 Mb/s; Upload: 882 Mb/s; RTT Latency: 3.1 ms)						
Download (Mb/s)	347	139	5[c]	138	439	6[d]
Upload (Mb/s)	260	111	146	132	489	5[d]
Additional RTT (ms)	0.2	0.5	0.8	0.3	0.2	0.5
Testbed deployment[b] (Throughput: 4.370 Mb/s; RTT Latency: 1.6 ms)						
Throughput (Mb/s)	211	76	131	83	577	155
Additional RTT (ms)	0.2	1.7	2.5	1.3	1.6	1.5
Security						
No cipher agility	✗	✗	✗	✗	✓	✓
Formally verified	✗	✗	✗	✗	✓	✗
No known weaknesses	✓	✓	✓	✗	✓	✓
No single point of failure	✓	✗	✗	✓	✓	✗
Configuration						
Central configuration	✗	✓	✓	✗	✗	✓
Central services	None	PKI	PKI	None	None	Discovery
Multiplexing						
Protocol[e]	GRE	VLAN	VLAN	VLAN	GRE	Native
Maximum number of networks	2^{32}	2^{12}	2^{12}	2^{12}	2^{32}	$> 2^{24}$
Additional packet size (Bytes)	4	4	4	4	4	0

a This is not documented and only based on observations during our benchmark
b Instead of distinct values for download/upload, testbed measurements only report one throughput value as the links were basically symmetrical
c Inconclusive due to a suspected implementation bug
d Inconclusive due to a known implementation bug
e For protocols without built-in network multiplexing support, we assume the most-efficient extension, depending on their operation mode

utilities ping and iperf3 in two different deployments, with two virtual machines each. In the first case we set them up on two different cloud platforms, and in the other case on dedicated hosts in our local testbed. For each deployment, we did some reference measurements to determine the baseline throughput and latency (see Table 1). All measurements were executed for 60 s and an average value was calculated over the whole time period.

The virtual machines of the cloud deployment were equipped with one virtual CPU and 2 GB of RAM each. WireGuard with a throughput of 439 Mb/s (down) and 489 Mb/s (up) as well as a round-trip overhead of only 0.2 ms is by far the best performing VPN solution in this scenario. IPsec comes in on the second place with only half of WireGuard's performance. OpenVPN, SoftEther and tinc rank on a comparable level with only a quarter of WireGuard's performance. ZeroTier turned out to be extremely slow while causing high CPU load on the sending host. This turned out to be a known performance issue with single CPU machines in current versions of ZeroTier [7]. A similar problem also manifested in the download measurements of SoftEther. Here, we were not able to find additional information or the limiting factor.

In the testbed deployment we used virtual machines with two CPU cores and 1 GB of RAM. This remedied the performance issues with ZeroTier and SoftEther. As the link quality in this setup was symmetrical, we only report one value for throughput. The trends from the previous results are also reflected in these measurements. WireGuard once again performs best, with 577 Mb/s. IPsec follows with 211 Mb/s and after that we can find two clusters with around 140 Mb/s (ZeroTier and SoftEther) and 80 Mb/s (tinc and OpenVPN).

Driven by the issues with the single core CPU, we also investigated if the tested VPN implementations make use of multi-core architectures. We could observe performance gains only with WireGuard and ZeroTier. For WireGuard, OpenVPN and tinc we found documentation that confirms our findings, for the others we can only rely on the observations during our measurements. Parallelizing strongswan (Debian's default IPsec implementation) is possible with the kernel module pcrypt, but we did not use any customizations during our tests.

3.3 Security

Our general security requirements – authentication of peers as well as integrity and confidentiality of transported data – can be provided by all tunnel protocols. Cipher agility denotes the negotiation of cipher algorithms between peers during the initial handshake. No cipher agility results in a simpler and more secure protocol, if the protocol is actively maintained. In case ciphers are broken, the whole software must be updated, but cipher configuration updates are at least just as burdensome. All VPNs support asymmetric authentication. IPsec, WireGuard, tinc and ZeroTier use asymmetric key pairs without certificates, whereas OpenVPN and SoftEther utilize a Public Key Infrastructure (PKI). In addition, IPsec, OpenVPN and SoftEther allow further authentication methods like pre-shared keys, passwords as well as external authentication protocols and frameworks. Regarding known weaknesses, tinc lists some issues allowing man-in-the-middle and chosen plaintext attacks, which were fixed in the preliminary release 1.1 [22]. However, this release has not yet been made stable since 2018. If we investigate possible failure points, it becomes evident that OpenVPN and SoftEther offer single points of failures due to their centralized structure. The same applies to their PKI, if certificates revocations are used, and to ZeroTier's discovery service. We found protocol verifications or cryptographic evaluations only for WireGuard and IPsec, with WireGuard being the only formally verified protocol. But even with those analyses, the varying encryption and authentication approaches make it hard to absolutely assess the security of the solutions.

3.4   Configuration Complexity

As configuration can be automated and its complexity is a rather subjective measure, we only assess the number of configuration updates required whenever peers are added or removed dynamically. Hereby, we can put all candidates in one of two groups. OpenVPN, SoftEther and ZeroTier use a centrally configured star topology and hereby need to connect to one host for reconfiguration. IPsec, tinc and WireGuard, on the other hand, can run on a mesh topology that requires all other peers to be contacted in order to advertise the updated configuration. In addition to that, ZeroTier requires an additional proprietary discovery service, which delivers the initial configuration or points to custom configuration servers. Also, OpenVPN and SoftEther suffer from additional configuration efforts with a PKI, if asymmetric authentication is assumed. OpenVPN and SoftEther could also use a custom authentication mechanism, but this would require additional implementation efforts. Using a pre-shared key is also no option in a star topology with dynamically joining and leaving nodes, as removed nodes could reconnect with the already known secret.

3.5   Network Multiplexing

To support multiple individual overlay networks, the VPN technology should support network multiplexing. For IPsec and WireGuard, GRE is able to create up to 2^{32} distinct tunnels between each host pair utilizing the GRE Key Extension, which adds an overhead of 4 bytes to each packet. OpenVPN, SoftEther and tinc have no built-in support for network multiplexing, but the application of VLAN offers 2^{12} virtual networks over any Ethernet network with a 4 byte overhead per packet. It would also be possible to use a distinct VPN with a unique UDP port for each individual network resulting in 2^{16} possible networks and no per-packet overhead. However, this approach would not scale very well as the configuration complexity would also increase with number of networks. In a similar way, ZeroTier's built-in network multiplexing supports up to 2^{24} networks without packet or large configuration overhead. In summary, all protocols support network multiplexing in some way, but with regards to the number of possible networks and their transport and configuration overhead, ZeroTier is the optimal approach, followed by IPsec and WireGuard using GRE, with a slightly larger number of available networks.

3.6   Conclusion

In summary, we see WireGuard in combination with GRE as the most promising VPN tunnel protocol. Mainly because of its performance results, but also because of its simple and secure design, which has been formally verified. We value the higher configuration efforts when peers are added or removed as well as the missing broadcast replication only as minor disadvantages that can be tolerated.

4   Approach

Figure 1 illustrates a high-level overview of our NetFed architecture for the automated federation of isolated network segments, showing two sample federated
networks spanning three sites. Networks are either bridged Ethernet or routed
dual-stack IPv4/6 networks, consisting of multiple virtual or physical network
segments inside a company site or cloud platform. The segments are connected
through federation agents (or peers), which run tunnels that forward the traffic
isolated from each other. NetFed knows two types of tunnels. Peer tunnels, which
connect two federation agents site-to-site, and neighbor tunnels, which connect
a federation agent with a host (or neighbor) in the same segment point-to-site.

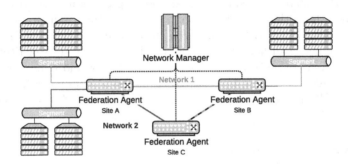

Fig. 1. High-level overview of two sample federated networks spanning three sites

At least one federation agent is placed in each site and all agents are connected with each other in a mesh topology. Additional agents could be utilized
to balance the load or isolate certain networks. Links can be deactivated in
order to ensure loop prevention and efficient routing. Federation agents run virtual switches and routers as GRE and WireGuard tunnel endpoints. A dynamic
configuration interface is exposed to the network manager. This central control
instance knows all federation agents and initializes the tunnels during startup
based on an external description or dynamically adapts the tunnel configurations
during runtime. The deployment of the federation agents is the responsibility of
the cloud orchestrator and not covered in this paper. We followed an agent-based
federation approach, as it constitutes a well-established approach and guarantees full control over the network segments without any vendor dependencies or
restrictions. Thus, our solution can be deployed to arbitrary cloud platforms and
computing environments.

4.1   Operation Modes

NetFed offers two operation modes – bridged and routed – to provide layer 2 and layer 3 federation. In bridged mode, the federation agents act as virtual switches in order to connect the isolated Ethernet fragments. This behavior is presented in Fig. 2 with Network 0 between Site A and Site B. This setup offers the highest flexibility and transparency, as it forwards any traffic and requires no further host configuration.

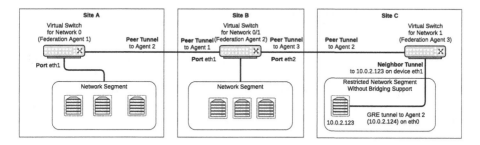

Fig. 2. Bridged mode: Peer tunnels between virtual switches connect the reachable hosts of network segments in Network 0; additional neighbor tunnels inside the local segment of Site C connect hosts to the virtual switch directly

However, some cloud platforms do not support BUM packets or do not forward layer 2 traffic originating from unknown/external MAC addresses. To cope with such platforms NetFed offers neighboring tunnels. One has to sacrifice the transparency property, since bridged mode with neighbor tunnels requires explicit host configuration. In this case, federation agents establish GRE tunnels to all hosts in the local segment, as illustrated in Fig. 2 with Network 1 between Site B and Site C.

The second mode NetFed can be used with is the routed mode. Here, the federation agents act as virtual routers for their network segment, as shown in Fig. 3. The data is forwarded based on configured routes. The routes for the remote networks must be enforced by the segment's default gateway or pushed to the hosts with DHCP.

4.2   Internal Networking

To achieve this flexibility, NetFed leverages the network protocol stack shown in Fig. 4(a) on its federation agents. At the bottom WireGuard serves as the VPN foundation. Therefore, every agent must be reachable from the Internet on WireGuard's de facto standard UDP port 51820 – directly or also indirectly through some NAT layer. To prevent address collisions with existing private IPv4 networks within some agent's environment, NetFed assigns IPv6's link-local addresses inside the WireGuard network, which can freely be chosen from

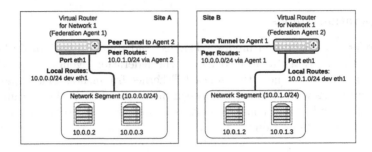

Fig. 3. Routed mode: Peer tunnels between virtual routers

the fe80::/64 address block and can carry an additional zone identifier [6]. This way, each federation agent gets assigned an IPv6 address with its numerical identifier mapped to the last 64 bits (e.g. agent with identifier 1 will be assigned fe80::1). With multiple ports, the additional identifier (e.g. fe80::1%eth0) ensures collision resistance.

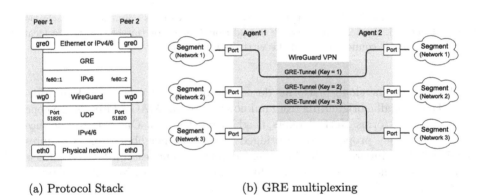

(a) Protocol Stack   (b) GRE multiplexing

Fig. 4. Internal networking: GRE over WireGuard

On top of a WireGuard VPN tunnel, multiple GRE tunnels can be established between each pair of federation agents. Figure 4(b) shows this behavior for three federated networks. Network multiplexing is achieved by simply putting the network's identifier into the GRE tunnel's key field [18]. For every federated network, a distinct virtual bridge device is created on each federation agent. By establishing selected tunnels between the agents, the network manager is able to shape the network topology based on external information such as link costs or traffic restrictions. Establishing tunnels between all federation agents forms a full mesh. In this case, additional protocols like the Spanning Tree Protocol [8] or Open Shortest Part First [18] can be used to prevent loops and optimize routing.

4.3   Deployment

In order to deploy NetFed, an external cloud orchestrator needs to provision the federation agents. This can be done by installing the federation agent software stack on the already existing gateways or by deploying the federation as virtual appliance, but we do not restrict NetFed to any particular infrastructure as code (IaC) technology. For every federation agent, its public IP address or hostname must be made available to the network manager. With this information at hand, the manager first establishes WireGuard VPN connections between the federation agents and then creates the peer tunnels to deploy the federated networks. The network manager only needs to be online during the initial deployment or whenever reconfigurations are needed. Future versions could replicate the federation agents to improve their reliability and scalability. Additional services like monitoring or policy enforcement could be integrated into the central network manager, which then should also be replicated to avoid a single point of failure.

5   Evaluation

We provide a prototype implementation for the federation agent, which is written in Python and implemented as command line agent. In the following we present our evaluation results in terms of functionality, security and performance.

5.1   Functionality

We tested the general functionality of our prototype implementation in an extended setup connecting multiple hosts in four different sites. With AWS and OpenNebula, we used a public and a private cloud, and further integrated two local network segments, one physical LAN and a virtualized network. NetFed is able to federate such networks in both modes. The bridged mode must make use of neighbor tunnels, since AWS and OpenNebula will drop packets with unknown source MAC addresses, as already described above.

However, during the functionality tests some issues with the maximum transmission unit (MTU) size occurred. Principally, the MTU sizes of all connected segments should match, and also be smaller than the WireGuard MTU without the GRE overhead, as packages exceeding this size will be silently dropped. Running Ethernet over GRE in our neighbor tunnels adds a combined overhead of 70 bytes if WireGuard runs on top of IPv6 (14 (Ethernet) + 8 (GRE) + 48 (IPv6, with Destination Options Header)) or 42 bytes in case of IPv4 (14 (Ethernet) + 8 (GRE) + 20 (IPv4)). Therefore, the MTU size of bridged networks must be set to the minimum of: the WireGuard network's MTU minus 70; the MTU sizes of the connected segments; and the MTU sizes of all connected segments running neighbor tunnels minus 70 (for IPv6 tunnels) or minus 42 (for IPv4 tunnels). With 1500 as the default Ethernet MTU, 1350 turned out to be a good choice to prevent fragmenting. This configuration option must be set on every host, what affects the transparency property in a negative way. It would be also possible to increase the WireGuard MTU on the agents only, but this would mean that WireGuard packets would be fragmented during their transport.

5.2 Security

The security guarantees of physical local networks should also hold for our federated networks. Thus, we performed a security analysis with attack tree modeling, which is not fully included due to length restrictions. The analysis is based on the following assumptions: (i) there is already an established trust relationship between the network manager and all federation agents that allows the manager to access the administrative interface of the agents via SSH; (ii) the network manager is never compromised, as its administrative access to the agents would compromise all federated networks; (iii) the underlying software stack is free of implementation bugs and provides it specified security properties; and (iv) the utilized strong cryptography is infeasible to break.

Following those assumptions, the integrity and confidentiality of the communication sent over federated networks is ensured through the authentication and encryption of the WireGuard VPN. The agent configuration in transit is protected in the same way by SSH. If an attacker gains control over a host in a network segment, either by compromising an existing host or by introducing a new host with the assistance of a compromised cloud platform, it can obviously read the traffic directed to that host and send traffic into all connected segments of that host's networks. Access to other federated networks, however, remains restricted. This corresponds to the behavior of physical networks.

Consequently, federation agents might constitute a more valuable attack target to attackers. But, introducing a new federation agent is a futile undertaking, since WireGuard requires an established trust relationship between all peers, in which all other need to learn the public key of a newly introduced peer. This trust can only be established by the network manager, which we assume to be secure. If an attacker compromises an existing federation agent, it can read and modify the traffic of all segments of the networks, to which this agent is connected, as well as introduce new traffic. Re-routing traffic by impersonating existing peers is, however, still not possible on compromised hosts, due to WireGuard's CryptoKey Routing [2].

All in all, it can be concluded that the security of NetFed heavily depends on the underlying components. We cannot fully prevent security breaches carried out by attackers that maliciously gained administrative access to cloud platforms or access to individual hosts, agents and their private keys. However, NetFed prevents attackers, without access to any host or agent in a federated network, from reading, manipulating or injecting packets in that network. And, attackers, with access to a host or agent, from reading, manipulating or injecting packets in other federated networks.

5.3   Performance

For the performance evaluation, we set up a federated network consisting of two segments with four hosts per segment. One segment was located in our private OpenNebula cloud (Passau, Germany) and the other segment was hosted in the eu-central-1 region of the public AWS cloud (Frankfurt, Germany). We run the tests with a bridged network using neighbor tunnels and a routed network.

Traffic Overhead. To determine the actual traffic overhead we sent one giga-byte of random data from one host in the one cloud to another host in the other cloud using the netcat utility. We measured the exchanged traffic on its way between the different hosts and responsible federation agents, as illustrated in Fig. 5. The results are shown in Table 2 with the TCP traffic between the two hosts as reference measurement. The main difference between the operation modes is represented by the 2.5% traffic overhead, which the neighbor tunnels add in bridged networks on the way from the host to the agent. The remaining overheads behave similar. GRE increases the data exchanged between the agents by 3.9% in the bridged setup and 3.2% in the routed set up. The IPv6-based WireGuard tunnel elevates those numbers to 17.0% and 15.1%

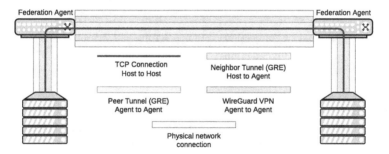

Fig. 5. Overview of the different types of nested tunnels in a federated network.

Table 2. Comparison of generated traffic when sending a fixed amount of random data over TCP. Relative deviations are in comparison to the TCP Host-to-Host traffic.

	Bridged setup	Routed setup
Payload	1024 MiB	1024 MiB
TCP Host-to-Host	1060 MiB (100%)	1060 MiB (100%)
All Host-to-Agent	1087 MiB (+2.5%)	1060 MiB (+0.0%)
GRE Agent-to-Agent	1102 MiB (+3.9%)	1094 MiB (+3.2%)
All Agent-to-Agent	1240 MiB (+17.0%)	1220 MiB (+15.1%)

Latency. We also investigated the influence of our tunnel network on latency using the same setups. For this purpose, we used ping to measure the round-trip time between two hosts in different clouds. We performed the measurements either with or without additional traffic, where one or multiple host pairs exchange data at a fixed rate or even unrestricted. We included once again a reference measurement without any federation. The results are shown in Table 3, from which we can see that the routed traffic is generally forwarded a little faster. This can be explained by the additional processing delay introduced by the GRE overlay. Apart from that, it also becomes clear that additional traffic on the network has a negative influence on the overall latency, which is most likely be caused by additional queuing delays. However, we cannot rule out minor deviations due to the external conditions the traffic experiences over the Internet.

Table 3. Latency (and standard deviation) between two hosts in different segments using a direct connection vs. a network federation setup with different levels of load.

	Bridged setup	Routed setup
Without tunnel	13.2 ± 2.8 ms	12.9 ± 3.7 ms
0 Mb/s	13.2 ± 1.6 ms	13.0 ± 2.6 ms
8 Mb/s	13.9 ± 3.1 ms	16.0 ± 8.6 ms
16 Mb/s	13.9 ± 2.6 ms	13.7 ± 4.8 ms
Full load (1 connection)	14.6 ± 3.4 ms	14.2 ± 4.8 ms
Full load (3 connections)	13.5 ± 2.2 ms	14.4 ± 6.2 ms

Throughput. We measured the total throughput of multiple host pairs exchanging data between two sites to determine throughput and the overhead of multiple connections. Measurements were done in both directions, with the OpenNebula hosts as clients and the AWS hosts as servers, so that Fig. 6 consequently represents the throughput as upload and download. Figure 6(a) shows that the overall throughput actually rises with more parallel connections. This counterintuitive behavior can be explained with the fairness property of TCP, which will be activated when multiple connections share a common bottleneck. In this case the congestion control algorithm tries to distribute the available bandwidth in fair shares over the competing connections, which results in a larger combined bandwidth than a single collection could obtain. In order to assess the actual overhead, we restricted the outgoing throughput of both agents to 10 Mb/s in order to create a non-shared bottleneck, as Fig. 6(b) illustrates. In bridged mode, we measured a throughput of 9.11 Mb/s (up) and 9.10 Mb/s (down), whereas in routed mode the throughput reached 9.21 Mb/s (up) and 9.26 Mb/s (down), regardless of the number of parallel connections. Hereby, the federated networks showed a relative network-bound overhead of about 9% for the bridged setup and 8% for the routed setup. It has to be noted that federation agents can in fact become bottlenecks, which is why the expected network load should be reflected in the agents' hardware configuration or the networks' topology.

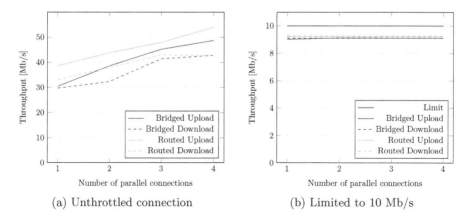

(a) Unthrottled connection   (b) Limited to 10 Mb/s

Fig. 6. Total throughput by number of parallel connections over a single tunnel

Neighbor Tunnels. So far we only investigated the communication between different segments. However, if neighbor tunnels are used, there is also an overhead on in-segment communication. Therefore, we measured the latency and throughput between a pair of hosts belonging to the same segment in our Open-Nebula environment – with and without neighbor tunnels. Without, we measured a throughput of 938 Mb/s and a round-trip latency of 0.50 ms. With tunnels, those values degraded to 602 Mb/s for throughput and 0.81 ms for latency. This local overhead must be considered in bridged inter-cloud operations.

6 Conclusion

In this work, we presented a fast and secure network federation approach that enables flexible and multi-cloud operations. From our analysis of existing tunneling protocols we selected WireGuard as the most secure and fastest-performing technology. The light-weight NetFed architecture is able to support a wide range of use case scenarios, while preserving network functionality, configuration transparency and cloud platform support. Our prototype implementation shows its practicability and the performance evaluation proves its efficiency. We still see room for improvements in various areas, such as cloud orchestration integration or an extended configuration management, but we leave this open as future work.

Acknowledgements. This work has been funded by the Deutsche Forschungsgemeinschaft (DFG, German Research Foundation) – 268730775 (OptSCORE).

References

1. Al-Shabibi, A., et al.: OpenVirteX: make your virtual SDNs programmable. In: Proceedings of the Third Workshop on Hot Topics in Software Defined Networking, HotSDN 2014, pp. 25–30. Association for Computing Machinery, New York, August 2014. https://doi.org/10.1145/2620728.2620741

2. Donenfeld, J.: WireGuard: next generation kernel network tunnel. In: Network and Distributed System Security Symposium (NDSS), February 2017. https://doi.org/10.14722/ndss.2017.23160

3. Gaul, C., Körner, M., Kao, O.: Design and implementation of a cloud-federation agent for software defined networking. In: 2015 IEEE International Conference on Cloud Engineering, pp. 323–328, March 2015. https://doi.org/10.1109/IC2E.2015.58

4. Goethals, T., Kerkhove, D., Van Hoye, L., Sebrechts, M., De Turck, F., Volckaert, B.: FUSE: a microservice approach to cross-domain federation using docker containers. In: Proceedings of the 9th International Conference on Cloud Computing and Services Science, May 2019

5. Google Cloud Platform: VPC network overview. https://cloud.google.com/vpc/docs/vpc. Accessed 18 Feb 2021

6. Hinden, R.M., Haberman, B.: Unique Local IPv6 Unicast Addresses. RFC 4193, October 2005. http://www.rfc-editor.org/rfc/rfc4193.txt

7. Holden, J.: CPU pegged at 100%, November 2019. https://github.com/zerotier/ZeroTierOne/issues/1079. Accessed 18 Feb 2021

8. Institute of Electrical and Electronics Engineers: IEEE Standard for Local and metropolitan area networks: Media Access Control (MAC) Bridges. IEEE Std. 802.1D-2004, pp. 137–179, June 2004. https://doi.org/10.1109/IEEESTD.2004.94569

9. Kimmerlin, M., Hasselmeyer, P., Heikkilä, S., Plauth, M., Parol, P., Sarolahti, P.: Network expansion in OpenStack cloud federations. In: 2017 European Conference on Networks and Communications (EuCNC), pp. 1–5, June 2017. https://doi.org/10.1109/EuCNC.2017.7980655

10. Levin, A., Barabash, K., Ben-Itzhak, Y., Guenender, S., Schour, L.: Networking architecture for seamless cloud interoperability. In: 2015 IEEE 8th International Conference on Cloud Computing. pp. 1021–1024, June 2015. https://doi.org/10.1109/CLOUD.2015.141

11. Mansouri, Y., Prokhorenko, V., Babar, M.A.: An automated implementation of hybrid cloud for performance evaluation of distributed databases. J. Netw. Comput. Appl. 102740 (2020). https://doi.org/10.1016/j.jnca.2020.102740

12. McKeown, N., et al.: OpenFlow: enabling innovation in campus networks. ACM SIGCOMM Comput. Commun. Rev. **2**, 69–74 (2008). https://doi.org/10.1145/1355734.1355746

13. Mechtri, M., Zeghlache, D., Zekri, E., Marshall, I.J.: Inter and intra cloud networking gateway as a service. In: 2013 IEEE 2nd International Conference on Cloud Networking (CloudNet), pp. 156–163, November 2013. https://doi.org/10.1109/CloudNet.2013.6710570

14. Medved, J., Varga, R., Tkacik, A., Gray, K.: OpenDaylight: towards a model-driven SDN controller architecture. In: Proceedings of the IEEE International Symposium on a World of Wireless, Mobile and Multimedia Networks 2014, pp. 1–6, June 2014. https://doi.org/10.1109/WoWMoM.2014.6918985

15. Moreno-Vozmediano, R., Montero, R.S., Huedo, E., Llorente, I.M.: Cross-site virtual network in cloud and fog computing. IEEE Cloud Comput. **2**, 46–53 (2017). https://doi.org/10.1109/MCC.2017.28

16. Moreno-Vozmediano, R., et al.: BEACON: a cloud network federation framework. In: Celesti, A., Leitner, P. (eds.) ESOCC Workshops 2015. CCIS, vol. 567, pp. 325–337. Springer, Cham (2016). https://doi.org/10.1007/978-3-319-33313-7_25

17. Moreno-Vozmediano, R., Montero, R.S., Huedo, E., Llorente, I.M.: Implementation and provisioning of federated networks in hybrid clouds. J. Grid Comput. **2**, 141–160 (2017). https://doi.org/10.1007/s10723-017-9395-1

18. Moy, J.: OSPF Version 2. RFC 2328, April 1998. http://www.rfc-editor.org/rfc/rfc2328.txt

19. Nadjaran Toosi, A., Buyya, R.: Virtual networking with azure for hybrid cloud computing in Aneka. In: Chaudhary, S., Somani, G., Buyya, R. (eds.) Research Advances in Cloud Computing, pp. 93–114. Springer, Singapore (2017). https://doi.org/10.1007/978-981-10-5026-8_5

20. Natarajan, S., Ramaiah, A., Mathen, M.: A software defined cloud-gateway automation system using OpenFlow. In: 2013 IEEE 2nd International Conference on Cloud Networking (CloudNet), pp. 219–226, November 2013. https://doi.org/10.1109/CloudNet.2013.6710582

21. Pepelnjak, I.: AWS Networking 101, June 2020. https://blog.ipspace.net/2020/05/aws-networking-101.html. Accessed 18 Feb 2021

22. Sliepen, G.: Tinc version 1.0.35 and 1.1pre17 released, October 2018. https://www.tinc-vpn.org/pipermail/tinc/2018-October/005311.html. Accessed 23 Apr 2021

23. Tai, S., Klems, M., Lenk, A., Kunze, M., Bermbach, D., Kurze, T.: Cloud federation. In: Proceedings of the 2nd International Conference on Cloud Computing, GRIDs, and Virtualization, Cloud Computing 2011. IARIA, September 2011

24. Wood, T., Gerber, A., Ramakrishnan, K.K., Shenoy, P., Van der Merwe, J.: The case for enterprise-ready virtual private clouds. In: Proceedings of the 2009 Conference on Hot Topics in Cloud Computing. HotCloud 2009, USENIX Association, USA, June 2009

25. Xu, Z., Di, S., Zhang, W., Cheng, L., Wang, C.: WAVNet: wide-area network virtualization technique for virtual private cloud. In: 2011 International Conference on Parallel Processing, pp. 285–294, September 2011. https://doi.org/10.1109/ICPP.2011.90

SpecK: Composition of Stream Processing Applications over Fog Environments

Davaadorj Battulga[1,2]([envelope]), Daniele Miorandi[2]([envelope]), and Cédric Tedeschi[1]([envelope])

[1] Univ Rennes, Inria, CNRS, IRISA, Rennes, France
{davaadorj.battulga,daniele.miorandi}@u-hopper.com
[2] U-Hopper, Trento, Italy
cedric.tedeschi@inria.fr

Abstract. Stream Processing (SP), i.e., the processing of data in motion, as soon as it becomes available, is a hot topic in cloud computing. Various SP stacks exist today, with applications ranging from IoT analytics to processing of payment transactions. The backbone of said stacks are Stream Processing Engines (SPEs), software packages offering a high-level programming model and scalable execution of data stream processing pipelines. SPEs have been traditionally developed to work inside a single datacenter, and optimised for speed. With the advent of Fog computing, however, the processing of data streams needs to be carried out over multiple geographically distributed computing sites: Data gets typically pre-processed close to where they are generated, then aggregated at intermediate nodes, and finally globally and persistently stored in the Cloud. SPEs were not designed to address these new scenarios. In this paper, we argue that large scale Fog-based stream processing should rely on the coordinated composition of geographically dispersed SPE instances. We propose an architecture based on the composition of multiple SPE instances and their communication via distributed message brokers. We introduce SpecK, a tool to automate the deployment and adaptation of pipelines over a Fog computing platform. Given a description of the pipeline, SpecK covers all the operations needed to deploy a stream processing computation over the different SPE instances targeted, using their own APIs and establishing the required communication channels to forward data among them. A prototypical implementation of SpecK is presented, and its performance is evaluated over Grid'5000, a large-scale, distributed experimental facility.

Keywords: Stream processing · Deployment · Geographically distributed platforms

1 Introduction

Stream Processing (SP) is a major research theme within the general area of big data infrastructures and applications. Practitioners, who need to deploy SP

Published by Springer Nature Switzerland AG 2021
M. Matos and F. Greve (Eds.): DAIS 2021, LNCS 12718, pp. 38–54, 2021.
https://doi.org/10.1007/978-3-030-78198-9_3

pipelines, are presented with different options, rather mature, in terms of available (typically open source) software stacks. The cornerstones of these stacks are stream processing engines (SPEs), such as Storm [32], Flink [7] and Spark streaming [33]. SPEs generally provide two main features: i) a *high-level programming model*, allowing developers to describe and code the intended behaviour, and ii) a *scalable execution model*, implemented by software able to deploy and monitor the application at run time.

Programmers define SP applications by combining operations to be applied on an incoming stream in a certain order. This combination can be linear (commonly referred to as a pipeline), but, more generally can be represented by a directed acyclic graph (DAG), whereby each vertex represent a single operation. Once implemented, such a program is deployed on the underlying computing infrastructure by the SP engine, thereby becoming a running *job*. The engine deploys the job over the compute nodes of the underlying infrastructure, trying to optimize application's throughput and resource usage. The main component supporting this deployment is commonly referred to as the *Job Manager*.

Datacenters, or more generally geographically-restricted infrastructures connecting compute nodes through a high-speed network are the natural target to deploy such jobs. Yet, with the advent of fog computing [19], we moved to a platform model made of a possibly large number of geographically distributed computing resources. This makes it difficult for a single Job Manager to remain efficient, due to the difficulties in maintaining an updated view over all possible available resources. The net result is that SPEs have some limitations when applied to fog computing scenarios, whereby data need to be processed in a coordinated fashion over a geographically distributed infrastructure. In a typical fog application, part of the processing is carried out directly close to the data origin (at the edge), aggregation steps are carried out at intermediate nodes (where data from different edges are joined), to be finally post-processed and stored in a more stable platform such as a Cloud [19]. This limitation calls for new execution models for SP applications over fog infrastructures. Until now, most works tackling this issue based their solution on revising scheduling policies by injecting some latency-awareness and some form of hierarchy into it. While such approaches are interesting, they present some limitation; furthermore, most of them stay at the prototype level.

This paper explores a radically different approach. Instead of revising existing SPEs, we advocate for a federated stream processing platform, able to combine multiple standard Job Managers (typically those provided by Flink, Storm or Spark Streaming), each one being responsible for the management of a geographically-restricted (local) portion of the infrastructure. Adopting this idea requires to revisit the traditional programming and execution models of SPEs. Considering geographically-distributed infrastructures will not only extend the range of computing platforms on which to deploy SP applications, but will also pave the way to the construction of SP applications through the composition of a set of ready-made SP Jobs. Similarly to the more traditional *service composition*, the notion of SP job composition carries the idea that developing complex SP applications out of the blue is not a reasonable option anymore. Such complexity should be handled by a higher-level programming model: the composition of existing SP jobs into a new *composite* SP application.

Let us explore the example of a road traffic monitoring application: the road traffic is sensed locally and a first cleaning of the data and the computation of real-time statistics about the traffic can be done locally (for instance to be offered to people in this area). Yet to be exploited further (e.g., for statistical purposes and to support the design and monitoring of transportation policies), data need to be aggregated at the regional/national level, which is typically done at a centralized Cloud-based location. This pipeline is composed of jobs that will strongly benefit from running over different sites: cleaning and local statistics at edges, and global statistics in a centralized Cloud. Finally, the user is at risk that those different jobs exist but were developed using different SPEs, in which case, there is a need to be able to have heterogeneous jobs composed.

This paper proposes a novel programming model for SP, based on the composition of existing SP Jobs, and their execution over a geographically-distributed computing infrastructure. We devise the SPECK framework bringing this proposal into reality: based on the description of the composite application to be deployed, SPECK starts each job composing the application over the resources of one computing site. Our assumption is that each computing site is equipped with an instance of a stream processing engine (a Flink Job Manager) able to deploy jobs over the local computing resources, and a message broker managing the needed message queues to transfer data and control messages between sites. SPECK provides two core APIs: the **Job Management API** focuses on the management of a single job. It allows to start, modify, and delete jobs in a unified fashion, regardless of the targeted SPE instance. The **Composition Management API**, given the description of a complex application composed of several jobs for which the code is available, deploys each job on the SPE instance specified for this job. This API supports dynamic on-the-fly reconfiguration/adaptation of the composition: The user simply needs to submit a new version of the description and SPECK will trigger all changes needed by contacting the SPE instances running jobs affected by the modification. SPECK was prototyped and deployed over the Grid'5000 large-scale testbed [2], where we evaluated its performance using real traffic traces.

Section 2 positions this work with respect to the relevant state of the art. Section 3 presents the programming and execution models of SPECK and details its usage, architecture and internals. Section 4 reviews the experimental results obtained over Grid'5000, focusing on scalability and on the ability of SPECK to bring the benefits of the Fog into reality when deploying SP applications at large scale. Section 5 concludes the paper, outlining a roadmap for the further development and integration of SPECK.

2   Related Work

Stream processing is gaining momentum, as application domains such as smart cities and the Internet of things are becoming mainstream. Stream processing engines represent the software response to the need for real-time analysis of large amount of data produced at a high rate [7,32,33].

Stream processing engines have adopted different programming models that can get categorized into two coarse-grain families. Low-level SP programming models, as for instance implemented by Storm [32], requires the user to code the application as an explicit directed acyclic graph of operators, the code of each of these operators being also left at the charge of the developer. While relatively cumbersome, this programming models brings about more flexibility and allows the user to define any operation. Higher-level SP programming models, as implemented by the Flink Datastream API [7], allows to express easily most pipelines by chaining predefined Flink operations in cascade.

Because we target environment where multiple running SPEs collaborate over a geographically-dispersed infrastructure (say one Flink *Job Manager* responsible for deploying and managing jobs over Cluster i, one Storm *Nimbus* responsible for deploying and managing jobs over Cluster j, *etc.*), we need to define programming abstractions able to express compositions of jobs, possibly running over different clusters and their dependencies). SpecK, presented in Sect. 3, given such a description, will be able to deploy and dynamically adapt such a composite application over such an environment.

A lot of work went into finding ways to optimize the deployment and placement of an application's operators over a computing platform, especially for cluster environments which are the natural playgrounds for traditional SPEs [16]. Yet, with the advent of Cloud computing, stream processing had the opportunity to deal with less constrained computing platforms and scale up and down dynamically as the velocity of the stream evolves [9,13,15,23].

With the advent of Fog computing [3,19], we are currently witnessing the emergence of works that will shape the fourth generation of stream processing platforms [4]: Stream processing is becoming highly distributed and deployed over hybrid Edge-Cloud platforms with a strong incentive to move processing at the edge where possible [24]. First, this leads to the development of light processing systems especially designed for the edge and its limited computing power [1,10,12,18,24]. These systems can be seen as lightweight SPEs. Choosing between different SPEs is not in the scope of the present work: the SpecK framework is designed so as favor SPE-agnosticism, so the execution of a composite application can be shared over SPE instances relying on different stacks.

A second series of research works was born from the need to consider Fog-like environments as the next natural playground for Stream Processing. They investigate scheduling strategies to place operators composing applications over geographically distributed compute resources, pursuing different metrics to optimize. Cardellini et al. [8] introduced a QoS-aware distributed scheduling algorithm taking into account the heterogeneous network capacity of the targeted platform. Frontier [22] explores strategies to optimize the performance and resilience of edge processing platforms for IoT, by dynamically routing streams according to network conditions. Planner [25] automates the deployment over hybrid platforms, taking decisions on what portion of an application graph should be taken care of at the edge, and what portion should stay in the Cloud, trying to minimize the network traffic cost. The work in [29] exhibits similar objectives while focusing on specific yet very common families of graphs found in data stream analytics, namely series parallel graphs. These works focus on modelling the placement problem and propose strategies to optimize certain metrics, statically or dynamically, they do require to modify the schedulers and deployers at the core of existing stream processing engines. While these works show the great vitality of the domain, they are mostly performance oriented. In this sense, they are quite orthogonal to the present work: SPECK does not intend to provide new scheduling strategies, but advocates for an alternative way to program and run stream processing applications in the Fog, through composition.

Automating software deployment over large scale platform is not new in itself. Tools have been proposed for platforms such as grids [11] or clouds [21]. Yet the problem of deploying stream processing platforms over Fog architectures is still widely open. To our knowledge, only few works have been presented on the topic. R-pulsar provides a user-level API for operator placement [14]. R-pulsar offers a programming model similar to Storm, but where the user can choose what operator has to be placed at the edge, and what operator has to be placed in the Cloud. Then, the framework decides on what precise node to place the operator. Also, standardizing the way to benchmark Fog-deployed data stream processing applications is explored in [27, 28].

To our knowledge, our closest related work is E2CLab [26]. E2CLab is a framework easing the deployment of SP applications over platforms interconnecting the whole range of possible computing resources, from IoT devices to HPC clusters. E2CLab relies on a high-level description of the whole deployment process, from the installation of the stacks to the execution of the jobs, thus facilitating large scale experiments over such platforms. SPECK differs from E2CLab in the sense that while E2CLab is a tool for experimenters and covers the whole deployment process, SPECK is end-user oriented and provides simplified interfaces for the description of the application. Also, while E2CLab targets complex initial deployments only, SPECK also supports on-the-fly adaptation.

3   SPECK: An SPE Coordinator

SPECK deploys and dynamically adapts stream processing applications built as a composition of independent stream processing jobs running over different stream processing stacks. The architectural framework it relies on provides two user interfaces, one to abstract out the details of the deployment of a single job, whatever its target SPE stack, one to coordinate the initial deployment and subsequent user-driven adaptations of compositions over multiple independently running stacks. Section 3.1 describes SPECK targeted underlying platform. Then, Sect. 3.2 adopts the user's viewpoint and describes SPECK usage. Finally, Sect. 3.3 exhibits a SPECK software prototype and its internals.

3.1 Targeted Platform

The present work targets infrastructures gathering geographically-dispersed computing resources, resources being grouped into what we refer to as a *computing site*. A computing site is typically a set of tightly coupled compute nodes, such as a cluster of small single-board computers located at the edge of the network. A larger datacenter, at the other end of the spectrum, can be seen as one site. All those sites are more and more aggregated into what the emerging *Edge-to-Cloud continuum* [5,6,20], the final objective being to be able to operate such a continuum in a unified manner. SPECK participates to this objective, focusing on stream processing applications.

Each site includes a running instance of a stream processing stack such as Storm, Flink or Spark streaming. This means that an orchestrator, commonly referred to as the *Job Manager*, is responsible to distribute the workloads submitted over the compute nodes of the site it is responsible of. The SPE instance constitutes the first software element we assume to be present on the sites. The second elements answer the need to link sites together so as to build the continuum: as SPE engines will be responsible only for portions of the applications deployed, different portions will run on resources of different sites. These jobs having dependencies, nodes from one site will have to communicate with nodes on another site. Inter-site communication is typically handled by Message Brokers (MB) such as Mosquitto [17], ActiveMQ [30] and Kafka [31].

Such an infrastructure is depicted in Fig. 1: each site, of different size reflecting its computing power, is equipped with its own instance of stream processing engine and message broker. As mentioned, some of these sites can be referred to as *Edges* (small sites in the picture) and will typically use edge-optimized stream processing engine such as Edgent [1]. One of these sites can be a *Cloud* (the bigger site in picture 1) and will be typically equipped with Cluster-ready stream processing engines such as Storm, Flink or Spark Streaming. We assume that direct communication between the sites is always possible. Security constraints that may appear fall outside the scope of the paper. Also, the choice of the specific message broker used locally at each site depends on local requirements and user preferences and is not discussed here.

As it is detailed in the following, SPECK acts as a coordinator between those sites to deploy composite SP applications over the whole infrastructure. The following sections review its usage, architecture and internal mechanisms.

3.2 SPECK Usage

SPECK acts as a coordinator between SPE instances, based on the user's input, as depicted in Fig. 2. It can be seen as a wrapper on top of a pool of available running SPE instances, to be exploited as specified by the user in its application's description. The interaction between SPECK and the users are one-way: the user pushes the description to SPECK. The interactions between SPECK and the SPE instances go in both directions, typically through HTTP.

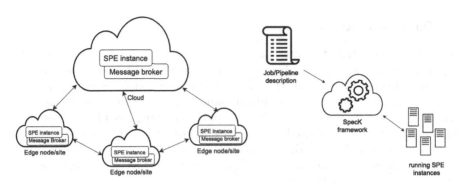

Fig. 1. SPECK targeted platform.   **Fig. 2.** SPECK overview

SPECK offers two interfaces to users. Firstly, it provides a **Job Manage-ment API**, a restful interface abstracting out the details of the flavour of the underlying specific Job Manager API: based on a simple description of a stream processing job to be deployed, this API deploys the job on whatever SPE is targeted for this job. It also supports adaptation: when the description of a job changes, this interface can stop, start and move jobs individually, again hiding the specifics of the underlying SPE. Secondly, on top of the Job Management API, SPECK provides the **Composition Management API**, able to manage a composition of jobs, typically expressed as a DAG of individual jobs. While the traditional granularity of DAGs in stream processing is an *operator*, SPECK han-dles DAGs of jobs, that themselves are internally possibly composed of several operators. The operators composing each job are not considered individually: each job is a black box with an input source and an output destination.

3.2.1   Job Management API

Within SPECK a job is described by three elements: i) the code it runs, ii) the SPE instance it runs on, and iii) its data source and sink. More precisely, a job description will contain the following elements. Firstly, the elements related to the job itself, namely: i) a (unique) **job name**, ii) an **entry class** which indicates the main class of a job's code, and iii) the **job path** which specifies the local path where to find the code of the job (typically a bytecode archive). Secondly, the SPE instance where to deploy the job needs to be specified, through the **SPE address**, represented by the IP address and the port of its Job Manager. Finally, information regarding the input and output data of the Job needs to be given: the two **message brokers** represented by their respective IP addresses and ports, managing its data source and sink respectively, and the two **data topics** identified by their respective names, where to read the incoming stream and where to write the outgoing stream. Given this description of the job, typ-ically encapsulated into a JSON description, the user can issue the following commands:

- POST /jobs - deploys and registers the job described
- GET /jobs - lists all running jobs
- GET /jobs/<job_name> - gets the details of job job_name
- DELETE /jobs/<job_name> - deletes the job job_name

The Job Management API is an SPE-agnostic block to start, get the status of and stop jobs, on top of which, job migration and monitoring can be implemented them. In particular, it paves the way for higher-level management programs such as the pipeline coordinator described in the next section.

3.2.2   Composition Management API

Let us now focus on the second interface provided to the users and which allows them to manage job compositions over geographically-distributed platforms. Let us consider the deployment of a simple composition, to be modified in a second step. Figure 3 illustrates the initial graph: the composition is a pipeline composed of four jobs, each to be deployed over a different site.

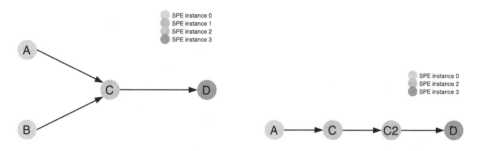

Fig. 3. Initial pipeline   **Fig. 4.** Adapted pipeline

More precisely, jobs A and B read their respective input streams from two different data *topics* managed by two distinct message brokers. They both have their output sent to a third topic managed by the broker of the third site. The third topic is read by Job C, which, on its turn, processes the data and sends the results via a message queue managed by one last message broker on Site 3 where the fourth Flink instance hosts Job D. Listing 1.1 gives the description of this pipeline as to be sent to the Composition API. We observe, for each job composing the pipeline, the elements mentioned in Sect. 3.2.1. As further described in Sect. 3.3, SpecK coordination module parses this file and, relying on the Job Management API, deploys the jobs as specified by the user. Note that, even if a job can read from a single input topic and write to a single output topic, by having multiple jobs writing their output into a common topic, any DAG can be specified.

Let us assume that the user, at some point, wishes to modify the pipeline for that of Fig. 4. It means that i) Job B gets removed, ii) Job C2 appears, as an extra processing step between C and D. Note that, consequently, SPE instance 1, which was hosting Job B is no longer part of the instances supporting the pipeline. A, C and D do not move. Let us assume that the user wants C2 to be grouped with C on SPE instance 2. Job C needs to be modified so as to redirect its output stream to Job C2. These changes are highlighted in Listing 1.2. Job B disappears, while job C2 (in green) is introduced. The information for the outgoing stream of C is modified (in red in Listing 1.1 and in cyan in Listing 1.2).

```
jobs:
  − job_name: A
    spe_address: http://172.16.39.7:8081/
    source_broker: tcp://172.16.39.7:1883
    sink_broker: tcp://172.16.192.18:1883
    source_topic: T−1
    sink_topic: T−C−filter
    entry_class: package.ExampleJob
    job_path: /usr/src/app/jars/test−1.jar

  − job_name: B
    spe_address: http://172.16.48.8:8081/
    source_broker: tcp://172.16.48.8:1883
    sink_broker: tcp://172.16.192.18:1883
    source_topic: T−2
    sink_topic: T−C−filter
    entry_class: package.ExampleJob
    job_path: /usr/src/app/jars/test−2.jar

  − job_name: C
    spe_address: http://172.16.192.18:8081/
    source_broker: tcp://172.16.192.18:1883
    sink_broker: tcp://172.16.177.7:1883
    source_topic: T−C−filter
    sink_topic: T-D-merger
    entry_class: package.ExampleJob
    job_path: /usr/src/app/jars/test−3.jar

  − job_name: D
    spe_address: http://172.16.177.7:8081/
    source_broker: tcp://172.16.177.7:1883
    sink_broker: tcp://172.16.177.7:1883
    source_topic: T−D−merger
    sink_topic: T−D−total
    entry_class: package.ExampleJob
    job_path: /usr/src/app/jars/test−4.jar
```

Listing 1.1. Initial pipeline.

```
jobs:
  − job_name: A
    spe_address: http://172.16.39.7:8081/
    source_broker: tcp://172.16.39.7:1883
    sink_broker: tcp://172.16.192.18:1883
    source_topic: T−1
    sink_topic: T−C−filter
    entry_class: package.ExampleJob
    job_path: /usr/src/app/jars/test−1.jar

  − job_name: C
    spe_address: http://172.16.192.18:8081/
    source_broker: tcp://172.16.192.18:1883
    sink_broker: tcp://172.16.192.18:1883
    source_topic: T−C−filter
    sink_topic: T-C2-filter
    entry_class: package.ExampleJob
    job_path: /usr/src/app/jars/test−3.jar

  - job_name: C2
    spe_address: http://172.16.192.18:8081/
    source_broker: tcp://172.16.192.18:1883
    sink_broker: tcp://172.16.193.22:1883
    source_topic: T-C2-filter
    sink_topic: T-D-merger
    entry_class: package.ExampleJob
    job_path: /usr/src/app/jars/test-4.jar

  − job_name: D
    spe_address: http://172.16.177.20:8081/
    source_broker: tcp://172.16.193.22:1883
    sink_broker: tcp://172.16.193.22:1883
    source_topic: T−D−merger
    sink_topic: T−D−total
    entry_class: package.ExampleJob
    job_path: /usr/src/app/jars/test−4.jar
```

Listing 1.2. Adapted pipeline.

3.3 SPECK Architecture and Internals

Figure 5 depicts the components of the SPECK architecture. It is composed of four interrelated components.

The client typically submits a complete pipeline of jobs by invoking the *composition management API* and passes it the pipeline description file. The composition API relies on the *pipeline coordinator*, a Python-based component which generates, for each job of the pipeline, the HTTP queries to be transmitted to the Job Management API described, as if they were coming directly from the user. The Job Management API is a REST API and was implemented using the Flask Python web framework.[1]

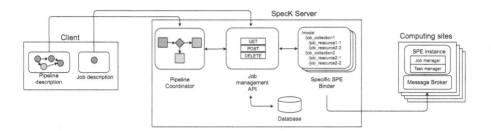

Fig. 5. SPECK software architecture.

The Job Management module is connected to the last two components: a database storing the state of the pipeline currently deployed, and a set of binders to different SPEs and MBs to make SPECK generic. When the Job Management API deploys a job, it records its description into the database, so when the user submits a modified version of the description of a pipeline, SPECK compares the running jobs described in the database with the newly submitted one and triggers the needed removals and introductions of jobs.

The actual deployment of jobs rely on SPE *binders*, each of them being able to communicate with a particular SPE flavour (Flink, Storm, *etc.*). As each SPE has its own API, basic commands such as starting, getting the status or stopping a job can differ depending on the specific SPE in use. SPE binders abstracts out this variability by taking care of formatting queries correctly for each SPE technology. In other words, SPECK also acts as a client sending queries to the Job Managers of available SPE instances on the sites of the infrastructure. Upon receiving the modified version of an existing pipeline, the same interactions take place. The coordinator compares the incoming jobs' arguments with the existing jobs description stored in the internal database and requests the status of jobs running on SPE instances via the Job Management API. It then decides whether jobs should be migrated to other SPE instance or not. Note that, doing so, only the necessary actions are performed. For instance, jobs that do not need to be migrated to another instance allow SPECK to save the cost of re-uploading the job. Again, all these movements are enforced by the Job Management API by communicating with the SPE instances using their specific APIs.

Remind that the sites composing the Fog are typically equipped with their own SPE and message broker instances. While this is not mandatory, using message brokers along with SPE in each instance not only allows to distribute the load of transmitting data between the computing sites, but also avoids unnecessary traffic between instances: the traffic between two jobs placed at the same site is kept local.

---

[1] https://flask.palletsprojects.com.

4 Experiments

The experimental campaign conducted has several objectives. Firstly, the scalability of the solution itself, the time it takes to deploy and modify large pipelines is evaluated in Sect. 4.1. Secondly, in Sect. 4.2, we place ourselves on top of a hybrid edge-cloud platform to show that SPECK can bring the benefits of such platforms into reality. The prototype of SPECK includes specific binders to Apache Flink SPE and to Mosquitto MB. Thus, we assume in the following that the computing sites are equipped with Flink and Mosquitto. This uniformity is desirable as it allows to focus on the validation of the functionalities and evaluating the performance of SPECK without having to estimate the influence of the specificity of SPE/MB technologies. The experiments were conducted over Grid'5000, a large-scale geographically-distributed computing platform bringing together thousands of computing cores grouped in clusters located in 8 different computing sites in France and Luxembourg [2].

4.1 Scalability and Overhead

We first evaluated the ability of SPECK to quickly deploy and modify large pipelines. These experiments were conducted on 6 instances distributed over 3 geographically-distant computing clusters (respectively located in Nantes, Lyon and Luxembourg). Each cluster includes two instances. The measured average network latency between clusters was of 18.6 ms. Each instance run its own Mosquitto MQTT broker and an Apache Flink Job Manager. Each Flink instance managed 24 to 32 Task slots to place the jobs on the workers of the cluster, depending on the number of cores available on the compute nodes, which made, depending on the experiment, a total of between 166 and 192 available task slots on the whole platform including the three distant clusters. We generated simple chains of between one and one hundred jobs. Each job consisted of a trivial SP program receiving an input from the previous job in the chain and passing it to the next one. The jobs composing these pipelines were deployed uniformly at random across the instances.

We measured the time elapsed for the initial deployment, modification, and removal of jobs, given in Fig. 6. For each configuration considered, 10 runs were executed, and the performance displayed was averaged over said 10 runs. We also report min and max over the set of runs whenever relevant. The green curve shows the time spent to initially deploy pipelines of sizes ranging from 1 to 100. The blue curve shows, once 100 jobs have been deployed, the time it takes to modify a number of jobs ranging from 1 to 100. Finally, the red curve shows the time taken to delete a variable number of jobs.

The main takeaways from this first experiment are the following: i) The modification of a large number of jobs is faster than its deployment: most of the time, it is better to modify the pipeline than to stop and restart it. ii) The time it takes to deploy, modify, delete jobs is linear in the number of jobs, showing that, at least up to a significant number of jobs, the system does not exhibit any scalability issue.

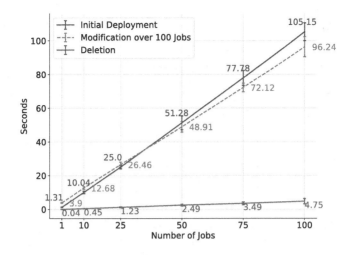

Fig. 6. Multiple deployment measurements

SPECK depends on a restful API. One common issue with restful services is that a large number of client requests may slow down (or even lead to the failure of) the underpinning server; yet SPECK does not create requests unless the user submits a new pipeline. In other words, SPECK does not generate any traffic unless the user emits requests, and the traffic generated is no more no less the traffic needed to deploy jobs. In other words, SPECK does not bring any measurable overhead in terms of traffic. The only measurable overhead is the disk space needed by SPECK to store the state of the deployed pipeline: As mentioned in Sect. 3.3, a persistent key-value store stores the state of the currently deployed jobs. The store is written on disk. Throughout all experiments the space used on disk remains very low. As an example, we mesured that a 1000-job pipelines only requires 754 KB.

4.2   Edge-to-Cloud Deployment

In order to validate the usage of the SPEC API in more realistic settings, we developed a Fog-targeted road-traffic monitoring application, consisting of 4 jobs, some of the jobs being duplicated over geographically distributed sites, making a total of 17 single-operator Flink Jobs. The dataset used included real-world data from 245,369 connected vehicles moving across Italy, and artificially expanded so as to increase the scale of the deployment and the velocity of the streams. This expansion does not means that artificial data were added, but that data were played at a higher rate than in the original dataset. The data are basically a list of cars passing by at specific points at specific times. Each time a car is detected at a sensor point, it is added in the stream.

The deployed pipeline is illustrated in Fig. 7. It is composed of four jobs, which aims at producing both timely statistics about the local road traffic and long term statistics at the global scale. The first type of statistics is supposed to

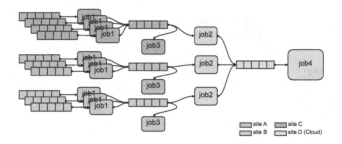

Fig. 7. Deployment of the application over multiple sites.

be generated locally, on each edge where data is ingested. The second type is for storage and later reuse and is thus typically computed in the Cloud. Each site includes its own Flink SPE and Mosquitto MQTT broker. Figure 7 illustrates its deployment over 3 edge sites and 1 cloud site. Let us review the four jobs: `Job 1` preprocesses the data received locally by filtering and cleaning them before they are injected into the rest of the pipeline. It removes erroneous data items or badly formatted ones. This cleaning is a stateless operation, not very time-consuming or compute-intensive and can typically be performed locally, close to where the data are *sensed*. As filtering can be done in parallel on each data source, we assume that one instance of Job 1 is deployed for each stream of data. `Job 2` is a forwarder: it collects data produced by Job 1 instances and sends them to the entry topic of Job 4 which will merge all data coming from the different sites. `Job 3` performs windowed statistics of data received locally on one site. It produces timely statistics about the recent - near real-time - local traffic. These statistics generation cannot be parallelized due to their stateful nature. In other words, there is a single instance of this job per site. `Job 4` is a merging operator which establishes global statistics over the data sent by the different sites, so later global post-processing can be conducted.

The benefits of such a deployment allowed by SPECK are twofold. By placing Job 1 at the edge, fewer data are sent across the network to Job 4, and faster data processing and monitoring rate is obtained when Job 3 runs closer to the source. To prove this, we focused on the performance of Job 3. We deployed two scenarios, both deployed using SPECK. In the *remote scenario*, Job 3 does not run on the same site where the data are generated. In the *local scenario*, Job 3 is placed on the same site where the data are generated. Then we gradually increased the data generation rate of the data we gathered from the real-world and compared the outcomes. Figure 8 shows the results. Having an ingestion rate of one message produced every 2ms already allows this benefit: as shown by Fig. 8(b), the local count of the car increases slower when done in the Cloud. The difference increases when the ingestion rate is 1 msg/ms (see Fig. 8(c)).

We then experimented with two global deployments, referred to as the *Fog* and the *Cloud* scenarios, respectively. In the **Fog scenario**, all 4 jobs were placed across A, B, C, D sites as shown in Fig. 7. Colors on the figure denotes the site where each job and message queues are located. In the **Cloud scenario** (Fig. 9),

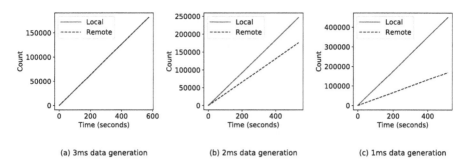

(a) 3ms data generation   (b) 2ms data generation   (c) 1ms data generation

Fig. 8. Data processing rate sample.

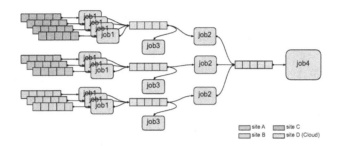

Fig. 9. Deployment of the application on a single site.

all 4 jobs are placed on site D, meaning the regionally generated data transit through the network to be directly processed on site D.

Figure 10 illustrates the output rate of each Job of the pipeline obtained in both deployment scenarios shown in Fig. 7 and Fig. 9. The X-axis gives the data input rate at each site. The Y-axis gives the benefit ratio of using the Fog scenario compared to the Cloud in terms of processing speed for Job 3 and 4, which provides local and global statistics, respectively. Here, processing speed is to be understood as the time taken to process a fixed amount of messages. Each deployment scenario was conducted for 15 min to measure the difference between the data processing rate of Fog and Cloud. The performance was averaged over 5 runs. The differential output rate can be expressed as $D = (100/F) * (F - C)$ where F is the amount of data processed in Fog scenario and C is the amount of data processed in Cloud scenario over these 15 min.

When a curve is above 0, data processing in Fog is quicker for this job. When a curve is below 0, it means the Cloud is quicker. Initially, when the data ingestion rate is low, the Fog deployment does not provide faster data processing rate compared to the Cloud for the final job (Job 4). This can be explained as in the Fog scenario, data need to traverse multiple MQTT brokers, each adding latency to the global data transmission from Edge to Cloud. Yet on the other hand, when we increased the ingestion rate up to 1 message sent per millisecond, data processing becomes closer on both scenarios due to the MQTT

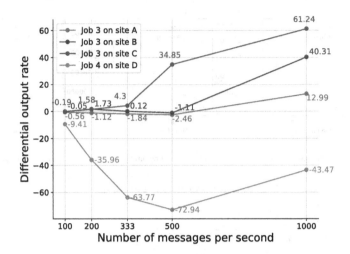

Fig. 10. Differential output rate.

broker message buffering. Also, we observed that the fog scenario compared to cloud gave better results for Job 3 which provides the local statistics, showing that multiple-site Job deployments benefit from SPECK.

5   Conclusion

While the Fog is increasingly cited as a key enabler for a new generation of latency-sensitive applications, reference architectures and concrete tools to fully benefit from it are still missing. In this work, we tackle the problem of how to effectively manage stream processing over a geographically distributed compute infrastructure. Our approach, SPECK is based on the idea of *composing* SPE instances, each one running their SPE of choice and managing local computing resources. By adding this further layer of coordination, we are able to effectively leverage locally-available resources, while providing application developers with an easy set of primitives to deal with, so as to facilitate the cumbersome process of deploying an SP pipeline over a large scale platform. Experiments with the SPECK prototype showed that it is able to effectively handle complex stream computations, coordinating the usage of locally-available resources over a geographically-distributed infrastructure with a limited overhead.

Future work will include enhancements in the programming language used to define computations and adding support for stateful operators, requiring a mechanism for managing state migrations. Also, we are moving to the performance and reliability aspects of SPECK. In particular, we are developing monitoring tools to automate migrations of jobs in function of the platform's conditions and users' performance requirements. Finally, we will extend the current SPECK implementation so it can support a larger set of SPE and message brokers.

References

1. Apache edgent. https://edgent.incubator.apache.org/
2. Grid'5000. https://www.grid5000.fr
3. Antonini, M., Vecchio, M., Antonelli, F.: Fog computing architectures: a reference for practitioners. CoRR abs/1909.01020 (2019). http://arxiv.org/abs/1909.01020
4. de Assunção, M.D., Veith, A.D.S., Buyya, R.: Distributed data stream processing and edge computing: a survey on resource elasticity and future directions. J. Netw. Comput. Appl. **103**, 1–17 (2018)
5. Balouek-Thomert, D., Renart, E.G., Zamani, A.R., Simonet, A., Parashar, M.: Towards a computing continuum: enabling edge-to-cloud integration for data-driven workflows. Int. J. High Perform. Comput. Appl. **33**(6), 1159–1174 (2019)
6. Beckman, P., et al.: Harnessing the computing continuum for programming our world, chap. 7, pp. 215–230. Wiley (2020)
7. Carbone, P., Katsifodimos, A., Ewen, S., Markl, V., Haridi, S., Tzoumas, K.: Apache flink: stream and batch processing in a single engine. Bull. IEEE Comput. Soc. Tech. Commit. Data Eng. **36**(4) (2015)
8. Cardellini, V., Grassi, V., Lo Presti, F., Nardelli, M.: Distributed QoS-aware scheduling in storm. In: Proceedings of the 9th ACM International Conference on Distributed Event-Based Systems, pp. 344–347 (2015)
9. Castro Fernandez, R., Migliavacca, M., Kalyvianaki, E., Pietzuch, P.: Integrating scale out and fault tolerance in stream processing using operator state management. In: ACM SIGMOD 2013, pp. 725–736 (2013)
10. Cheng, B., Papageorgiou, A., Bauer, M.: Geelytics: enabling on-demand edge analytics over scoped data sources. In: 2016 IEEE International Congress on Big Data (BigData Congress), pp. 101–108 (2016)
11. Claudel, B., Huard, G., Richard, O.: TakTuk, adaptive deployment of remote executions. In: Kranzlmüller, D., Bode, A., Hegering, H., Casanova, H., Gerndt, M. (eds.) Proceedings of the 18th ACM International Symposium on High Performance Distributed Computing, HPDC 2009, Garching, Germany, 11–13 June 2009, pp. 91–100. ACM (2009). https://doi.org/10.1145/1551609.1551629
12. Fu, X., Ghaffar, T., Davis, J.C., Lee, D.: Edgewise: a better stream processing engine for the edge. In: 2019 USENIX Annual Technical Conference (USENIX ATC 19), pp. 929–946. USENIX Association, Renton, July 2019
13. Gedik, B., Schneider, S., Hirzel, M., Wu, K.L.: Elastic scaling for data stream processing. IEEE Trans. Parallel Distrib. Syst. **25**(6), 1447–1463 (2013)
14. Gibert Renart, E., Da Silva Veith, A., Balouek-Thomert, D., De Assunção, M.D., Lefèvre, L., Parashar, M.: Distributed operator placement for IoT data analytics across edge and cloud resources. In: 2019 19th IEEE/ACM International Symposium on Cluster, Cloud and Grid Computing (CCGRID), pp. 459–468 (2019)
15. Gulisano, V., Jiménez-Peris, R., Patiño-Martínez, M., Soriente, C., Valduriez, P.: StreamCloud: an elastic and scalable data streaming system. IEEE Trans. Parallel Distrib. Syst. **23**(12), 2351–2365 (2012)
16. Lakshmanan, G.T., Li, Y., Strom, R.: Placement strategies for internet-scale data stream systems. IEEE Internet Comput. **12**(6), 50–60 (2008)
17. Light, R.A.: Mosquitto: server and client implementation of the MQTT protocol. J. Open Sour. Softw. **2**(13), 265 (2017)
18. Liu, F., Tang, G., Li, Y., Cai, Z., Zhang, X., Zhou, T.: A survey on edge computing systems and tools. Proc. IEEE **107**(8), 1537–1562 (2019)

19. Mahmud, R., Kotagiri, R., Buyya, R.: Fog computing: a taxonomy, survey and future directions. In: Di Martino, B., Li, K.C., Yang, L., Esposito, A. (eds.) Internet of Everything, pp. 103–130. Springer, Singapore (2018). https://doi.org/10.1007/978-981-10-5861-5_5
20. Milojicic, D.: The edge-to-cloud continuum. Computer **53**(11), 16–25 (2020)
21. Nicolae, B., Bresnahan, J., Keahey, K., Antoniu, G.: Going back and forth: efficient multideployment and multisnapshotting on clouds. In: Proceedings of the 20th International Symposium on High Performance Distributed Computing (HPDC), pp. 147–158 (2011)
22. O'Keeffe, D., Salonidis, T., Pietzuch, P.: Frontier: resilient edge processing for the internet of things. Proc. VLDB Endow. **11**(10), 1178–1191 (2018)
23. Peng, B., Hosseini, M., Hong, Z., Farivar, R., Campbell, R.: R-storm: resource-aware scheduling in storm. In: Proceedings of the 16th Annual Middleware Conference, Middleware 2015, pp. 149–161 (2015)
24. Pisani, F., Brunetta, J.R., Martins Do Rosario, V., Borin, E.: Beyond the fog: bringing cross-platform code execution to constrained IoT devices. In: 2017 29th International Symposium on Computer Architecture and High Performance Computing (SBAC-PAD), pp. 17–24 (2017)
25. Prosperi, L., Costan, A., Silva, P., Antoniu, G.: Planner: cost-efficient execution plans placement for uniform stream analytics on edge and cloud. In: 2018 IEEE/ACM Workflows in Support of Large-Scale Science (WORKS), pp. 42–51 (2018)
26. Rosendo, D., Silva, P., Simonin, M., Costan, A., Antoniu, G.: E2Clab: exploring the computing continuum through repeatable, replicable and reproducible edge-to-cloud experiments. In: Cluster 2020 - IEEE International Conference on Cluster Computing, Kobe, Japan, pp. 1–11, September 2020
27. Silva, P., Costan, A., Antoniu, G.: Investigating edge vs. cloud computing trade-offs for stream processing. In: 2019 IEEE International Conference on Big Data (Big Data), pp. 469–474 (2019)
28. Silva, P., Costan, A., Antoniu, G.: Towards a methodology for benchmarking edge processing frameworks. In: 2019 IEEE International Parallel and Distributed Processing Symposium Workshops (IPDPSW), pp. 904–907 (2019)
29. da Silva Veith, A., de Assunção, M.D., Lefèvre, L.: Latency-aware placement of data stream analytics on edge computing. In: Pahl, C., Vukovic, M., Yin, J., Yu, Q. (eds.) ICSOC 2018. LNCS, vol. 11236, pp. 215–229. Springer, Cham (2018). https://doi.org/10.1007/978-3-030-03596-9_14
30. Snyder, B., Bosanac, D., Davies, R.: Introduction to apache ActiveMQ. Active MQ in action, pp. 6–16 (2017)
31. Thein, K.M.M.: Apache kafka: next generation distributed messaging system. Int. J. Sci. Eng. Technol. Res. **3**(47), 9478–9483 (2014)
32. Toshniwal, A., et al.: Storm@twitter. In: Proceedings of the 2014 ACM SIGMOD International Conference on Management of Data, SIGMOD 2014, pp. 147–156. Association for Computing Machinery, New York (2014). https://doi.org/10.1145/2588555.2595641
33. Zaharia, M., Das, T., Li, H., Hunter, T., Shenker, S., Stoica, I.: Discretized streams: fault-tolerant streaming computation at scale. In: 24th ACM SIGOPS Symposium on Operating Systems Principles (SOSP 2013), Farmington, USA, pp. 423–438, November 2013

Fault Tolerance and Big Data

ASPAS: As Secure as Possible Available Systems

Houssam Yactine[1]([⊠]), Ali Shoker[2], and Georges Younes[1]

[1] HASLab, INESC TEC, University of Minho, Braga, Portugal
{houssam.a.yactin,georges.r.younes}@inesctec.pt
[2] VORTEX Colab, Porto, Portugal
ali.shoker@vortex-colab.com

Abstract. Available-Partition-tolerant (AP) geo-replicated systems trade consistency for availability. They allow replicas to serve clients' requests without prior synchronization. Potential conflicts due to concurrent operations can then be resolved using a conflict resolution mechanism if operations are commutative and execution is deterministic. However, a Byzantine replica can diverge from deterministic execution of operations and break convergence. In this paper, we introduce ASPAS: As Secure as Possible highly Available System that is a Byzantine resilient AP system. ASPAS follows an optimistic approach to maintain a single round-trip response time. It then allows the detection of Byzantine replicas in the background, i.e., off the critical path of clients requests. Our empirical evaluation of ASPAS in a geo-replicated setting shows that its latency in the normal case is close to that of an AP system, and one order of magnitude better than classical BFT protocols that provide stronger (total ordering) guarantees, unnecessary in AP systems.

Keywords: Availability · Integrity · Consistency · CRDT · BFT

1 Introduction

In the context of the CAP theorem [14], an Available-Partition-tolerant (AP) geo-replicated system trades consistency for availability. The design follows *optimistic replication* with a relaxed consistency model [18,22,27] where a replica immediately replies to the client without prior synchronization with other replicas. The essence is to reduce the response delay to a single round-trip between a replica and a client. This is desired in latency-sensitive applications where a soft (stale) state is accepted. Nevertheless, concurrent updates can lead to inconsistency that must be resolved (in the background).

This paradigm is recently getting attention with the advent of conflict resolution mechanisms as Last-Writer-Wins, Cloud Types, and Conflict-free Replicated DataTypes (CRDTs) [2,5,25]. Such conflict resolution mechanisms ensure *Strong Eventual Consistency (SEC)* [24] that guarantees convergence across system replicas if operations are designed to be commutative and only if faults are

Published by Springer Nature Switzerland AG 2021
M. Matos and F. Greve (Eds.): DAIS 2021, LNCS 12718, pp. 57–73, 2021.
https://doi.org/10.1007/978-3-030-78198-9_4

benign (see Definition 1 in Sect. 3.1 for details). The idea is to relax the replica's state from being totally ordered log to a partially ordered log (POLog) [2]. Being commutative, executing operations in the POLog will lead to equivalent states if replicas are deterministic. Since it is impractical to synchronize or "pause" an AP system to do this integrity check, it is acceptable for concurrent clients at distinct replicas to (temporarily) observe different states. This makes it hard to differentiate a deterministic execution of concurrent operations in a partial order from a non-deterministic execution caused by a Byzantine (a.k.a., arbitrary or malicious) [20] replica. This can lead to permanent system divergence.

An intuitive option to address the Byzantine problem is to assess the feasibility of classical BFT protocols [1,8,10,16,29] to an AP system. This approach was followed in OBFT [9] where the authors deferred the synchronization (consensus) of replicas, executing concurrent operations, to epochs where the entire system is "paused". A similar approach was followed in Zeno [26] that reduced the quorum size under network partitions, but imposed total ordering within a partition before replying to clients. Unfortunately, these approaches are not preferred in AP systems where the expected latency is a single round-trip.

In this paper, we introduce a novel As Secure as Possible AP System (ASPAS) that guarantees Strong Convergence (of SEC) and provides Byzantine security without compromising availability. As shown in Fig. 1, ASPAS runs a frontend layer composed of loosely connected application servers (appservers) that can serve clients' requests without prior synchronization. The replica of an appserver is a datatype following the SEC model, e.g., a CRDT, in order to ensure convergence despite concurrent operations. A correct client connects to a single associated appserver. After executing the client's operation locally, the appserver propagates the request to other appservers (in the background) using a Reliable Causal Broadcast [3,4,15] (RCB). Delivered operations via the RCB are then executed in a deterministic way by correct appservers. In the backend, and to detect Byzantine appservers, correct appservers asynchronously forward their operations to a BFT cluster (see Fig. 1). This process is decoupled from the client-appserver communication to maintain the desired latency in AP applications, i.e., a single round-trip delay. The BFT cluster is responsible for extracting, out of the different appserver POLogs, a log of *stable* operations: non-concurrent operations that are already delivered and executed by all appservers. The BFT cluster then generates a log "certificate" that ensures the log integrity up to a common state version across appservers. The BFT cluster sends the certificate to correct appservers that piggy-back it to clients asserting the integrity of data up to that state version.

An alternative possible design to the three-tiered design of ASPAS (in Fig. 1) is a two-layered design using Secure RCB [7,15,21]. Such RCB protocols are quorum-based and, thus, require synchronization before replying to clients which increases the latency. Therefore, the prospective design ends up having another layer (but running on the same appservers this time) for arbitration, i.e., another BFT protocol to compare stable partially ordered log versions up to some offset. This coupling of delivery and arbitration on the same appserver leads to several

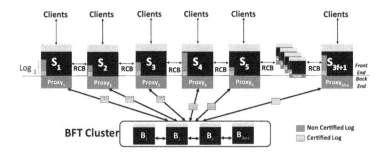

Fig. 1. ASPAS architecture.

drawbacks, among them: (1) Classical BFT protocols scale linearly $O(N)$ with the number of appservers N in the system. It is more reasonable to decouple the execution layer from the arbitration layer as in ASPAS where the arbitration protocol runs on a smaller set of $n \ll N$ BFT servers. (2) Imposing high inter-replica delays (e.g., up to 100ms in geo-scalable settings) on the BFT protocol in the arbitration layer. This inter-replica overhead can be mitigated significantly if the BFT protocol runs in a well connected cluster as we do in ASPAS. (3) Imposing more memory and computational overhead on appservers due to the heavy-weight cryptographic and messaging work in BFT protocols. ASPAS offloads this overhead to the BFT cluster, and thus keeps appservers dedicated to serving clients' requests.

The three-tier design of ASPAS allows different clients to choose their level of security based on their desired freshness and availability-security tradeoff (hence the name "As Secure As Possible"). It can provide high security as close as classical BFT protocols, or high availability as close as AP systems, and a wide spectrum of options in between. However, this entails two main challenges we solve in ASPAS. The first is generating a consistent certificate despite the execution of operations in different orders on different appservers (a native pattern in AP systems). The second is to prevent the appserver from sending certificates or use different logs for different clients. This is important since client's requests in AP systems are handled by only one appserver (without consensus).

ASPAS can be used in any geo-replicated application that adopts SEC [24] and tolerates a window of unconfirmed operations. In fact, SEC-based applications trade consistency (i.e., a correctness property) for availability in the fault-recovery model. Following the same analogy, we argue that these applications also favor availability over Byzantine integrity (i.e., a correctness property) provided that the system state eventually converges. In addition, an end-user client is guaranteed to be notified of a Byzantine fault and get a correct state within a predefined tolerance window of operations. Note that this is commonly accepted in several SEC-based applications, e.g., social networks functionalities like: number of Likes, number of comments, list of comments, recommended media, number of Ads, shopping carts, real time collaborative editing, etc., as long as the system eventually converges to a correct state that the client can observe. Non end-user stateful applications can also roll-back recent changes if required. This is very common in AP-based applications where the client plays the role of a cache or *Edge* computing node that is used as backend to end-user applications. This is driven by Edge systems in open volunteer networks like Guifi.net monitoring that used to monitor the network state, and Content Delivery Networks where a cache is used to boost the reply to end-user browsers.

We implemented ASPAS using BFT-SMaRt [1] as a backend BFT Cluster due to its well tested Java implementation (but any classical BFT protocol can be used). We conducted an empirical evaluation using YCSB benchmark workloads [11] in geo-replicated setting. We compared ASPAS with OBFT [9] as a state of the art protocol of the same SEC-based class, and with baseline configurations: AP system alone, and BFT protocol alone. The results show that the normal case latency of ASPAS is close to classical AP systems, and one order of magnitude lower than classical BFT protocols in the geo-replicated settings.

The rest of the paper is organized as follows. We start with presenting the most related works in Sect. 2. We then present the problem definition and ASPAS as a proposed solution in Sect. 3. Next, we present the empirical evaluation in Sect. 4, and we conclude in Sect. 5.

2   Related Work

Byzantine Fault Tolerant (BFT) protocols often follow quorum-based State Machine Replication (SMR) [1,8,10,16,23,29] to ensure total ordering despite the existence of a fraction f (out of $2f + 1$ or more) Byzantine replicas. These protocols, including the more scalable ones in the Blockchain realm [17,29], are known of their high latency due to the cost of consensus. This encouraged the introduction of more relaxed agreement protocols whose latency is low enough to be used in AP systems. To provide Byzantine tolerance under partitions, Zeno [26] lets clients of different partitions to miss the updates of replicas under network partitions until it heals. However, Zeno exhibits a consensus overhead by imposing total ordering of updates within the same partition before replying to clients. On the contrary, ASPAS maintains a single round-trip latency as it makes use of CRDTs to resolve conflicts and delegates the (costly) consensus entirely to the background. Similarly, in the more practical work [13] for hardening Cassandra against Byzantine failures, a Write request is confirmed only after obtaining signed responses from a quorum of nodes—in the critical path of clients' requests. In ASPAS, the client never blocks on Writes; it applies them locally and delegates the integrity checking to a background process. Furthermore, Byzantine reliable causal broadcast (BRCB) protocols such as [3,4,15,21] are used to propagate updates to different replicas despite the presence of Byzantine replicas. Such protocols do not guarantee SEC by default, because a Byzantine replica can execute local operations incorrectly to impede convergence. Including execution will again require a costly quorum-based protocol.

The most related work to ours is OBFT [9], which is an AP system that tries to ensure SEC under Byzantine faults. Since concurrent updates on different replicas may lead to conflicts, OBFT periodically "pauses" client's requests until it achieves convergence. Although it matches the different message logs and uses CRDTs to ease the merging, as we do in ASPAS, this is done in a blocking way which is unacceptable in AP applications. ASPAS avoids fiddling with the client-appserver message exchange to maintain low latency, and delegates the integrity checking to a backend BFT cluster off the critical path of clients requests.

3   ASPAS Protocol

3.1   Problem

Modern geo-replicated AP systems trade consistency for availability. They support concurrent Write/Read operations, which allows client applications to observe—as fast as possible—different states at different replicas. Despite this, the entire system should not be broken, by diverging permanently, and thus it follows the Strong Eventual Consistency (SEC) [24] model to eventually ensure convergence.

Definition 1 (Strong eventual consistency (SEC)). *An object is* Strongly Eventually Consistent *if the following properties are satisfied:*

- *Eventual delivery: An update delivered at some correct replica is eventually delivered to all correct replicas:* $\forall i, j : f \in c_i$ *then* $\Diamond f \in c_j$
- *Termination: All method f executions terminate.*
- *Strong Convergence: Correct replicas that have delivered the same updates, even in different orders, have equivalent state:* $\forall i, j : c_i = c_j$ *then* $s_i \equiv s_j$.

As depicted in Definition 1, the Strong Convergence (third) property of SEC extends the Eventual Consistency [22,27] model by stating that the execution of the same set of operations in different partially ordered logs should lead to an equivalent state. However, this (equation $c_i = c_j$ then $s_i \equiv s_j$) holds true only if the execution is deterministic, which cannot be guaranteed if the executing replica is Byzantine. Therefore, the presence of a single Byzantine replica can render the entire system convergence impossible.

As a simple example in a social network application, different clients on different replicas may *forever* view different lists of comments for the same post, even if no actions affect that post any more. Notice that this is even harder to detect when the AP system is in action due to Eventual Consistency and the lack of consensus between replicas.

3.2   System and Fault Models

We address ASPAS, a three-tier system model (sketched in Fig. 1) composed of frontend and backend. The frontend follows the geo-replicated AP system model in which $3f + 1$ appservers are geographically located and fully replicated where at most f appservers are assumed to be Byzantine. Replicated data is assumed to

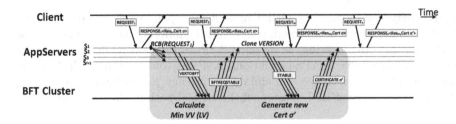

Fig. 2. Messages exchange pattern showing normal update operation and the certification steps between appservers and BFT cluster in background .

satisfy SEC [24], e.g., CRDTs [2,25]. CRDTs are backed by partially ordered logs defined using appservers' Version Clocks [19]. In ASPAS, every client has connections to all appservers, but issues its requests to a single appserver, likely the closest one. In the backend, appservers propagate the received operations to each other using a Reliable Causal Broadcast (RCB) [3]. Appservers also push their requests to a BFT cluster that runs a classical BFT SMR protocol, e.g., [1,8]. The cluster is composed of $3b+1$ BFT replicas (bftservers), where at most $b << f$ of them are assumed to be Byzantine. The network may (not infinitely) fail to deliver, corrupt, delay, or reorder messages. Byzantine appservers, replicas, and clients may either behave arbitrarily, i.e., in a different way to their designed purposes, or just crash and recover (benign faults). A strong adversary coordinates Byzantine replicas or appservers to compromise the replicated service and thus bring the appservers to inconsistent states. However, we assume that the adversary cannot break cryptographic techniques like: collision-resistant hashes, encryption, and signatures. We also assume all nodes to have unique identities and cryptographic keys distributed through a trusted mechanism.

3.3   An Overview of ASPAS

ASPAS is composed of a frontend and backend. The frontend runs a loosely coupled geo-replicated AP service over dozens of appservers, to which clients issue their requests. The backend runs a smaller black-box BFT cluster, to which appservers send their operation logs to assert their consistency up to a certain version. To thwart blocking and delays in the AP service, these two layers are completely decoupled and operate concurrently; clients only interact with appservers, i.e., they are agnostic of the BFT cluster.

As depicted in Fig. 2, ASPAS runs two concurrent phases: *Normal operation* and *Certification* (presented next in detail). The former represents the normal operation of an AP system: a client sends its requests to a single associated appserver at a time (to avoid Byzantine clients issuing different requests to different appservers). The appserver replies to the client immediately, and then propagates the operations to its counterpart appservers. The latter executes (or merge) these operations locally. Using CRDTs techniques, convergence is guaranteed as long as appservers are not Byzantine. To guard against Byzantine

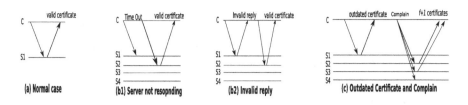

Fig. 3. Different messaging patterns of ASPAS.

appservers (that can cause divergence), correct appservers piggyback a "certificate": a signed message issued by the BFT cluster in the certification phase to assert a consistent appserver state up to a certain version. In the certification phase, appservers periodically send their (partially-ordered) logs to the BFT cluster. The latter issues a certificate to correct appserver whose logs are matching to a certain (incremental) state version. Choosing the version and extracting the corresponding logs are explained in the mechanisms: **Stable versions** and **Log extraction** in the Sect. 3.6.

In the case of an invalid certificate, i.e., unauthentic, non-matching or outdated, the client launches a Complaining process (see the **Complaining** mechanism in Sect. 3.6) to notify about possible Byzantine appserver and switch to another associated one. An outdated certificate is defined per client via a Byzantine tolerance threshold (τ): the maximum number of unconfirmed operations the client can tolerate, until a new certificate arrives. On the other hand, if the certificate is valid but demonstrates a prior inconsistent state observed by clients (which occurs due to a Byzantine appserver or due to concurrency in AP systems), the latter can make different decisions, e.g., notify users or roll-back. This is out of the scope of our work.

3.4 Normal Operation Phase

At the beginning, a client gets assigned an associated appserver s. It establishes a session with s by sending its desired tolerance threshold τ. The appserver stores τ and broadcasts it with the client unique ID to all other appservers. When the client c_i invokes a new operation o, it sends a REQUEST($\langle$lastReq$\rangle^{\alpha}_{c_i}, s$) message to s; where lastReq contains the last sequence number of client's requests, the client identifier c_i and the operation o. $\langle\rangle^{\alpha}_{c_i}$ is the encrypted security token (e.g. digital signature and hash digest) signed with the private key α of c_i. Upon receipt of a valid client REQUEST, s processes the new operation, assigns it a new version vector VV, updates its vector clock, and sends RESPONSE($\langle$LastRes[n]$,\sigma'\rangle^{\alpha}_{s_j}, c_i$) to the client; where LastRes[n] is the corresponding result with a sequence number n and σ' is the appserver's last *certificate*. When the client receives RESPONSE from the associated appserver, it checks its validity (i.e., authenticity, integrity, and sequence nb). Otherwise, as shown in the Figs. 3.b1 and 3.b2, if the client associated a slow appserver or received a number of invalid messages, it *complains* and switches to another appserver (see the **Complaining** mechanism in Sect. 3.6).

In the case of an update operation, the appserver signs and broadcasts the client's REQUEST, via the RCB, to the other appservers. Once receiving REQUEST, other appservers process it and update their vectors clocks. The execution of a new operations triggers the certification phase (see next Sect. 3.5).

3.5 Certification Phase

This phase aims at generating consistent certificate versions across appservers. It occurs in parallel with the Normal phase to avoid any delays in the critical path of clients' requests. As sketched in Fig. 2, for every executed REQUEST, an appserver sends a VERTOBFT(m,$\langle\sigma\rangle_{s_j}^{\alpha}$,$B$)) message to the BFT cluster. The BFT cluster, waits for specific TimeOut epochs trying to collect VERTOBFT messages, then computes a common *stable last version* (LV) as described below. Note that this delay is acceptable being not in the critical path of client's requests. If the LV is equal to a previous LV, the BFT cluster ignores it and repeats the process by waiting for new VERTOBFT messages. Otherwise, the BFT cluster sends a BFTREQSTABLE($\langle$LV$\rangle_B^{\alpha}$,S) to all the appservers asking them for a corresponding state to the LV. Since a convergent state requires all the logs of appservers in an AP systems, the presence of a single Byzantine appserver can affect liveness— but not correctness. However, liveness only affects the more conservative clients, i.e., whose τ is very small due to freshness requirements. These clients may be blocked waiting for a new certificate, while the other clients operate normally.

Once an appserver receives a request BFTREQSTABLE from the BFT cluster, it may already have the exact state version stored. This occurs when LV matched a previous operation VV it executed. If not, the appserver generates such a state using the *Log extraction* mechanism, described below. Afterwards, the appserver sends the generated state in a STABLE($\langle\sigma\rangle_{s_j}^{\alpha}$,$B$)) message to the BFT cluster, asking for a new certificate that represents a new stable system snapshot. When the BFT cluster receives at least $f + 1$ valid matching states from the appservers via messages of type STABLE, within a defined TimeOut, it generates a new certificate that contains signed hash digests of the appservers (having matching STABLE), and multicasts it as a CERTIFICATE($\langle\sigma'$,STABLE$\rangle_B^{\alpha}$,$CorrectS$) message to these correct appservers only. Late correct appservers can still ask for this certificate version within a predefined timeout. This has no impact on correctness as the late appserver can receive a newer certificate that covers the current operations.

Finally, once a new certificate σ' is received, an appserver checks its validity, updates its old certificate σ with a new one σ' if valid, and starts including it in the future replies to clients.

3.6 ASPAS Mechanisms

Stable Versions. This mechanism is used by the BFT cluster proxy process to agree on a specific stable version for which a new certificate will be generated. This is required in AP systems since appservers run at different speeds. As operations are applied in different (partial) orders on different replicas, it is necessary to compute a common *stable last version* (LV) according to the received VERTOBFT from at least $2f + 1$ appservers. LV guarantees that all operations in the causal past of this version are executed. In particular, the BFT cluster proxy process tries to generate LV in a periodic fashion. The technique is fairly simple: it tries to match the recent version vectors (of operations) received from appservers and then calculates the minVV by computing the minimum of every index apart (in vector clock, every index corresponds to an appserver's index [18]), a condition that the new computed minVV should be greater than the last old one. Since the minVV is less than or equal all VVs, it means that all corresponding appservers are in a future state of minVV. Therefore, they will be able to generate a corresponding state. We have constrained the new calculated minVV (or what we called LV) to be strictly greater than the last previous one to avoid attacks from Byzantine appserver. The latter may try to send old versions (i.e., small VV) to prohibit generating new certificates. In addition, very high versions sent by Byzantine appservers will be ignored by the minVV function.

Log Extraction. Appservers need a way to extract a STABLE state corresponding to the last stable version LV in BFTREQSTABLE, requested by the BFT server proxy. This extraction is needed as an appserver may have never passed through this exact state, although it is included in the final one (a normal behavior in commutative data types). To this end, we used Pure CRDTs [2] that retain a partial ordered log (POLog) of operations. This simplifies the generation of a materialized state using the operations of the POLog, a process we call *Cloning*. The idea is to "clone" the state of the current data type by simply extracting all operations in a POLog having timestamps t' such that $t' \leq t$ (i.e., causally related as per the Lamport's happens-before relation [19]). Any re-execution of this POLog extract will result with the same state since concurrent operations commute. Therefore, appservers can re-execute these operations with $VV \leq LV$ to result a STABLE state that must be equal on all correct appservers. Due to lack of space, we refer the reader to Pure CRDTs [2] for more information if desired.

Complaining. Complaining is the mechanism through which a client can "complain" about a potential Byzantine appserver behavior. A client can complain in two cases. The first case is upon receiving a message that holds an invalid or outdated certificate, as shown in Fig. 3.c. In this case the client sends a COMPLAIN($\langle$N$_{Complain}$,PROOF$\rangle_{c_i}^\alpha$,$S-s$) message to all appservers excluding its associated one. The COMPLAIN includes the complain's sequence number N$_{Complain}$ and a PROOF:=($\langle\langle\tau$,seqNb$_i$,σ,$\sigma'\rangle_s^\alpha\rangle_{c_i}^\alpha$) of complain correctness. The PROOF contains the agreed client's configurable tolerance threshold τ signed by the associated appserver, the appserver reply's sequence number seqNb$_i$, the old and new certificate digests σ and σ'. A correct appserver can verify the correctness of the COMPLAIN by checking if seqNb$_i > \tau$ and $\sigma = \sigma'$. This proof verification is necessary to avoid Byzantine clients from using fake complaints as a DOS attack to blacklist correct appservers. Furthermore, it is used as an evidence to detect/block Byzantine clients with high threat rate. As a result of verification, the correct appservers can detect and blacklist a Byzantine appserver, and reply to the client with a BLACKLIST($in=\langle bList,\sigma\rangle_{s_j}^\alpha$) message. When a client receives $f+1$ matching and valid BLACKLIST messages as a response to its COMPLAIN request, it updates its blacklist accordingly and switches to a new appserver. The client also rollbacks its state to the last correct certificate (if necessary) and resumes sending REQUEST to the new associated appserver in the normal case. The second case of COMPLAIN occurs when the client collects $f + 1$ mismatching replies INSPECTREPLY($in=\langle\sigma\rangle^{\alpha}_{s_r}$) from different $f + 1$ correct appservers according to its INSPECTION. To avoid fake COMPLAIN requested by a Byzantine client, the latter should piggyback the INSPECTION results as a proof of truth PROOF:=($\langle\langle rndState,\sigma\rangle^{\alpha}_{s_r}\rangle^{\alpha}_{c_i}$).

Inspection. Inspection is a mechanism used by clients in a periodic fashion to make sure an appserver is not using two different logs in the backend and frontend. In ASPAS, to support various security levels for different clients, each client has to define its "tolerance threshold" τ during which it can operate until a new certificate arrives. This requires the client to hold a fairly small log of operations (smaller than τ) for which it has the ability to rollback. While a certificate is always generated according to causal order of operations (delivered via the RCB), any client with $\tau > 1$ will only receive certificates in intervals. However, certificate versions are stable versions that may not correspond to operations on all appservers (as shown in **Stable versions** mechanism in Sect. 3.6). Consequently, there is a need to make sure that received states between two consecutive certificates are correct. Indeed, a Byzantine appserver may assign the same VV to multiple clients' requests, while only pushes one of them to the BFT cluster. To fool the clients, the appserver can send them wrong replies joint with a correct certificate that holds the only pushed one to the BFT cluster. Inspection starts by having each client to periodically select a random non-certified reply from the appserver (rndState) in its log. Then, it sends an INSPECTION($\langle rndState\rangle^{\alpha}_{c_i}$,$S$) request to all the appservers, asking for a confirmation of correctness. The client should collect at least $f + 1$ matching INSPECTREPLY($in=\langle\sigma\rangle^{\alpha}_{s_r}$) from the appservers for its requested INSPECTION; otherwise, it will assume its associated appserver as Byzantine. In this case, it sends a COMPLAIN to the other appservers. This random INSPECTION stands as an accountable approach to prevent the misbehavior of appservers. For that, if the number of concurrent clients on the service is high, a Byzantine appserver will be blacklisted even if the rate of inspection is low. Notice that inspection should be used according to a well configured policy (defined time, number of times...) to prevent Byzantine clients from using it as a DOS attack to overload the network. Furthermore, inspection is not crucial to maintain system convergence, it is just an additional mechanism to guarantee as much as possible the correctness of client's received replies. Clients tending for high security over latency can minimize τ to one, or use a classical BFT system.

4   Evaluation

4.1   Implementation

Code. We implemented ASPAS as a Proof of Concept of 5K Java LOC. We opted for Java to have a smooth integration with the BFT-SMaRt library [1], used as the BFT Cluster. The implementation included a thin client, modular proxies (as described in Fig. 1), and appserver including a basic Reliable Broadcast protocol [3]. Being modular, ASPAS can use any classical BFT protocol, like [8, 10, 29], as a backend as long as it exposes the same BFT-SMaRt API. This is required to integrate with the BFT proxies of ASPAS.

DataTypes. We experimented ASPAS using the Counter and Set datatypes following the Pure CRDT model [2]. These two datatypes are widely used in many AP applications. As a single example on social network applications, counters can implement the number of actions: likes, dislikes, comments, views, Ads, etc.; and sets can implement collections of recommended videos, comments, posts, etc. In addition, experimenting counters and sets helps us diversify the payload size of requests and replies (although this had little impact on our results). We plan to opensource the code after refactoring.

4.2 Experimental Settings

Testbed. We prepared an experimental environment that is very close to reality using Emulab [28]. Emulab is a good choice because it allows using real machines for processes, and interestingly allows emulating the network delays using intermediary physical machines which gives the same experience as in geo-replicated link delays and router's queuing. We avoided using Grid5000 since it allows sharing the machines for several experiments which induces ambiguity to the results and makes it harder to reproduce and compare against.

Machines. We used up to 100 physical commodity real machines at Emulab each having two 8-core CPUs with RAM between 8 GB and 16 GB, five Ethernet 10Gb NICs, and running 64-bit Ubuntu OS. These properties allowed us to run up to 50 client processes or 10 appserver processes on the same machine. The BFT cluster was deployed on four machines to run BFT-SMaRt bftservers.

Networks. One third of these machines were used by Emulab as intermediary delay machines to mimic a real delay in geo-replicated settings. To mitigate the interference across layers and overloading network interfaces (as done in real settings), we used a different network for each layer: frontend, BFT cluster, appservers, and backend (as shown in Fig. 1). Otherwise explicitly stated, we configured the network round-trip delays considering the estimated geo-replicated intra- and inter-continental average delays [12]: 70 ms for the frontend network (clients and appservers), 70 ms to 110 ms as variant average delay for the appservers network and backend network (appservers and bftservers), and 10 ms for the BFT cluster (since it is not necessary to be geo-replicated). We could have explicitly used different delays within the same network to mimic a real geo-replicated case, but we did not see a significant impact on the evaluation.

4.3   Evaluation Methodology

Metrics and Benchmarks. The evaluation focuses on measuring the latency of ASPAS being the most significant Key Performance Indicator in AP systems. In addition, we also measure the throughput considering: the number of simultaneous clients with different payloads (without batching), and execution times. We assume $b = 1$ faulty bftservers out of $3b + 1$ in the BFT cluster unless otherwise stated. We experimented the Counter and Set datatypes via microbenchmarks and YCSB [11] read/write workloads. In all cases, clients issue a sufficiently big number (up to 10K) of requests to stabilize the network queues. We did not aim to saturate the network being unrealistic in geo-replicated settings. We remove the outliers during the system warm-up and cool-down phases to measure the steady case. We ran each experiment at least five times. Latencies measured at each client are used to compute the average latency. Throughput is measured at the appservers and summed up.

Compared Protocols. We compared ASPAS with OBFT [9] as a state of the art BFT protocol for AP systems. To understand the overhead of Byzantine tolerance, we compared ASPAS to two baseline configurations representing the ASPAS extremes: (1) an AP system without any BFT backend or cryptography overhead, and (2) a system running a BFT protocol, e.g., BFT-SMaRt in our case. Even if sometimes deemed to provide "eventual" consistency, we do not compare with recent, classical BFT protocols [6,26,29]. However, these protocols are complementary to ASPAS because they can be used as backend instead of BFT-SMaRt if they can improve the BFT cluster functionality.

Compared ASPAS Configurations. In addition, to understand the performance-security tradeoffs of ASPAS, we considered five ASPAS configurations summarized in Table 1. ASPAS1, ASPAS2, and ASPAS3 are the most interesting configurations as they represent reasonable proportions of different levels of security by clients. We argue that the percentage of $\tau = 1$ is not very low considering AP systems (which is not the common paradigm for conservative applications). ASPAS0 and ASPAS4 are used for the sake of the experiments and in special cases (e.g., under a problem in the backend or system under attack, respectively); therefore, these are not sought to be normal-case ASPAS configurations.

Table 1. The five ASPAS interesting configurations.

Configuration	% $\tau = 1$	% $\tau = 1000$	% $\tau = \infty$
ASPAS0	0%	0%	100%
ASPAS1	5%	50%	45%
ASPAS2	3%	30%	67%
ASPAS3	0%	100%	0%
ASPAS4	100%	0%	0%

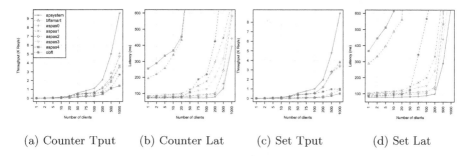

(a) Counter Tput   (b) Counter Lat   (c) Set Tput   (d) Set Lat

Fig. 4. Throughput and latency microbenchmarks for Counter and Set datatypes with payloads 128B and 4 KB, respectively with fixed $f = 3$ and $b = 1$.

4.4 Latency and Throughput Microbenchmarks

Counter. Figures 4b and 4a show that the latency (resp., throughput) of ASPAS, as the number of clients increase, are close to that of the optimal baseline AP System (apsystem) in most configurations (for $f = 3$). The latency of both ASPAS and apsystem range between 72 ms and 400 ms as the number of clients reaches 1000. This is consistent with a round-trip request/reply with link delay 70 ms with few clients, and expected for 1000 clients since we ran up to 50 client processes on each machine. The same pattern also noticed for the throughput that exceeds 5K req/s with 1000 clients. The figure shows that the apsystem can scale a bit more than ASPAS, but we could not add more clients due to the limited number of machines. This result is expected as appservers do extra work by communicating with the BFT cluster, even if in the background.

Considering OBFT [9], as state of the art SEC-based protocol, its latency is slightly lower than ASPAS with few clients. This is not surprising since OBFT uses less secure HMAC-symmetric keys of 6Bytes length and SHA1 digests. However, OBFT's latency starts to increase significantly with 10 clients and more. Indeed, OBFT uses periodic (every 1000 requests) synchronization between appservers to resolve conflicts, which is, contrary to ASPAS, blocking to the client. For the same reason, the throughput of OBFT is the lowest compared to ASPAS and apsystem. This result is an evidence that using a modular approach like ASPAS to check the Byzantine behaviours in the background is less complex and maintains the desired low latency in AP Systems.

On the more conservative baseline, BFT-SMaRt only scales up to 100 clients with almost double the latency of apsystem and ASPAS0 in geo-replicated setting i.e., 70 ms round-trip delay. This is expected due to the extensive two round-trip messaging pattern of the BFT-SMaRt protocol. As expected, the latency of ASPAS4 is higher than BFT-SMaRt as confirmed in the figures since all clients requests in ASPAS4 are only served after a certificate is requested from the BFT cluster (which incurs additional round-trip delay of 70 ms). This was consistent with the results with few clients where the latency difference was around 78 ms.

Interestingly, the latency and throughput of ASPAS in most configurations are very close to apsystem. As expected, the latency of ASPAS0 is a little higher

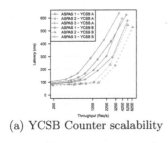
(a) YCSB Counter scalability

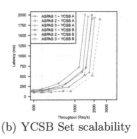
(b) YCSB Set scalability

Fig. 5. Scalability under YCSB A and B workloads

than apsystem due to the overhead of SHA256 hashing and RSA signatures (used by BFT-SmaRt). The results show that as the number of clients with $\tau = 1$ increases, e.g., in ASPAS1 and ASPAS2, the latency (resp, throughput) increases (resp., decreases). This is referred to the impact of high delays of clients with $\tau = 1$ that follow the strong consistency. We also observed that ASPAS2 outperforms ASPAS3 (where all clients set $\tau = 1000$), due to the high proportion of clients with $\tau = \infty$ (i.e., never block) that dominates the effect of the 3% clients with $\tau = 1$. The result of ASPAS3 is promising as ASPAS scales up to 500 clients with throughput and latency close to the optimal baseline apsystem.

Set. Figures 4d and 4c convey the microbenchmarks on the set datatypes. We noticed the same patterns as in the counter case with lower scalability. This is expected since the set payload is set to 4 KBytes which incurs additional Cryptographic overhead (using SHA256). The large payload overhead also dominates other protocol's factors which reflects the observation that all ASPAS configurations and OBFT curves are closer than the counter case.

Another observation is that the latency and throughput get worse much faster than the counter case. In fact, the increase in the payload size causes delays in the systems that also delays the certificate at the BFT cluster. Therefore, a fraction of the clients will reach the threshold τ and thus wait some milliseconds for the certificate. The average latency shown on the graphs reflects this certificate delay overhead which we discuss further in the following sections. Finally, we expected the latency of OBFT to be worse than the counter case with more concurrent clients (i.e., leads more conflicts). This is because it uses a sophisticated process to have appservers agree on a correct state and undo incorrect ones [9].

4.5 Scalability with YCSB Benchmark

To understand the behaviour of ASPAS with real workloads, we experimented it using the YCSB benchmark [11] considering Read/Write percentages for both Counter and Set cases. We only focused on the most three realistic configurations of ASPAS, i.e., ASPAS1, ASPAS2 and ASPAS3. We omit the comparison with other protocols as the results we got are very consistent with those in the previous section. We have used two widely used YCSB workloads: workload A (YCSB A) as an update-heavy scenario with 50% read and 50% update, and the workload B (YCSB B) as a read heavy scenario with 95% read and 5% update. In both scenarios, the request distribution is set to *zipfian*.

Counter: In Fig. 5a, i.e., the counter datatype, the results we obtained are consistent with those in the microbenchmark case: the three ASPAS configurations scale up to 500 clients where the latency stays below 450 ms, with throughput 3680 req/s in the worst case (ASPAS1). Again, this is considered acceptable in Internet-based geo-replicated applications. We believe this could be lower in reality as we ran 50 clients on a single machine in this scenario. Even in this case, the latency remains realistic although the throughput of the protocol no longer improves when the appservers get overloaded and the broadcast cost across appserver gets higher. This is also consistent with another observation that the scalability with YCSB B is around 20% better than YCSB A in all configurations; which is expected since with lower update rate in YCSB B, less load is imposed on the system as no broadcast is needed. On the other hand, we noticed the same pattern as in the microbenchmark results where ASPAS2 outperforms ASPAS1 as it includes more clients with $\tau = \infty$ (favor availability) and less clients are conservative (with $\tau = 1$). This phenomenon is expected since clients with $\tau = \infty$ do not have to wait for a certificate, whereas those with $\tau = 1$ wait on every update. However, ASPAS3's scalability remains lower than ASPAS2 although no clients with $\tau = 1$ exist, but as the clients with $\tau = \infty$ (which have the lowest latency) also disappear in the system, the average latency increases slightly, but not as worse as ASPAS1.

Set: The results for the set datatype are conveyed in Fig. 5b. The first salient observation is that the curves are closer to those in the Counter case in all ASPAS configurations and both YCSB A and B. The reason is referred to the domination of the request sizes in the Set (4 KB) over other factors in the system. What supports this explanation is the low throughput in the case of the set despite the acceptable latency: although the latency is not significantly higher than the counters case (where the link delay is a main factor), the throughput (between 2000 and 3000 req/s) is significantly lower that of the counter case (6400 req/s).

5   Conclusion

In this paper, we presented ASPAS: a Byzantine resilient AP system that ensures Strong Eventual Convergence despite Byzantine behaviors. ASPAS provides backend Byzantine faults detection off the critical path of clients requests, being a requirement for highly available applications. ASPAS also provides a client-based spectrum of tradeoffs between availability and Byzantine security, which is convenient for deployments with mixed application security requirements. Although ASPAS does not affect the liveness of non Byzantine-sensitive clients, it could temporarily block conservative clients that require high freshness. Unfortunately, this is an intrinsic property of AP systems themselves, even in the crash-recovery model, that could be solved via full replication (i.e., mirroring) at the application server level.

Acknowledgments. This work is co-financed by the National Funds through the Portuguese funding agency, FCT - Fundação para a Ciência e a Tecnologia, within project UIDB/50014/2020; and the "NORTE-06-3559-FSE-000046 - Emprego altamente qualificado nas empresas – Contratação de Recursos Humanos Altamente Qualificados (PME ou CoLAB)" financed by the Norte's Regional Operational Programme (NORTE 2020) through the European Social Fund (ESF).

References

1. Bessani, A., Sousa, J., Alchieri, E.: State machine replication for the masses with BFT-SMART. In: Proceedings of the 44th IEEE/IFIP International Conference on Dependable Systems and Networks. IEEE (2014)
2. Baquero, C., Almeida, P.S., Shoker, A.: Making operation-based CRDTs operation-based. In: Distributed Applications and Interoperable Systems - International Conference, DAIS 2014, pp. 126–140 (2014)
3. Birman, K., Schiper, A., Stephenson, P.: Lightweight causal and atomic group multicast. ACM Trans. Comput. Syst. **9**(3), 272–314 (1991). https://doi.org/10.1145/128738.128742, http://doi.acm.org/10.1145/128738.128742
4. Bracha, G.: Asynchronous byzantine agreement protocols. Inf. Comput. **75**(2), 130–143 (1987)
5. Burckhardt, S., Gotsman, A., Yang, H., Zawirski, M.: Replicated data types: specification, verification, optimality. In: ACM Sigplan Notices, vol. 49, pp. 271–284. ACM (2014)
6. Cachin, C.: Architecture of the hyperledger blockchain fabric. In: Workshop on Distributed Cryptocurrencies and Consensus Ledgers, vol. 310 (2016)
7. Cachin, C., Kursawe, K., Petzold, F., Shoup, V.: Secure and efficient asynchronous broadcast protocols. In: Kilian, J. (ed.) Annual International Cryptology Conference, vol. 2139, pp. 524–541. Springer, Heidelberg (2001). https://doi.org/10.1007/3-540-44647-8_31
8. Castro, M., Liskov, B.: Practical byzantine fault tolerance and proactive recovery. ACM Trans. Comput. Syst. **20**(4), 398–461 (2002). https://doi.org/10.1145/571637.571640, http://doi.acm.org/10.1145/571637.571640
9. Chai, H., Zhao, W.: Byzantine fault tolerance for services with commutative operations. In: Proceedings of the 2014 IEEE International Conference on Services Computing, SCC 2014, pp. 219–226. IEEE Computer Society, Washington, DC, USA (2014). https://doi.org/10.1109/SCC.2014.37, http://dx.doi.org/10.1109/SCC.2014.37
10. Clement, A., et al.: Upright cluster services. In: Proceedings of the ACM SIGOPS 22nd Symposium on Operating Systems Principles, pp. 277–290. ACM (2009)
11. Cooper, B.F., Silberstein, A., Tam, E., Ramakrishnan, R., Sears, R.: Benchmarking cloud serving systems with YCSB. In: Proceedings of the 1st ACM symposium on Cloud computing, pp. 143–154. ACM (2010)
12. Couto, R.S., Secci, S., Campista, M.E.M., Costa, L.H.M.: Latency versus survivability in geo-distributed data center design. In: 2014 IEEE Global Communications Conference, pp. 1102–1107. IEEE (2014)
13. Friedman, R., Licher, R.: Hardening cassandra against byzantine failures. In: Aspnes, J., Bessani, A., Felber, P., Leitão, J. (eds.) 21st International Conference on Principles of Distributed Systems (OPODIS 2017). Leibniz International Proceedings in Informatics (LIPIcs), vol. 95, pp. 27:1–27:20. Schloss Dagstuhl-Leibniz-Zentrum fuer Informatik, Dagstuhl, Germany (2018). https://doi.org/10.4230/LIPIcs.OPODIS.2017.27, http://drops.dagstuhl.de/opus/volltexte/2018/8642

14. Gilbert, S., Lynch, N.: Brewer's conjecture and the feasibility of consistent, available, partition-tolerant web services. ACM SIGACT News **33**(2), 51–59 (2002)
15. Guerraoui, R., Kuznetsov, P., Monti, M., Pavlovic, M., Seredinschi, D.A.: Scalable byzantine reliable broadcast (extended version). arXiv preprint arXiv:1908.01738 (2019)
16. Kotla, R., Alvisi, L., Dahlin, M., Clement, A., Wong, E.: Zyzzyva: Speculative byzantine fault tolerance. ACM Trans. Comput. Syst. **27**(4), 7:1–7:39 (2010)
17. Kwon, J.: Tendermint: Consensus without mining. Draft v. 0.6, fall 1(11) (2014)
18. Lamport, L.: Time, clocks, and the ordering of events in a distributed system, pp. 558–565. ACM (1978)
19. Lamport, L.: Time, clocks, and the ordering of events in a distributed system. Commun. ACM **21**(7), 558–565 (1978)
20. Lamport, L., Shostak, R., Pease, M.: The byzantine generals problem. ACM Trans. Program. Lang. Syst. **4**(3), 382–401 (1982). https://doi.org/10.1145/357172.357176
21. Malkhi, D., Merritt, M., Rodeh, O.: Secure reliable multicast protocols in a WAN. Distrib. Comput. **13**(1), 19–28 (2000)
22. Saito, Y., Shapiro, M.: Optimistic replication. ACM Comput. Surv. (CSUR) **37**(1), 42–81 (2005)
23. Schneider, F.B.: Replication management using the state-machine approach, distributed systems (1993)
24. Shapiro, M., Preguiça, N., Baquero, C., Zawirski, M.: A comprehensive study of convergent and commutative replicated data types (2011)
25. Shapiro, M., Preguiça, N., Baquero, C., Zawirski, M.: Conflict-free replicated data types. In: Defago, X., Petit, F., Villain, V. (eds.) Proceedings of the 13th International Conference on Stabilization, Safety, and Security of Distributed Systems. pp. 386–400. SSS 2011, Springer, Heidelberg (2011). https://doi.org/10.1007/978-3-642-24550-3_29, http://dl.acm.org/citation.cfm?id=2050613.2050642
26. Singh, A., Fonseca, P., Kuznetsov, P., Rodrigues, R., Maniatis, P.: Zeno: eventually consistent byzantine-fault tolerance. In: Proceedings of the 6th USENIX Symposium on Networked Systems Design and Implementation, NSDI 2009, pp. 169–184. USENIX Association, Berkeley, CA, USA (2009). http://dl.acm.org/citation.cfm?id=1558977.1558989
27. Vogels, W.: Eventually consistent: building reliable distributed systems at a worldwide scale demands trade-offs? Between consistency and availability. Queue **6**(6), 14–19 (2008)
28. White, B., et al.: An integrated experimental environment for distributed systems and networks. ACM SIGOPS Oper. Syst. Rev. **36**(SI), 255–270 (2002)
29. Yin, M., Malkhi, D., Reiter, M.K., Gueta, G.G., Abraham, I.: Hotstuff: BFT consensus with linearity and responsiveness. In: Proceedings of the 2019 ACM Symposium on Principles of Distributed Computing, pp. 347–356 (2019)

Portable Intermediate Representation for Efficient Big Data Analytics

Giannis Tzouros, Michail Tsenos, and Vana Kalogeraki[✉]

Department of Informatics, Athens University of Economics and Business,
Athens, Greece
{tzouros,tsemike,vana}@aueb.gr

Abstract. To process big data, applications have been utilizing data processing libraries over the last years, which are however not optimized to work together for efficient processing. Intermediate Representations (IR) have been introduced for unifying essential functions into an abstract interface that supports cross-optimization between applications. Still, the efficiency of an IR depends on the architecture and the tools required for compilation and execution. In this paper, we present a first glance at a framework that provides an IR by creating containers with executable code from structures of data analytics functions, described in an input grammar. These containers process data in query lists and they can be executed either standalone or integrated with other big data analytics applications without the need to compile the entire framework.

1 Introduction

Over the last ten years, massive amounts of information is generated constantly by social media, digital stores, weather stations, traffic sensors, e-commerce, healthcare, smart cities etc. The data created by the aforementioned data domains can be transferred for storage and further processing.

To manage big data, modern applications deploy libraries and algorithms for various big data computations, including aggregates, top-K results, nearest neighbor machine learning, etc. On the other hand, the evolution of applications introduces new types of data that require combinations of existing libraries and/or new libraries, which may lead to performance and efficiency challenges when executing on CPU resources. To deal with these issues, compilers utilize Intermediate Representation (IR) to provide universal computing functions and allow cross optimizations between different libraries and algorithms. [1]. An Intermediate Representation provides an abstraction for otherwise incompatible libraries, which hides details about the target execution platform and expresses data tasks under a unique interface. However, the deployment of Intermediate Representations can be complicated depending on the tools required and the scope of a framework. This problem leads to adaptability issues regarding deploying the representations on diverse environments and portability issues due to potential file size of the source code of each representation.

© IFIP International Federation for Information Processing 2021
Published by Springer Nature Switzerland AG 2021
M. Matos and F. Greve (Eds.): DAIS 2021, LNCS 12718, pp. 74–80, 2021.
https://doi.org/10.1007/978-3-030-78198-9_5

To address those problems, we present a framework that provides an Intermediate Representation created in Java, which takes as input a context-free grammar with computing function structures and creates portable containers via an extended SableCC compiler[1] that execute the functions described in the grammar. The containers are easily deployable over multiple environments and can be deployed easily on multiple data processing frameworks, potentially improving their compilation and execution times, but also on multi-cluster serverless environments, supporting parallel execution, optimizing resource usage.

2   Design and Challenges

The objective of our framework's intermediate representation is to compile computational functions from different libraries described in a hand-made grammar into a unified abstraction and convert them into portable containers. Our framework's design goals are to provide support for different high-level programming languages and multiple data analytics applications, compatibility with software optimizations for efficient execution and portability and autonomy support for containers so that they can be used without recompiling the main framework.

2.1   Design Objectives

More specifically, there are the following three design objectives: First, the containers must include an operational code which can be executed in multiple networking environments, including serverless environments, and must support standalone usage by the client or a variety of applications. Secondly, our framework must ensure that the output data of a container will be ready for use with other containers without any extra changes, in order to optimize execution and reduced processing times between operations. Finally, big data functions inside a container must be available for execution as many times as possible without having to build the entire code of the framework. The containers must be created by the Intermediate Representation only once, so that they can operate as standalone executables on multiple environments.

3   System Architecture

Our Intermediate Representation Container framework consists of the following components: The Intermediate Representation which captures the structures of the functions described in a grammar, the runtime environment which implements the functions captured in the IR into abstraction instances, the SableCC backend compiler which constructs containers based on the function instances made by the compiler and the portable containers deployed in multiple data environments and execute computations on input queries. The architecture and the synergy between the components of the framework is shown on Fig. 1.

---

[1] https://sablecc.org/.

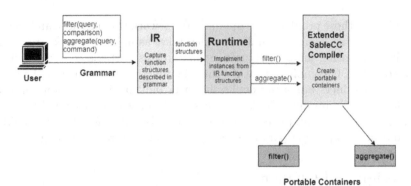

Fig. 1. The architecture of our framework: The IR that captures the function structures of an input grammar, the runtime environment that generates executable code from the IR instances and the extended SableCC compiler which generates serverless portable containers with the generated code.

3.1   Intermediate Representation Model

Our framework creates an IR which collects the most essential functions from different applications and programming languages described in a grammar and integrate them into a single concept, containing universal functions, ready to use in various big data environments. The functions within our framework's IR must contain well structured semantics in order to be later on converted as container executables via the backend compiler.

To convert data analytics functions, our framework's Intermediate Representation takes as input a grammar created by the user, which includes names and structures for these functions.

Data Model. The grammar contains two categories of data types: **Scalars**, which are data objects with finite values (int, long, double etc.), and **Lists**, which accommodate multiple values of one or more Scalar types into a single data object (String of multiple char values, dynamic array of numeric values, strings or key-value pairs). The data types are used as parameters for the functions described in the grammar. We chose these data types because they are common in the majority of functions and operations throughout most popular programming languages.

Functions. Based on the input grammar, our framework's Intermediate Representation utilizes operators that describe big data analytics functions. All functions take as input a query list with multiple entries, where each entry contains one or more Scalar values either as a key-pair or as a CSV line with more than 2 values. For certain functions, the user or device must insert one or more Scalar values as parameters required by the appropriate function. Currently, our IR supports the following big data functions:

filter(query, comparison): The operation takes as input a query list and a string that describes the filtering requirement of a variable compared to a numeric value and returns a new query list that contains any of the previous query entries that satisfy the entered requirement.

aggregate(query, command): Outputs a computational result for a variable's values within a query list, depending on the value of the string *command*. The *command* string supports the following entries: average, count, sum, median, standard deviation, minimum, maximum, mode and range.

valueScore(query): Outputs the number of occurrence of a value for every entry in the input query list. Namely, how many times each value appears through the entire query.

topKValue(query, k): Outputs the top k entries from the input query in a descending order [2] based on the value of a variable

topKScore(query, k): Similar to *valueScore*, this operation outputs the top k entries from the input query list in a descending order based on the frequency a value occurs.

nearestNeighbor(query, x, y, k, g1, g2): This operation implements the most common nearest neighbor technique: the k-Nearest Neighbor classification algorithm [3]. To classify a target object with coordinates x and y, the function computes the distance (Euclidean or Hamming) between the object and every entry in the query list that belongs either of the groups *g1* or *g2*. Next, the function sorts all computed distances in ascending order, from the entry closest to the object. Finally, the function gathers the top k entries from the list and, depending on the group the majority these entries are, the object is classified to the winning group.

3.2 Runtime Environment

Our framework supports a runtime environment to generate code for function structures captured by the Intermediate Representation. The runtime is developed in Java and takes the main ideas of the cached function: input, computations and output/result and recreates the main operations of the function in Java.

3.3 Backend Compiler

Our framework uses an extended version of the SableCC backend compiler. Due to the fact that SableCC compiles grammars only for lexical, syntax and semantic purposes, we enhanced its functions by converting the executable code created by the runtime for every function in the Intermediate Representation into JAR executable files and, next, enclosed the JARs into portable containers which can run in multiple environments. These containers execute their included code when they take a query list and any required parameters as input, as indicated by the function's structure in IR.

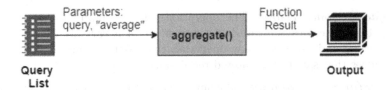

Fig. 2. Architecture of a serverless container that describes its functionality as well as the input data and the output target.

3.4 Serverless Containers

The containers, created from the backend compiler described above, are able to run on either single computers, server clusters or as serverless functions in a cloud provider such as IBM Cloud Functions, Amazon AWS, or in a private cloud with OpenFaas². The container packages up application code and all its dependencies so the application can run in any environment. A container can be replicated and each replica can be referenced as an active instance of the application. In Fig. 2 you can see the execution process of a single container created by our compiler. By choosing the Serverless computing model [4], we have a lower operational and deployment cost due to its unique pricing policy based on a *pay-as-you-use* model. The cloud provider allocates instances on demand, so the number of active instances can be selected either by the application user, or can be adapted dynamically according to the number of requests. During periods of high load the number of active instances is adapted automatically in order to compensate the increased traffic and during extended periods of inactivity the number of active instances can be decreased to zero and release any resource that where allocated.

4   Related Work

Our framework's objective is to unify Intermediate Representation, code compilation and distributed computing into one abstraction, providing Intermediate Representation to gather essential functions from different libraries and languages into one abstraction layer, accessible by any system regardless of its network environment or architecture. To accomplish that objective, our work must provide services and operations that extend or improve on techniques from existing IR implementations. More specifically, LLVM [5] and OpenCL [6] implement low-level language independent Intermediate Representation for uniting and compiling code portions written in different libraries or languages, whereas Weld [7] improves upon the previous works by making the IR compatible with parallel distributed systems using loop fusion and loop tiling. For our framework, we need to gather the structures of the most essential functions from widely used languages and libraries and describe them in a single grammar file from which our work will construct its Intermediate Representation.

---

² https://github.com/openfaas/faasd.

Certain IR frameworks focus only on certain languages or systems, like LINQ [8] which provides IR exclusively for .NET framework systems and PinaVM [9] which utilizes IR for verification of programs written in SystemC [10], a C++ library focused on modeling of systems at different levels of abstractions ranging from functional description to cycle-accurate modeling.. Our framework initially provides IR for queries written in Python, but in the future we can add support for other widely used languages, such as Java, C++ and JavaScript. Also, other frameworks utilize IR for different applications i.e. Halide [11] uses IR to improve image processing, the approach of Vatavu et al. [12] uses IR for detection of 3D models in a traffic road and IF [13] deploys IR on Specification and Description Language (SDL) telecommunication systems. Our framework's IR creates containers that are deployable with a wide range of applications through multiple data environments, including the applications mentioned above.

There are several implementations of runtime systems that generate code for function structures, such as HyPer [14] and LegoBase [15]. These systems, however, are restricted to the relational model and are often difficult to implement in different systems because they need to generate imperative code directly from multiple operators. Our framework contains operators written in Java for constructing code for a series of supported functions.

Container deployment is a well known technique used by implementations like Docker [16], Kubernetes [17] and Firecracker [18] for optimizing code execution on distributed systems. Faasd is an OpenFaas fork, which offers a lightweight portable FaaS engine which can run anywhere, from AWS to small low powered computers, such as Raspberry Pi. In our framework we generate images that are compatible with the Containerd runtime. In this way the user can easily choose the environment that he wants to deploy the function which can scale from its home desktop to fully distributed over Docker Swarm or Kubernetes.

5   Conclusion

In this paper we have presented a framework that utilizes intermediate representation for providing a unique abstraction for functions from multiple libraries or languages and creates portable containers based on these functions, which can be executed standalone by users or applications on multiple environments, without requiring to compile the framework's entire code each time.

Acknowledgements. This research has been supported by the European Union through the H2020 952215 TAILOR project.

References

1. Zhao, J., Nagarakatte, S., Martin, M.M., Zdancewic, S.: Formalizing the llVM intermediate representation for verified program transformations. In: Proceedings of the 39th annual ACM SIGPLAN-SIGACT symposium on Principles of programming languages, pp. 427–440 (2012)

2. Soliman, M.A., Ilyas, I.F., Chang, K.C.C.: Top-k query processing in uncertain databases. In: 2007 IEEE 23rd International Conference on Data Engineering, pp. 896–905. IEEE (2007)
3. Guo, G., Wang, H., Bell, D., Bi, Y., Greer, K.: KNN model-based approach in classification. In: Meersman, R., Tari, Z., Schmidt, D.C. (eds.) OTM 2003. LNCS, vol. 2888, pp. 986–996. Springer, Heidelberg (2003). https://doi.org/10.1007/978-3-540-39964-3_62
4. Lin, X.C., et al.: Serverless boom or bust? An analysis of economic incentives. In: USENIX (2020)
5. Lattner, C., Adve, V.: LLVM: a compilation framework for lifelong program analysis & transformation. In: International Symposium on Code Generation and Optimization, 2004. CGO 2004, pp. 75–86. IEEE (2004)
6. Stone, J.E., Gohara, D., Shi, G.: OpenCL: A parallel programming standard for heterogeneous computing systems. Comput. Sci. Eng. **12**(3), 66 (2010)
7. Palkar, S., et al.: Weld: a common runtime for high performance data analytics. In: Conference on Innovative Data Systems Research (CIDR), pp. 45 (2017)
8. Meijer, E., Beckman, B., Bierman, G.: LINQ: reconciling object, relations and xml in the. net framework. In: Proceedings of the 2006 ACM SIGMOD international conference on Management of data, pp. 706–706 (2006)
9. Marquet, K., Moy, M.: PinaVM: a SystemC front-end based on an executable intermediate representation. In: Proceedings of the tenth ACM international conference on Embedded software, pp. 79–88 (2010)
10. Black, D.C., Donovan, J., Bunton, B., Keist, A.: SystemC: From the Ground Up, vol. 71. Springer Science & Business Media, Heidelberg (2009)
11. Ragan-Kelley, J., et al.: Halide: decoupling algorithms from schedules for high-performance image processing. Commun. ACM **61**(1), 106–115 (2017)
12. Vatavu, A., Nedevschi, S.: Real-time modeling of dynamic environments in traffic scenarios using a stereo-vision system. In: 2012 15th International IEEE Conference on Intelligent Transportation Systems, pp. 722–727. IEEE (2012)
13. Bozga, M., et al.: If: an intermediate representation for SDL and its applications. In: SDL 1999, pp. 423–440. Elsevier (1999)
14. Neumann, T.: Efficiently compiling efficient query plans for modern hardware. Proc. VLDB Endowment **4**(9), 539–550 (2011)
15. Klonatos, Y., Koch, C., Rompf, T., Chafi, H.: Building efficient query engines in a high-level language. Proc. VLDB Endowment **7**(10), 853–864 (2014)
16. Docker. https://www.docker.org
17. Brewer, E.A.: Kubernetes and the path to cloud native. In: Proceedings of the sixth ACM symposium on cloud computing, pp. 167–167 (2015)
18. Agache, A., et al.: Firecracker: lightweight virtualization for serverless applications. In: 17th {usenix} symposium on networked systems design and implementation ({nsdi} 20), pp. 419–434 (2020)

Distributed Algorithms

Shared-Dining: Broadcasting Secret Shares Using Dining-Cryptographers Groups

David Mödinger$^{(\boxtimes)}$, Juri Dispan, and Franz J. Hauck

Institute of Distributed Systems, Ulm University, 89081 Ulm, Germany
{david.moedinger,juri.dispan,franz.hauck}@uni-ulm.de

Abstract. We introduce a combination of Shamir's secret sharing and dining-cryptographers networks, which provides $(n - |\text{attackers}|)$-anonymity for up to $k - 1$ attackers and has manageable performance impact on dissemination. A k-anonymous broadcast can be implemented using a small group of dining cryptographers to first share the message, followed by a flooding phase started by group members. Members have little incentive to forward the message in a timely manner, as forwarding incurs costs, or they may even profit from keeping the message. In worst case, this leaves the true originator as the only sender, rendering the dining-cryptographers phase useless and compromising their privacy. We present a novel approach using a modified dining-cryptographers protocol to distributed shares of an (n, k)-Shamir's secret sharing scheme. All group members broadcast their received share through the network, allowing any recipient of k shares to reconstruct the message, enforcing anonymity. If less than k group members broadcast their shares, the message cannot be decoded thus preventing privacy breaches for the originator. We demonstrate the privacy and performance results in a security analysis and performance evaluation based on a proof-of-concept prototype. Throughput rates between 10 and 100 kB/s are enough for many real applications with high privacy requirements, e.g., financial blockchain system.

Keywords: Network protocol · Privacy protocol · Dining cryptographers · Secret sharing · Peer-to-Peer networking

1 Introduction

In recent years, the general public has become more interested in privacy issues, even leading to strong privacy-protection regulation, e.g., the general data protection regulation (GDPR) of the European Union. This increased interest led to a rekindling of privacy research, especially for financially-sensitive information.

Several cryptocurrencies attempt to provide unlinkable transactions for their users [8,9]. Unfortunately, many of these approaches neglected the underlying network's privacy and focused on the public information accessible through the

© IFIP International Federation for Information Processing 2021
Published by Springer Nature Switzerland AG 2021
M. Matos and F. Greve (Eds.): DAIS 2021, LNCS 12718, pp. 83–98, 2021.
https://doi.org/10.1007/978-3-030-78198-9_6

blockchain. Researchers showed that transactions can still be deanonymized through the network [2,7]. This network deanonymization led to even better identification, as internet-protocol (IP) addresses can be matched to real-world identities compared to public keys.

Various projects tackled this issue of network identification. Monero [9] applies Kovri[1], a garlic-based routing scheme. In previous work, we proposed a protocol based on dining-cryptographers (DC) groups, where only a part of the whole network perform a DC protocol, to realize a broadcast protocol with strong privacy guarantees [11]. Chaum's dining-cryptographers groups [3] have been used by other state-of-the-art protocols such as Dissent [4,13] and k-anonymous groups [1].

Although DC groups provide very strong privacy, their efficient usage for broadcast communication requires additional protocols layered on top of the DC network, e.g., a flood-and-prune broadcast. This creates additional risks, as non-cooperating participants in the layered protocol might force the true origi-nator to step up and jeopardize their anonymity. In previous systems, timeouts were used to detect nodes responsible to broadcast but failed to do so. Groups then had to punish or exclude these misbehaving nodes. A better system would incentivize nodes to participate instead of only punish when misbehaving. Proper incentives become even more important under stricter scrutiny, as misbehaving nodes might refuse cooperation selectively or drag out processes unnecessarily, leaving the true originator to forfeit their anonymity guarantees and start the flooding themselves. Therefore, we designed a system where messages can only be read when enough participants cooperate to cross a threshold, enforcing the anonymity guarantees of the protocol throughout the network.

Our contribution is a novel system combining dining-cryptographers groups and (n, k)-Shamir's secret sharing. Our system prevents identification of the orig-inator in the presence of up to $k-1$ attackers in the DC group for a given security parameter $k < n$ with a DC group size of n. Broadcasting the shares requires at least k participants, leading to enforced k-anonymity during the broadcast. Lastly, we provide a proof-of-concept implementation and its evaluation.

The structure of this paper is as follows: In Sect. 2, we give an overview of the basic building blocks and the background of this paper. We propose our k-resistant solution to broadcast messages using a DC-protocol and Shamir's secret sharing in Sect. 3. We provide proof of our scheme's security and privacy in Sect. 4, while an evaluation of the performance of our scheme can be found in Sect. 5. Lastly, in Sect. 6, we discuss possible applications of our scheme.

2   Background

In this section, we discuss the required background for this paper. First and foremost, this encompasses the notation, scenario, and attacker model and the algorithmic and mathematical concepts used in this paper, i.e., Chaum's dining-cryptographers protocol and Shamir's secret-sharing scheme.

---

[1] See https://gitlab.com/kovri-project/kovri.

2.1   Notation and Scenario

For this paper, we will restrict the discussion to groups of nodes that interact as peers, e.g., a peer-to-peer network. Hereby, the network is further segregated into a group of n participants, who form a group $G = g_1, \ldots, g_n$. Each participant g_i is identified by its index i.

Participants create various messages. The message a participant g_i creates and wants to broadcast is denoted by m_i. Intermittent messages created to be sent throughout the protocol by g_i and received by g_k are denoted as M_i. Throughout the paper, we use $\oplus$ to denote the bitwise XOR.

The group has various requirements for their network communication. A group needs pairwise authenticated connections between all nodes to prevent network manipulation. Further, nodes need to be able to create a securely shared secret between each pair of nodes. The assumptions are easily satisfied by modern networks using mTLS and generally available cryptographic libraries.

2.2   Dining-Cryptographers Protocol

Chaum's dining-cryptographers protocol [3] allows a participant in a group to broadcast a message with perfect sender anonymity. This means that an attacker attempting to identify the sender of a message deducts that all non-colluding participants have an equal probability of being the sender of the message.

Conceptually, the dining-cryptographers protocol performs a distributed computation of the bitwise XOR function $\bigoplus_{i=1\ldots n} m_i$ where each participant provides one input value m_i. In case participant g_k is sending a message m_k and every other participant is using $m_{i \neq k} = 0$, each member computes

$$m_{out} = \bigoplus_{i \in 1 \ldots n} m_i = 0 \oplus 0 \oplus \cdots \oplus m_k \oplus \cdots \oplus 0 = m_k. \tag{1}$$

To compute a bitwise XOR, and therefore hide the true sender, all messages need to have the same length. This requirement can be lifted by application of preparing communication steps as used by Dissent [13]. At most one message is allowed to be non-zero, otherwise, the resulting message m_{out} would be the XOR of all input messages and therefore unreadable. A common attack has an attacker transmit random values, interrupting the communication of all nodes. This is addressed in modern networks and will be discussed in Sect. 4.4.

A node that does not intend to send anything uses $m_i = 0$ as an input message. The protocol as described in Algorithm 1 is run by every node separately, broadcasting one message per-protocol run.

Please note, that all secrets $s_{i,j}$ are symmetrical, i.e., $s_{i,j} = s_{j,i}$, and are shared between pairs of nodes g_i, g_j. The result $m_{out} = \bigoplus_{i=1\ldots n} M_i$ contains every index combination $i \neq j$ exactly once. Therefore, all secret pairs $s_{i,j}, s_{j,i}$ eliminate each other $s_{i,j} \oplus s_{j,i} = 0$.

Dining-cryptographers protocols are a well-known privacy-preserving primitive for network communication. They are applied in small groups of nodes in

---

Algorithm 1. Dining Cryptographer Protocol as executed by node g_{self}.

Input: Participants $g_1, g_2, \ldots, g_n$, message m_{self} of length ℓ
Output: Message $m_{out} = \bigoplus_{k=1\ldots n} m_k$ which is the same across all participants
1: Establish shared random secrets $s_{\text{self},i}$ of length ℓ with each member $g_i, i \neq$ self
2: $M_{\text{self}} = m_{\text{self}} \oplus \bigoplus_{i=1\ldots n, i \neq \text{self}} s_{\text{self},i}$
3: Send M_{self} to $g_i \ \forall i \in \{1 \ldots n\} \setminus \{\text{self}\}$
4: Receive M_i from $g_i \ \forall i \in \{1 \ldots n\} \setminus \{\text{self}\}$
5: $m_{out} = \bigoplus_{i=1\ldots n} M_i = \bigoplus_{i=1\ldots n} \left(m_i \oplus \bigoplus_{j=1\ldots n, j \neq i} s_{i,j} \right) = \bigoplus_{i=1\ldots n} m_i$

---

various modern protocols [1,4,11,13]. Dissent [4,13] applies them as its communication protocol in the core anonymity network. Von Ahn et al. [1] and also we, in previous work [11], use them as group components to provide strong sender anonymity. So their security properties are relevant for modern designs as well.

Using DC networks for implementing a broadcast will be very inefficient for large groups. To mitigate this, a reasonably-sized sub-group could run a DC protocol. Some of the members then start a flood-and-prune broadcast to reach all other group members, e.g., as we laid out in [10]. However, care has to be taken on how the flood-and-prune phase is started so that it does not reveal the originator or the entire group composition.

2.3 Shamir's Secret Sharing

Lastly, we introduce Shamir's secret sharing [12]. The scheme splits a message into n shares so that k with $1 \leq k \leq n$ shares are required to reconstruct the original message. This is often called a (n, k) threshold scheme.

Any polynomial $f = \sum_{i=0}^{k-1} a_i x^i, a_{k-1} \neq 0$ of degree $k-1$ is unambiguously defined by any k points [5] and can be reconstructed from them. Given n distinct points of f with $\forall i \neq j : x_i \neq x_j$, we can denote the set as:

$$\{(x_1, f(x_1)), (x_2, f(x_2)), \ldots, (x_n, f(x_n))\}. \tag{2}$$

The original polynomial can be recovered from any subset of points of size k. Lagrange interpolation provides the formula to recover the original polynomial, which works over the real numbers as well as over fields $\mathbb{Z}_p$, making all operations over integers modulo p. This leads to the same result independent of the chosen points [5] and is computed by:

$$f(x) = \sum_{i=1}^{k} f(x_i) \mathcal{L}_i(x), \tag{3}$$

$$\mathcal{L}_i(x) = \prod_{j=1, j \neq i}^{k} \frac{x - x_j}{x_i - x_j}. \tag{4}$$

Given a message $m \in \mathbb{Z}_p$ we now want to construct a polynomial $f \in \mathbb{Z}_p[x]$, the polynomial space over the given integers. The degree of f is $\deg(f) = k - 1$

and $f(0) = m$. A polynomial can be constructed easily by choosing integers $r_1, \ldots, r_{k-1} \in \mathbb{Z}_p \backslash \{0\}$ randomly and computing

$$f(x) = m + \sum_{i=1}^{k-1} r_i x^i. \tag{5}$$

It is easy to see that $f(0) = m$, as all other coefficients will be eliminated, and it holds that the degree of f is $k - 1$. The required n secret shares can then be computed as

$$s_i = (i, f(i)), i \in \{1, \ldots, n\}. \tag{6}$$

A Galois field $\mathrm{GF}(2^n)$ of suitable size is used to implement Shamir's secret sharing efficiently, usually $\mathrm{GF}(2^8)$. A notable property of these fields is that the addition of elements is equivalent to bitwise XOR of their binary representation.

2.4   Goal

Our honest peers' goal is to broadcast a message within the network while maintaining sender anonymity, i.e., at least $k-1$ other nodes should be indistinguishable from them as the originator, where k depends on the parameters chosen in the system. Honest nodes will strictly follow the protocol, as their goal is to broadcast messages correctly.

The primary goal of the attacker is to identify the participant sending the message. Attackers follow the semi-honest model, i.e., they follow the protocol, with a small modification: They are allowed to refuse cooperation in the flood and prune broadcasting phase. They will combine all knowledge they can acquire throughout the protocol, e.g., all messages they receive. Attackers cannot manipulate the network, compromise other nodes, and solve computationally-infeasible problems such as encryption schemes. Section 4.4 details additional measures and their applicability with malicious attackers.

3   Secret-Shared Dining-Cryptographers Protocol

Within a large network, consider a group of size n, where one participant wants to transmit a message into the entire network. We change the broadcast of the message to all participants into the transmission of n distinct parts while still using a dining-cryptographers broadcast. The parts are created using a (n, k) Shamir's secret-sharing technique. Each part is transmitted simultaneously during a modified dining cryptographer round, resulting in each participant ending up with a single share of the message. The values of n and k required for the secret-sharing are system parameters, i.e., they are known beforehand and stay the same in the whole system.

Our protocol consists of three phases, which are shown in Fig. 1. In the first phase, named Split, a given message m is split into n secret shares. To split the message, we chose $k - 1$ random numbers $r_1, \ldots, r_{k.1}$. To create a random polynomial f which evaluates as $f(0) = m$, we use $f(x) = m + \sum_{i=1}^{k-1} r_i x^i$. We compute the secret shares $s_i = (i, f(i) \mod p)$ for all $i \in [1, n]$.

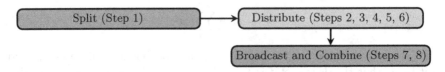

Fig. 1. The three phases of the protocol and their corresponding steps in Algorithm 2.

In the following phase (the distribution phase), each of the n participants of the network then receives a unique share of the secret. As described above, the DC protocol can only be used to make anonymous broadcasts, but not to send individual messages to certain participants anonymously. We can modify the protocol in such a way that this becomes possible. The modified DC protocol version is shown in Algorithm 2, note that a node that does not intend to send anything still proceeds with $m_{\text{self}} = 0$. Further note that participants not part of the group just execute Step 8 of Algorithm 2. The key modification compared to the original DC protocol as described by Chaum [3] (shown in Algorithm 1) is that Step 3 no longer makes a broadcast but transmits individual messages to other participants. The impact of this change is discussed in Sect. 4.

Algorithm 2. Modified DC protocol as executed by node g_{self}.

Input: Participants $g_1, g_2, \ldots, g_n$, message m_{self} of length ℓ
Output: Message $m_{\text{self},out}$, the message transmitted to this entity
1: Split m_{self} into n parts $m_{\text{self},1}, \ldots, m_{\text{self},n}$ using the secret-sharing scheme
2: Establish shared random secrets $s_{\text{self},i}$ of length ℓ with each member $g_i, i \neq$ self
3: $M_{\text{self},i} = m_{\text{self},i} \oplus \bigoplus_{j=1\ldots n, j \neq \text{self}} s_{\text{self},j} \; \forall i \in \{1 \ldots n\}$
4: Send $M_{\text{self},i}$ to $g_i \; \forall i \in \{1 \ldots n\} \setminus \{\text{self}\}$
5: Receive $M_{i,\text{self}}$ from $g_i \; \forall i \in \{1 \ldots n\} \setminus \{\text{self}\}$
6: $m_{\text{self},out} = \bigoplus_{i=1\ldots n, j \neq \text{self}} M_{i,\text{self}}$
7: Broadcast $m_{\text{self},out}$ to all network participants
8: Reconstruct m_{out} after receiving $k - 1$ other shares

The output of the distributed XOR function that participant g_h computes is no longer $m_{out} = \bigoplus_{i=1\ldots n} m_i$ but rather $m_{h,out} = \bigoplus_{i=1\ldots n} m_{i,h}$. Each member must now broadcast the message $m_{h_o ut}$ throughout the network.

If at least k participants broadcast their message, every recipient can decode the original message. If $k - 2$ or fewer participants broadcast the message, no one can decode the message. When exactly $k - 1$ participants broadcast, only non-broadcasting participants of the group can decode the message, as they possess the last share required to decrypt the message themself. Verifying the correctness of the result is omitted for the simplicity of the presentation. It would require application-level integrity protection, i.e., there needs to be a way to ensure a message is valid for the application using the protocol.

3.1   Correctness

For the protocol's correctness, we assume all participants execute the DC protocol correctly, no errors occurred, and everyone used a (n, k) Shamir's secret sharing technique. In a first step, we show that participants can reconstruct the sum of all Shamir's secret sharing points from the messages received in the DC protocol. From this, we reconstruct the original message $m_i \neq 0$ in a second step, given a successful sharing round.

Recovering the Sum of All Shared Points. The i-th participant receives the $n - 1$ messages $M_{1,i} \dots M_{i-1,i} M_{i+1,i} \dots M_{n,i}$. Further, they create the message $M_{i,i}$ themselves. Each message has the form:

$$M_{h,i} = m_{h,i} \oplus \bigoplus_{j \in \{1 \dots n\} \setminus \{h\}} s_{h,j}. \tag{7}$$

Therefore, the combination through XOR of all receives messages is

$$\bigoplus_{h \in \{1 \dots n\}} M_{h,i} = \bigoplus_{h \in \{1 \dots n\}} \left(m_{h,i} \oplus \bigoplus_{j \in \{1 \dots n\} \setminus \{h\}} s_{h,j} \right)$$

$$= \left(\bigoplus_{h \in \{1 \dots n\}} m_{h,i} \right) \oplus \underbrace{\left(\bigoplus_{h \in \{1 \dots n\}} \bigoplus_{j \in \{1 \dots n\} \setminus \{h\}} s_{h,j} \right)}_{=0, \text{ as } s_{h,j} \oplus s_{j,h} = 0} \tag{8}$$

$$= \bigoplus_{h \in \{1 \dots n\}} m_{h,i}.$$

As $m_{h,i}$ was created through the Shamir's secret sharing protocol, they have the form $m_{h,i} = p_h(i)$. Here p_h is the polynomial created by participant h to split their message. The polynomial is created over the Galois field $GF(2^8)$, a field with characteristic 2. In fields of characteristic 2, XOR and addition are equivalent. Therefore, it holds that the transformation allowing interoperability between Shamir's secret sharing and an XOR based dining-cryptographers network is possible:

$$\bigoplus_{h \in \{1 \dots n\}} m_{h,i} = \bigoplus_{h \in \{1 \dots n\}} p_h(i) \overset{\text{over } GF(2^q)}{=} \sum_{h \in \{1 \dots n\}} p_h(i). \tag{9}$$

Reconstruction of the Shared Message. In this second step, we show that receiving k distinct results allows us to reconstruct the protocol's original message input. We assume that the flooding mechanism, or any appropriate sharing protocol, correctly distributed k shares to all participants. Without loss of generality, we assume a participant received the first k messages:

$$\sum_{h \in \{1...n\}} p_h(1), \ldots, \sum_{h \in \{1...n\}} p_h(k). \tag{10}$$

We saw in the section on Lagrange interpolation, that polynomial interpolation is uniquely possible with k evaluation points $p(1), \ldots, p(k)$ for a polynomial p of degree $deg(p) = k - 1$. We interpret our received messages as points of a polynomial p_Σ :

$$p_\Sigma(i) := \sum_{h \in \{1...n\}} p_h(i). \tag{11}$$

Polynomial interpolation is unique with the given degree restrictions, and polynomial addition cannot increase the degree of the resulting polynomial. It holds, therefore, that:

$$p_\Sigma = \sum_{h \in \{1...n\}} p_h. \tag{12}$$

Evaluation and addition is commutative for polynomials, i.e., $(f + g)(x) = f(x) + g(x)$. Lastly, assume the messages are encoded at evaluation position s.

$$p_\Sigma(s) = \left(\sum_{h \in \{1...n\}} p_h \right)(s) = \left(\sum_{h \in \{1...n\}} \underbrace{p_h(s)}_{=m_i} \right) \tag{13}$$

If at most one message $m_i \neq 0$ exists, the reconstruction of the message is successful. Otherwise, the sum of all non-zero messages is restored.

4   Security and Privacy Evaluation

We assume a group size of n participants using a secure (n, k)-secret sharing scheme for this evaluation. We restrict ourselves to group communication, as the flood and prune broadcast has no interesting privacy or security properties.

4.1   Goal

Let $M_i = (M_{i,1}, \ldots, M_{i,n})$ be the vector of messages created by node i in a system with n participants, and Setup the creation of groups and distribution of keys and parameters. Let f be the function combining such a vector into the intended message, i.e., the combination algorithm of the secret sharing scheme. Within the formalisation, we denote the previously presented Algorithm 2 as Algorithm 2, which is used to create all messages $M_{i,j}$. Let the probability of $k - 1$ attackers A successfully identify a node ℓ sending a message be denoted by:

$$P\left[f(M_\ell) \neq 0 \,\middle|\, \begin{array}{c} pp \leftarrow \text{Setup}(\lambda, k, f) \\ M_i := M_{i,j}, i, j \in \{1 \ldots n\} \leftarrow \text{Alg2}(pp) \\ \ell \in \{1, k+1, \ldots, n\} \leftarrow A(pp, M_{i,j}, j \in \{2 \ldots k\}) \end{array}\right]. \quad (14)$$

We call our scheme $(n, k-1)$ secure if this probability is only negligibly different from selecting a participant out of the $n - k + 1$ non attackers at random, i.e.,

$$\left| P - \frac{1}{n - k + 1} \right| < \text{negl}(\lambda). \quad (15)$$

Informally, this definition is true when $k - 1$ colluding nodes cannot identify the originator of the message within the set of $n - |\text{attackers}|$ non-colluding nodes. But once k nodes cooperate, no guarantees are made.

4.2   Semi-Honest Model

To show our scheme fulfills the previous definition, let there be $k - 1$ colluding attackers present in the group, which follow the semi-honest model. Assume, without loss of generality as the nodes can be renumbered, that the victim has index 1 and the attackers' index 2 through k.

These colluding participants can collect $k - 1$ messages $M_{i,j}$ of the form $M_{i,j} = m_{i,j} \oplus \bigoplus_{h \in \{1 \ldots n\}} s_{i,h}$ by any participant i and the honest reconstruction of p_Σ, which provides the transmitted message m and the sum of all point evaluations. To identify the originator, the attackers need to compute any $m_{1,j}$ of the victim or, equivalently, their aggregate key $\bigoplus_j s_{1,j}$. The original proof of Chaum holds for directly reconstructing $\bigoplus_j s_{1,j}$, so we will focus on $m_{1,j}$. Note that $m_{1,j} = p_1(j)$ is equivalent, where the polynomial p_1 has degree $deg(p_i) = k - 1$ and the form

$$p_i(x) = \sum_{\ell=1}^{k} a_\ell x^{\ell-1}. \quad (16)$$

Given $k - 1$ messages $M_{1,2} \ldots M_{1,k+1}$ and $i \neq j$ we can see that it holds that

$$
\begin{aligned}
M_{1,i} \oplus M_{1,j} &= \left(m_{1,i} \oplus \bigoplus_{h \in \{1 \ldots n\}} s_{1,h} \right) \oplus \left(m_{1,j} \oplus \bigoplus_{h \in \{1 \ldots n\}} s_{1,h} \right) \\
&= m_{1,i} \oplus m_{1,j} \oplus \left(\bigoplus_{h \in \{1 \ldots n\}} s_{1,h} \oplus \bigoplus_{h \in \{1 \ldots n\}} s_{1,h} \right) \quad (17) \\
&= m_{1,i} \oplus m_{1,j} \oplus \bigoplus_{h \in \{1 \ldots n\}} \underbrace{\left(s_{1,h} \oplus s_{1,h} \right)}_{=0} = m_{1,i} \oplus m_{1,j}
\end{aligned}
$$

As XOR and addition are equivalent over base fields of characteristic 2, which we use, and that $m_{i,j} = p_i(j)$, we can see that

$$m_{1,i} \oplus m_{1,j} = p_1(i) + p_1(j). \tag{18}$$

Note that this only holds for even combinations, i.e., we cannot create $p_1(2) + p_1(3) + p_1(4)$. All combinations with an even number of parts can be constructed as a linear combination of combinations of two parts. Therefore, using this equation, we can create only $k - 2$ linearly independent equations:

$$[p_1] = \begin{cases} \sum_{i=1}^k 2a_i 2^{i-1} 3^{i-1} & = & p_1(2) + p_1(3) \\ \vdots & & \vdots \\ \sum_{i=1}^k 2a_i (k-1)^{i-1} k^{i-1} & = & p_1(k-1) + p_1(k) \end{cases} \tag{19}$$

The attackers can reconstruct the transmitted message $m = p_\Sigma(0)$ by following the protocol normally. Removing all attacker polynomials $p_2 \ldots p_k$ leaves

$$p_\Sigma - \sum_{j=2}^k p_j = p_1 + \sum_{j=k+1}^n p_j =: p_{\text{remains}}. \tag{20}$$

Using this and applying the strategy to compute $[p_1]$ on all non-colluding participants allows the attackers to create the following matrix

$$\begin{bmatrix} [p_1] & [0] & \cdots & [0] & S_1 \\ [0] & [p_{k+1}] & & [0] & S_{k+1} \\ \vdots & & \ddots & & \vdots \\ [0] & [0] & & [p_n] & S_n \\ 1 \ldots 1 & 1 \ldots 1 & \ldots & 1 \ldots 1 & p_{\text{remains}} \end{bmatrix} \tag{21}$$

All entries $[p_i]$ represent the previous equation systems with their respective solution vectors $S_i = (p_i(2) + p_i(3), \ldots, p_i(k-1) + p_i(k))$ generated from the messages $M_{i,j}$. Each block $[p_i]$ and $[0]$ have $k-2$ rows, while the final row models p_{remains}, where all coefficients are present exactly once. All further derivations of p_{remains} would not be linearly independent equations. There is no further relation between the remaining polynomials $p_1, p_{k+1}, \ldots, p_n$, as all are chosen independently at random.

Solving the equations for a single participant leaves us with $k - 2 + 1$ rows ($[p_i]$ and p_{remains}) and k indeterminants $a_1, \ldots, a_k$ and therefore k columns. The full matrix has $(n - k + 1) \times (k - 2) + 1$ rows and $k \times (n - k + 1) + 1$ columns. Using the Rouché–Capelli theorem, i.e., if for a system of equations $Ax = b$ there is a unique solution iff $rank(A) = rank(A|b)$, this results in infinitely many solutions, i.e., ambiguous reconstruction, and further breaks the security assumption of the base secret sharing protocol.

If a message can be verified after decryption, an exhaustive search for solutions is possible. The underlying field size determines the cost for an exhaustive search, i.e., the field size corresponds to λ in our previous definition. Absent any notes identifying correct solutions, all solutions to the system of equations are equally valid and likely, i.e., any of the $n - k + 1$ possible victims might be the sender with equal probability $P[f(M_\ell) \neq 0] = \frac{1}{n-k+1}$.

4.3   Outside Observers

Outside observers cannot determine the origin of a broadcast as long as secure channels are used, as all participants have to send data of the same size for each transmission. Similar to classical DC networks, no guarantees can be retained when the channels are no longer secure.

4.4   Modern DC Malicious Mitigations

While attackers act semi-honest in the previous evaluation, modern dining-cryptographers protocols apply various mechanisms to deal with collisions of multiple sent messages, fairness, and robustness issues of the protocol [1,6].

To increase fairness the protocol can apply $2n$ slots, where every participant may use at most one slot at a time, which they chose randomly. Participants create commitments on each secret share they create, to prevent cheating. Each commitment is broadcast to the whole group. When more than n slots are occupied, a zero-knowledge proof allows every honest participant to show their innocence. As long as every participant uses at most one slot, any participant has a fair chance of at least $\frac{1}{2}$ to transmit their message.

Lastly, the most problematic case, selective non-participation, can be combated by pre-emptively sharing all secrets in encrypted form with the group. If any node claims another refuses to send their messages to them, any other node can take over by forwarding the encrypted shares.

These techniques can be applied to our proposed protocol to make it resistant to malicious participants. Slots can be easily introduced by applying the secret splitting per slot, not on the full message. Commitments can be created in the same form as by von Ahn et al. [1]: each slot provides its own commitments. The zero-knowledge proof of fairness by von Ahn et al. can be extended as easily: The opening of commitments is combined with a reconstruction of the secret shares into the actual message. This message has to be zero.

5   Performance Evaluation

5.1   Methodology

We implemented a prototype simulation that can simulate both the original DC protocol and our modified version. The simulation is available online[2] and written in Java. We use built-in synchronization utilities to model the communication and synchronization of participants. For threshold cryptography, we

---

[2] https://github.com/vs-uulm/thc-in-dc-simulation.

used the open-source library shamir[3] in version 0.7.0. The Shamir library uses a Galois field $GF(2^8)$ as a base field. The library provides two methods, split and join, of combined complexity of $\mathcal{O}(\ell \cdot (n + k^2))$.

We ran this implementation 10 to 30 times for each combination of parameters. We aggregated the measured throughput and computed the average and standard deviation.

Network latency is simulated, but we set it to 0 to prevent influence on the measured variable when not specified. To mitigate our results' distortion due to runtime optimization attempts by the Java virtual machine, we ran a warm-up phase before each test. In this warm-up phase, 100 runs were performed that are not included in our results.

We compared the modified DC protocol, denoted as Broadcast, to Chaum's original version's performance, denoted as DC Phase in graphs. We investigated several core issues:

- The size ℓ of the transmitted message,
- the scaling behaviour of the protocol, i.e., increasing n,
- the performance impact of variable k values,
- the influence of network latency.

For the performance evaluation, we consider a simple collaboration protocol in place of the broadcast to reduce simulation effort. Participants send their shares to the $k-1$ following participants, based on an established order of group participants, e.g., sorted by increasing public keys. As all participants compute the same subgroups, the minimum number of messages are sent. See Algorithm 3. We opted not to evaluate a full flooding approach, as this would shift the focus from the modifications we performed and the performance characteristics of flooding approaches are well known.

Algorithm 3. Combine protocol to emulate broadcast.

Input: Message part m_i, Group members $g_1, g_2, \ldots, g_n$, number of shares k
Output: Message m_{out}
1: Send m_i to g_j $\forall j \in \{i + a \mod (n + 1) \mid a \in \mathbb{N}, 1 \le a \le k - 1\}$
2: Receive m_r from $g_r \forall r \in \{x \mid \exists a, 1 \le a \le k - 1 : x + a \mod (n + 1) = i\}$
3: **return** m_{out} from the $k - 1$ received messages and m_i.

5.2   Message Size ℓ

Both the original DC protocol and our modified protocol transmit a message of the fixed-length ℓ each round. We want to keep ℓ as close as possible to the actual length of the information we want to send.

---

[3] https://github.com/codahale/shamir.

Messages longer than ℓ can be split into multiple messages, increasing overhead and, therefore, decreasing throughput. If the information is shorter than ℓ, it can be padded with 0-bytes to make it size ℓ, leading to the transmission of more data than necessary, producing overhead as well.

We show the results of this overhead in Fig. 2. We varied ℓ from 32 B to 32 kB with $n = 10$ and a given real message size of 8 kB. We chose the relevant parameters for this benchmark with regard to the potential use for our proposed system in the field of cryptocurrencies. Therefore we picked sizes applicable to groups [11] and transaction sizes, validating our assumption that the performance is at its peak when ℓ is roughly equal to the size of the information to transmit. Results for varying sizes of n (not shown) lead to the same validation.

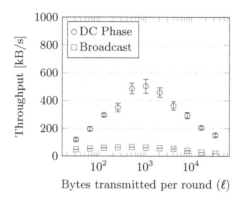

Fig. 2. The measured throughput and its standard deviation while increasing ℓ for $n = 10$, $k = 3$ and the size of m is 8 kB.

5.3   Network Size n

While the message complexity for the core DC protocol is identical in both schemes, a round of the modified version of the DC protocol needs additional messages in the cooperation phase. When keeping k constant, the modified version of the protocol requires $\mathcal{O}(n)$ more transmissions than the original protocol. We see in Fig. 3a, this makes a significant difference for a low number of participants. Both versions of the protocol are of overall complexity $\mathcal{O}(n^2)$, so the linear performance penalty becomes less of a concern when n grows larger.

The increased number of sent messages is only one reason for the worse performance of our system. The time for performing one round of the protocol can be divided into two parts: time spent communicating and time spent for calculations. Our system requires a larger amount of computations compared to the classical DC protocol. In addition to performing the core DC functionality, it also splits and joins the messages to transmit using a secret-sharing scheme, resulting in the strong performance difference seen in Fig. 3a.

5.4   Network Delay

To investigate less optimal environments, we simulated our scheme using a delay of >0 ms. The gap in performance between the original DC protocol and our system is notably smaller. The results of adding a delay of 100 ms are shown in Fig. 3b respectively, but simulations with intermediate values show similar results. We chose 100 ms as a typical representation of internet communication delay, but in real-world scenarios, it can be considerably smaller.

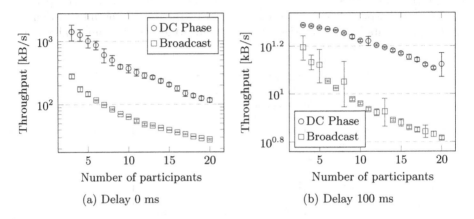

Fig. 3. Measuring throughput in DC protocol runs over networks of various sizes. Variable n, $k = 3$, $\ell = 8$ kB.

Note that when adding delay, our system only improves relative to the original dining-cryptographers protocol. The absolute performance of both approaches suffers under message transmission delay. We measured throughput rates of 13.58 kB/s for $n = 4$ and 9.12 kB/s for $n = 10$ with a delay of 100 ms.

5.5   Number of Shares k

Lastly, the value of k is the number of message shares needed to restore a message and significantly impacts the protocol. This impact is due to participants needing to compute additional methods and perform additional $k - 1$ transmissions to receive the shares. Figure 4 shows the results of benchmarking our system with $n = 10$, $\ell = 8$ kB and $k \in \{3, \ldots, 10\}$. As expected, increasing k decreases our system's performance.

6   Applications

As we have seen, our version of a DC protocol typically achieves throughput rates between 10 kB/s and 100 kB/s. A real-world application for our system lies in the anonymous transmission of transaction data for blockchains, e.g., in an

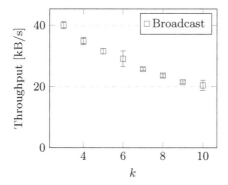

Fig. 4. Measuring network throughput while varying parameter k. The other parameters are kept constant with $n = 10$ and ℓ as well as the size of the transmitted information as $8\,kB$.

environment like the one proposed in [11]. Such transaction data are typically of size $< 1\,kB$, whereas group sizes are between $n = 4$ and $n = 10$ and transmission delay is around $100\,ms$.

Many blockchain systems produce only a few transactions per second, despite thousands of nodes participating. Separating these into groups for privacy is unlikely to lead to any groups that require more than one transaction per second. Therefore, every system that can achieve speeds of >1 transactions made per second is suitable for application in a system as the one proposed in [11]. Our system is well-suited for such a task, as it can efficiently work with this load.

7   Conclusion

In this work, we proposed a combination of the classical dining-cryptographers protocol and Shamir's secret sharing to enforce anonymity during a broadcast process. This problem arises during a broadcast, as nodes that already received the message might refuse further cooperation. We showed that the protocol is computational secure in the number of shares k, maintaining $n - |attackers|$-anonymity for at most $k - 1$ attackers.

Our system provides a first, unoptimized solution, so further work could improve the system's performance and flexibility. In our simulation, this results in throughput rates between $10\,kB/s$ and $100\,kB/s$ for a full broadcast simulation and over $500\,kB/s$ with reasonable privacy settings. These performance results show our system is viable for a wide range of applications, such as blockchain-transaction dissemination in peer-to-peer networks.

References

1. von Ahn, L., Bortz, A., Hopper, N.J.: K-anonymous message transmission. In: 10th ACM SIGSAC Conference on Computer and Communications Security (CCS), pp. 122–130. ACM, New York (2003)

2. Biryukov, A., Khovratovich, D., Pustogarov, I.: Deanonymisation of clients in Bitcoin P2P network. In: ACM SIGSAC Conference on Computer and Communications Security (CCS), pp. 15–29. ACM, New York (2014)

3. Chaum, D.: The dining cryptographers problem: unconditional sender and recipient untraceability. J. Cryptol. **1**(1), 65–75 (1988)

4. Corrigan-Gibbs, H., Ford, B.: Dissent: accountable anonymous group messaging. In: 17th ACM SIGSAC Conference on Computer and Communications Security (CCS), pp. 340–350. ACM, New York (2010)

5. Gasca, M., Sauer, T.: Polynomial interpolation in several variables. Adv. Comput. Math. **12**(4), 377 (2000). https://doi.org/10.1023/A:1018981505752

6. Golle, P., Juels, A.: Dining cryptographers revisited. In: Cachin, C., Camenisch, J.L. (eds.) EUROCRYPT 2004. LNCS, vol. 3027, pp. 456–473. Springer, Heidelberg (2004). https://doi.org/10.1007/978-3-540-24676-3_27

7. Koshy, P., Koshy, D., McDaniel, P.: An analysis of anonymity in bitcoin using P2P network traffic. In: Christin, N., Safavi-Naini, R. (eds.) FC 2014. LNCS, vol. 8437, pp. 469–485. Springer, Heidelberg (2014). https://doi.org/10.1007/978-3-662-45472-5_30

8. Miers, I., Garman, C., Green, M., Rubin, A.D.: Zerocoin: anonymous distributed e-cash from Bitcoin. In: IEEE Symposium on Security and Privacy (SP), pp. 397–411, May 2013

9. Möser, M., et al.: An empirical analysis of traceability in the Monero blockchain. In: Proceedings on Privacy Enhancing Technologies Symposium (PoPETs 2018), vol. 3, pp. 143–163 (2018)

10. Mödinger, D., Hauck, F.J.: 3P3: strong flexible privacy for broadcasts. In: 4th International Workshop on Cyberspace Security (IWCSS 2020) (2020)

11. Mödinger, D., Kopp, H., Kargl, F., Hauck, F.J.: A flexible network approach to privacy of blockchain transactions. In: IEEE 38th International Conference on Distributed Computing Systems (ICDCS), pp. 1486–1491, July 2018

12. Shamir, A.: How to share a secret. Commun. ACM **22**(11), 612–613 (1979)

13. Wolinsky, D.I., Corrigan-Gibbs, H., Ford, B., Johnson, A.: Dissent in numbers: making strong anonymity scale. In: 10th USENIX Conference on Operating Systems Design and Implementation (OSDI), pp. 179–192. USENIX Association, Berkeley (2012)

UCBFed: Using Reinforcement Learning Method to Tackle the Federated Optimization Problem

Wanqi Chen[1,2](✉) and Xin Zhou[1,2]

[1] Institute of Software, Chinese Academy of Sciences, Beijing, China
{wanqi2020,zhouxin}@iscas.ac.cn
[2] University of Chinese Academy of Sciences, Beijing, China

Abstract. Federated learning is a novel research area of AI technology that focus on distributed training and privacy preservation. Current federated optimization algorithms face serious challenge in the aspects of speed and accuracy, especially in non-i.i.d scenario. In this work, we propose UCBFed, a federated optimization algorithm that uses the Upper Confidence Bound (UCB) method to heuristically select participating clients in each round's optimization process. We evaluate our algorithm in multiple federated distributed datasets. Comparing to most widely-used FedAvg and FedOpt, the UCBFed we proposed is superior in both the final accuracy and communication efficiency.

Keywords: Federated learning · Upper Confidence Bound · Distributed learning · Optimization

1 Introduction

Federated learning is an emerging field in machine learning research. In the federated setting, training data remained distributed in a large number and variety of edge devices, such as computers, smart phones and many other IOT devices. Data in those devices might be useful for training a global model to accomplish specific missions, such as image classification, object detection and others. However, due to privacy, liability, cost and some other issues, it's not allowed to move this data together in the federated setting.

There are many open challenges in federated learning research, such as increasing communication-efficiency [9], preserving users' privacy [3] and defensing against malicious attacks [13]. In this work we address the speed and accuracy of federated optimization, especially in heterogeneous (non-i.i.d) situation.

In this paper, we propose a new algorithm called UCBFed. Instead of selecting clients randomly in each round in popular method like FedAvg [10], UCBFed uses the Upper Confidence Bound (UCB) method [1] which is originally designed

© IFIP International Federation for Information Processing 2021
Published by Springer Nature Switzerland AG 2021
M. Matos and F. Greve (Eds.): DAIS 2021, LNCS 12718, pp. 99–105, 2021.
https://doi.org/10.1007/978-3-030-78198-9_7

for multi-armed bandit problem in Reinforcement Learning. The UCB algorithm take both history "rewards" and number of times that one client has been chosen into account to determine which client will be chosen in a specific round. To define the "reward", referring to the experience of FedReID [14], we use cosine distance of the last layer of backbone network between old global model and newly trained client model as a metric. We also use this metric as the weight when aggregate models from clients, replacing "the number of data cases in each clients" used by FedAvg algorithm. The remainder of this paper is organized as follows. In Sect. 2, we provide an simple overview of related work. In Sect. 3 we propose our UCBFed algorithm and describe two main components of the algorithm. In Sect. 4 the comparison among baseline algorithms and ours is presented. Finally, we expound our conclusion and future work that need to continue in Sect. 5.

2   Related Work

2.1   Federated Learning

The very beginning of the federated learning research is from 2015, with the first publications on federated averaging (FedAvg). There are many research directions in this area, including improving accuracy and speed of federated optimization, reducing the communication burden during the federated process and protect users' privacy in federated settings. For the first direction, many algorithms including FedProx [8] and SCAFFOLD [6] use information from central model to "correct" the local updates. Then, methods such as model compression and model pruning are applied to the reduction of communication cost. Finally, Bagdasaryan [2], Wang [11] and Zhu [13] investigate many aspects about how to attack and defense of the federated learning.

There are different scenarios of federated learning. In horizontal federated learning, different clients have data that have same features but different IDs. On the contrary, in vertical scenario, different sets of data have same IDs but different features. And in transfer federated learning, both features and IDs are different.

Horizontal Federated Learning. In this paper, our work focus on horizontal federated learning. The problem can be formulated as follows:

Consider a scenario with C clients. The ith client has D_i samples. Let z_i be the data domain of each client and $L(w, z_i)$ be the likelihood function of ith client, then:

$$\arg\max_{w} f(w) = \sum_{i=1}^{C} \frac{D_i}{\sum_{i=1}^{C} D_i} L(w, z_i)$$

FedAvg. In FedAvg algorithm, each client train local model using local data in multiple batches and upload the gradients to the server. Then the server will weight averaging all the gradients using local data size as the weight. Then server will transfer back the weights to client and start next rounds of training. Though FedAvg is successful in several fields, it still has some space for improvement. As our work concerns, the FedAvg selects clients randomly in each round, ignoring the quality of each client's data. Unavoidably it will harm the result of optimization. Therefore our work present a strategy to choose client in each round.

2.2 Multi-armed Bandit Problem

The multi-armed bandit problem can be described as follows:

The multi-armed bandit has $K \in N^+$ levers and the reward delivered by each bandit is associated with a distribution $R_i \in B = \{R_1, ..., R_K\}$. The player repeatedly plays one lever per round and observes the associated reward. The aim is to maximize the sum of rewards collected by players.

To solve the multi-armed bandit problem, an algorithm should tackle with a trade-off between two choices: exploit the levers that have better history rewards or explore those levers that are rarely visited.

Several algorithms have been proposed, including ϵ-greedy algorithm, Thompson sampling, Upper Confidence Bounds (UCB) and more.

Upper Confidence Bound (UCB) Algorithm. In UCB algorithm, each lever a has a metric A_t given by:

$$A_t = \arg\max_a [\frac{H_t(a)}{N_t(a)} + c\sqrt{\frac{\log t}{N_t(a)}}]$$

$H_t(a)$ is the sum of history rewards of the lever at time step t and $N_t(a)$ is the number of times that the level has been selected before. Finally, c is a control variable that controls the level of exploration.

During each round t, UCB algorithm plays the lever that has the maximum value of A_t and updates A_t of all levers.

3 The Proposed UCBFed Algorithm

3.1 Cosine Distance Weight (CDW)

To apply UCB thought to the process of choosing participating clients, we need a metric to define the "quality" of each client's training result. A simple yet effective idea is to use the amount of information or the change that a single client contributes to the model. Hence, inspired by the work of FedReID [14], We choose Cosine Distance Weight (CDW) as the metric. CDW measures the information that a client has learned by the cosine distance between the outputs of feature extraction parts of the model before and after client training process.

Algorithm 1: UCBFed. S is the set of all clients. K is the number of clients that participate in a round; B is the local minibatch size, E is the number of local epochs, and η is the learning rate. D is data size of all clients

---

1 **Server executes:**
2   Initialize w_0
3   Initialize: $\forall c_i \in S, H_t(c_i) \leftarrow 0, N_t(c_i) \leftarrow 0$
4   **for** *each round t=1,2...,T* **do**
5   **for** $c_i \in S$ **do**
6           $A_t(c_i) = \frac{H_t(c_i)}{N_t(c_i)} + \beta\sqrt{\frac{\log t}{N_t(c_i)}}$
7   **end**
8       $S_t \leftarrow$ clients that have top K largest A_t
9   **for** *each client* $c_k \in S_t$ *in parallel* **do**
10           $w_{t+1}^k, CDW_{t+1}^k \leftarrow ClientUpdate(k, w_t)$ $N_{t+1}(c_k) \leftarrow N_t(c_k) + 1$
11   **end**
12   update H_t using Algorithm 3
13       $w_{t+1} \leftarrow \sum_{k=1}^K \frac{CDW_{t+1}^k}{\sum_{j=1}^K CDW_{t+1}^j} w_{t+1}^k$
14   **end**
15 **ClientUpdate:**
16   **for** *each local epoch* **do**
17   **for** *batch* $b \in$ *training data* **do**
18           $w \leftarrow w - \eta\nabla l(w; b)$
19   **end**
20   **end**
21    $CDW_k \leftarrow$ computing CDW using Algorithm 2
22   return CDW_k to server

3.2 Reward Allocation

Once a round of client training process is finished and the server gets all participating clients' CDWs, we can allocate actual rewards to these clients based on the metrics. UCBFed gives those clients which have the largest CDW a positive reward ($+1$) while other clients can only get zero rewards.

3.3 Clients Selection and Model Aggregating

After we get reward and CDWs of participating clients, we can start to aggregate the client models into a new global model and select the participating clients in the next round. The algorithm is generally based on FedAvg but has two improvements. First, instead of random selecting clients in each round, we choose the clients that have the largest Upper-Confidence-Bound value A_t; Second, instead of using data size as the weight of weight averaging process of model aggregating, we use a CDW-based weight.

The full process of the UCB algorithm is in Algorithm 1.

4   Experiments

We evaluate our **UCBFed** algorithm in multiple datasets. We compared our algorithm with the most widely used algorithm–**FedAvg** and **FedOpt**. UCBFed has shown promising results in various datasets.

4.1   Experiments Details

Datasets and Setup. We run experiments on three different datasets: EMNIST [4], SHAKESPEARE [8] and CIFAR-100 [7]. These datasets have been already used in different works in these areas before. **EMNIST** is an handwritten character classification datasets. It's collected from 3400 different writers; **Shakespeare** dataset is a next-word prediction task on *The Complete Works of William Shakespeare* and each speaking role corresponds to a device; Finally, **CIFAR100** is a tiny image classification dataset consists of 100 classes of 60000 samples. And for the federated setting experiment it is divided into 500 parts and each part corresponds to a device. Statistic are summarized in Table 1.

Table 1. Summaries of models using in different tasks

Dataset	Device	Training samples	Testing samples
Shakespeare	143	413629	103477
CIFAR-100	500	50000	10000
EMNIST	3400	671585	77483

Federated Models. In this experiments we train different models in different datasets in federated settings using UCBFed and FedAvg. More specifically, we use a simple deep convolution network on **EMNIST** dataset and a simple LSTM network on **Shakespeare** dataset. A ResNet-18 network is adopted on CIFAR-100 mission to represent the scenario that a complicated network is trained using federated settings. In federated scenarios, computing resources of client devices are usually limited, hence the batch-size might be very small. In this case, traditional Batch Normalization may lose its efficiencies. So we use batch-size-irrelevant Group Normalization [12] instead of Batch Normalization in ResNet-18 network.

Implementation. We implement our experiments code based on FedML framework [5]. More specifically, we use the single-machine stimulation environment the framework provided to demonstrate our experiment. Based on FedAvg codes, we modify the process of client sampling and weight averaging. For all tasks, we set $\alpha = 0.8$ and $E = 5$. Other hyperparameters are summarized in Table 2.

Table 2. Summaries of hyperparameters

Dataset	Learning rate	Device per round	Total round
Shakespeare	0.8	10	200
CIFAR-100	0.001	10	1000
EMNIST	0.03	50	1000

Metrics. For each task, we evaluate our algorithms using two metrics. First is the highest accuracy that an algorithm can achieve. Another commonly used metric in federated optimization area is the communication cost for reaching a specific accuracy target. In this experiment, the communication cost of each round is equal between UCBFed and FedAvg. Hence, we use the communication round before reaching a specific accuracy target as an equivalent.

4.2   Experiment Results

As it has shown in Table 3 and Table 4, UCBFed is superior than FedAvg in all three tasks. Comparing to FedOpt, UCBFed has achieved better highest accuracy. However, in the aspect of communication round, UCBFed takes more round to achieve the target accuracy than FedOpt in EMNIST and CIFAR-100.

Table 3. Highest accuracy

Dataset	UCBFed (ours)	FedAvg	FedOpt
Shakespeare	**0.519**	0.513	0.386
EMNIST	**0.851**	0.849	0.834
CIFAR-100	**0.264**	0.235	0.224

Table 4. Communication round of reaching a specific accuracy target

Dataset (target accuracy)	UCBFed (ours)	FedAvg	FedOpt
Shakespeare (0.5)	**35**	115	N/A
EMNIST (0.8)	55	60	**50**
CIFAR-100 (0.2)	185	445	**130**

5   Conclusion and Future Works

In this work, we have proposed UCBFed, a federated learning algorithm that tackles the speed and accuracy of federated optimization. UCBFed uses the

Upper Confidence Bound (UCB) method to select the participating clients of each round to improve the quality of optimization. In our experiment UCBFed shows significantly better result than FedAvg. It indicates that UCBFed improves the convergence behavior of federated learning in realistic heterogeneous network.

The future work includes the application to various and complicated federated scenarios, including federated object detection and ReId. Then, it is interesting to find if there are better metrics to replace CDW. Finally, the combination of UCBFed and model personalization is also an interesting research point.

References

1. Auer, P.: Using upper confidence bounds for online learning. In: Proceedings 41st Annual Symposium on Foundations of Computer Science, pp. 270–279. IEEE (2000)
2. Bagdasaryan, E., Veit, A., Hua, Y., Estrin, D., Shmatikov, V.: How to backdoor federated learning. In: International Conference on Artificial Intelligence and Statistics, pp. 2938–2948. PMLR (2020)
3. Bonawitz, K., et al.: Practical secure aggregation for privacy-preserving machine learning. In: Proceedings of the 2017 ACM SIGSAC Conference on Computer and Communications Security, pp. 1175–1191 (2017)
4. Cohen, G., Afshar, S., Tapson, J., Van Schaik, A.: EMNIST: extending MNIST to handwritten letters. In: 2017 International Joint Conference on Neural Networks (IJCNN), pp. 2921–2926. IEEE (2017)
5. He, C., et al.: FedML: a research library and benchmark for federated machine learning. arXiv preprint arXiv:2007.13518 (2020)
6. Karimireddy, S.P., Kale, S., Mohri, M., Reddi, S.J., Stich, S.U., Suresh, A.T.: Scaffold: stochastic controlled averaging for on-device federated learning. arXiv preprint arXiv:1910.06378 (2019)
7. Krizhevsky, A., Hinton, G., et al.: Learning multiple layers of features from tiny images (2009)
8. Li, T., Sahu, A.K., Zaheer, M., Sanjabi, M., Talwalkar, A., Smith, V.: Federated optimization in heterogeneous networks. arXiv preprint arXiv:1812.06127 (2018)
9. Lin, Y., Han, S., Mao, H., Wang, Y., Dally, W.J.: Deep gradient compression: reducing the communication bandwidth for distributed training. arXiv preprint arXiv:1712.01887 (2017)
10. McMahan, B., Moore, E., Ramage, D., Hampson, S., Arcas, B.A.: Communication-efficient learning of deep networks from decentralized data. In: Artificial Intelligence and Statistics, pp. 1273–1282. PMLR (2017)
11. Wang, H., et al.: Attack of the tails: yes, you really can backdoor federated learning. arXiv preprint arXiv:2007.05084 (2020)
12. Wu, Y., He, K.: Group normalization. In: Ferrari, V., Hebert, M., Sminchisescu, C., Weiss, Y. (eds.) ECCV 2018. LNCS, vol. 11217, pp. 3–19. Springer, Cham (2018). https://doi.org/10.1007/978-3-030-01261-8_1
13. Zhu, L., Liu, Z., Han, S.: Deep leakage from gradients. In: Advances in Neural Information Processing Systems, pp. 14774–14784 (2019)
14. Zhuang, W., et al.: Performance optimization of federated person re-identification via benchmark analysis. In: Proceedings of the 28th ACM International Conference on Multimedia, pp. 955–963 (2020)

Trusted Environments

KEVLAR-TZ: A Secure Cache for ARM TRUSTZONE
(Practical Experience Report)

Oscar Benedito[1], Ricard Delgado-Gonzalo[1] (ID), and Valerio Schiavoni[2(✉)] (ID)

[1] CSEM, Neuchâtel, Switzerland
{obo,rdg}@csem.ch
[2] University of Neuchâtel, Neuchâtel, Switzerland
valerio.schiavoni@unine.ch

Abstract. Edge devices are increasingly in charge of storing privacy-sensitive data, in particular implantables, wearables, and nearables can potentially collect and process high-resolution vital signs 24/7. Storing and performing computations over such data in a privacy-preserving fashion is of paramount importance. We present KEVLAR-TZ, an application-level trusted cache designed to leverage ARM TRUSTZONE, a popular trusted execution environment available in consumer-grade devices. To facilitate the integration with existing systems and IoT devices and protocols, KEVLAR-TZ exposes a REST-based interface with connection endpoints inside the TRUSTZONE enclave. Furthermore, it exploits the on-device secure persistent storage to guarantee durability of data across reboots. We fully implemented KEVLAR-TZ on top of the OP-TEE framework, and experimentally evaluated its performance. Our results showcase performance trade-offs, for instance in terms of throughput and latency, for various workloads, and we believe our results can be useful for practitioners and in general developers of systems for TRUSTZONE. KEVLAR-TZ is available as open-source at https://github.com/mqttz/kevlar-tz/.

Keywords: Caching · Edge devices · TrustZone · TEE · OP-TEE

1 Introduction

Wearable and Internet-of-Things (IoT) devices are becoming increasingly pervasive in modern society. It is predicted that by the year 2025 there will be more than 600 million wearable devices deployed and connected worldwide [9], and according to Cisco up to 500 billion IoT devices by 2030 [4]. These devices continuously produce data from a wide range of sensor types: inertial sensors (*e.g.*, accelerometers, gyroscopes) [12], biopotential (*e.g.*, electrocardiography) [14], optical (*e.g.*, photopletysmography) [42], biochemical (*e.g.*, pH) [17], *etc.* Combinations of such sensors allow for the monitoring of the health statuses of the users, ranging from the user's physical activity [19] to the detection of cardiac abnormalities [21]. The nature of this data is intrinsically privacy-sensitive. Applications and system designers must protect it from malicious attackers,

© IFIP International Federation for Information Processing 2021
Published by Springer Nature Switzerland AG 2021
M. Matos and F. Greve (Eds.): DAIS 2021, LNCS 12718, pp. 109–124, 2021.
https://doi.org/10.1007/978-3-030-78198-9_8

including those with physical access, from accessing and possibly unveiling them. Similarly, IoT devices are regularly used to monitor and record privacy-related data. Examples include motion sensors (*e.g.*, in the case of a smart-home deployment, revealing for instance the presence of humans indoors [34]), power-consumption meters (*e.g.*, potentially revealing the habits of a household), weather sensors (*e.g.*, a key asset in farming used to decide on optimal irrigation levels [35]), *etc.*. The vast majority of such applications deal with the insertion and retrieval of data from/to a dedicated, and preferably persistent, memory area. The mentioned operations are typically offered by key-value stores, *e.g.*, software libraries or services that allow to put and get values associated with unique identifiers (*i.e.*, the keys), for later retrieval, similar to a *caching* mechanism. Note that such libraries are vastly known in literature (*i.e.*, [13,27], *etc.*), extensively studied [24] and find usage in several and diverse application domains. Noteworthy, the result of confidential computations (*e.g.*, edge-based privacy-preserving machine-learning model training, just to name one) must also be stored and retrieved following the same access patterns. Hence, the content of such memory area must be shielded.

The need for stringent data privacy guarantees, such as the mentioned shielding, usually comes at the cost of computational overhead. This is the case of full homomorphic encryption (HE) [23], a purely software-based approach to compute and operate over encrypted data. However, recent work [25] has shown how state-of-the-art HE implementations [26] still result in orders of magnitude slowdown even for simple arithmetical operations, and major breakthroughs are yet to be seen for HE to become a viable solution.

The introduction and widespread adoption in the last few years of trusted execution environments (TEE) for consumer- and server-grade devices offers an opportunity to combine the need for privacy with the ones of viable performance. TEEs provide a hardware-supported mechanism to maintain the privacy and integrity of data while allowing for efficient and transparent protection from malicious attackers or compromised operating systems. Such protected areas are commonly referred to as *enclaves*, and they represent the main programming abstraction supported by the large majority of available TEEs. Notable examples include Intel®SGX [16], AMD Secure Encrypted Virtualization (SEV) [30] for server-grade as well as cloud-based deployments [5,6] and ARM TRUSTZONE [11,37] for more edge-centric scenarios, the focus of this work.

In this practical experience report paper, we present KEVLAR-TZ, an efficient trusted cache application for ARM TRUSTZONE with support for non-volatile secure storage. KEVLAR-TZ exposes an easy-to-use REST interface to facilitate the integration with existing systems, protocols, and third-party devices. The network connection endpoints are established within the TRUSTZONE enclave. Finally, KEVLAR-TZ is designed to exploit the secure storage implemented by some TRUSTZONE-enabled systems, allowing for secure data durability.

The main **contributions** of this work are twofold. First, we present the design and implementation of KEVLAR-TZ, a secure cache for ARM TRUSTZONE. Second, we describe in detail our implementation and evaluate it using real-world data, including a performance comparison with an emulator, showcasing the performance-tradeoffs that practitioners must face.

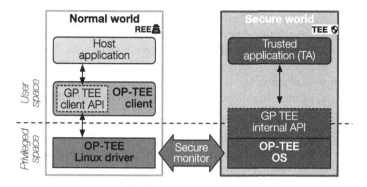

Fig. 1. Architecture of OP-TEE to realize trusted applications leveraging TRUSTZONE. GP: GlobalPlatform [7], a standardization effort for TEEs.

Roadmap. The rest of this paper is organized as follows. Section 2 provides relevant background material on TEEs, TRUSTZONE and trusted applications in general, including some of the underlying libraries and systems used in our evaluation. We present the architecture of KEVLAR-TZ in Sect. 4, detailing some of its implementation details in Sect. 5. Section 6 presents our in-depth performance evaluation of the KEVLAR-TZ prototype, using micro- and macro-benchmarks as well as real-world data. We survey related work in Sect. 7, before concluding and devising future work in Sect. 8.

2 Background

Trusted Execution Environments (TEEs). A trusted execution environment is a hardware-protected part of the processor. Depending on the specific version and implementation, a TEE can guarantee confidentiality, integrity and protection against several types of attacks for code and data executed and processed within it. Currently, there exist several hardware-based technologies that enable physical isolation of different execution environments available in a wide range of CPUs, including ARM TRUST-ZONE [1,11,37], Intel®SGX [16], AMD SEV [30], and RISC-V Keystone [31]. While we expect more TEE options to surface in the coming years, we focus on ARM TRUST-ZONE in the reminder of the paper, highlighting its main features and programming framework.

TRUSTZONE. TRUSTZONE is a hardware feature implemented in ARM processors since 2004 [10]. It enables physical separation between two different execution environments: the trusted side (known as the TEE or *secure world*) and the untrusted side (known as the REE or *normal world*). The TRUSTZONE protects the integrity and confidentiality of the code run inside the *secure world* from an attacker with physical access to the device, a malicious kernel or a high-privileged software. Programs hosted inside the TRUSTZONE, known as Trusted Applications, can leverage additional TRUSTZONE functionalities such as secure persistent storage with the use of APIs.

Op-Tee. The Open Portable Trusted Execution Environment (Op-Tee) is an open source operating system with native support for the TrustZone. Op-Tee implements two APIs compliant with the GlobalPlatform [7] specifications: the TEE Internal Core API [3], which is exposed to the Trusted Applications, and the TEE Client API [2], which defines how a client in the REE should communicate with the TEE. The TEE can run alongside a Linux-based operating system (such as a GNU/Linux distribution or AOSP) as the untrusted OS.

Trusted Application. Trusted Applications (TAs) run inside the *secure world*, making use of the TEE kernel to access system resources. TAs can act as a service for applications running on the *normal world* as well as for other TAs. When using Op-Tee, Trusted Applications are implemented in C and they can leverage the TEE Internal Core API implemented by Op-Tee, which offers several services, including trusted storage and cryptographic, time and arithmetical operations. KeVlar-Tz is an application that runs on the TEE, so it is a Trusted Application. When using KeVlar-Tz, we can do so from another TA (if we are running it on the TEE) or from a normal application running in the REE. The design of trusted applications for Op-Tee is depicted in Fig. 1.

Trusted Persistent Storage. Op-Tee provides the Trusted Storage API for Data and Keys as part of the TEE Internal Core API [3]. This API can be used by Trusted Applications to access a secure storage which is only accessible to that particular TA and that is persistent between reboots. The data is stored encrypted and signed on the disk, to prevent it from being accessed or tampered with by any other application. The data can later be transparently accessed in cleartext by the TA. KeVlar-Tz exploits this by saving the encryption keys using a public ID, which are the value and key (respectively) in the key-value storage. When an untrusted application needs to use an encryption key, it sends the key's ID and KeVlar-Tz retrieves it.

MQTT and `mosquitto`. The Message Queuing Telemetry Transport (MQTT) is a lightweight, publish-subscribe network protocol, suited for communication in environments with few resources and low network bandwidth. MQTT has two types of entities: the broker and the clients. The clients can publish messages to a topic or subscribe to one of them, while the broker is a server that forwards each incoming message to all the subscribers of its topic. `mosquitto` is an open source implementation of the MQTT broker developed and maintained by the Eclipse Foundation, which also provides a C library for implementing MQTT clients, as well as one implementation of both a subscriber client and a publisher client.

MQT-Tz. MQT-Tz [40] is a fork of `mosquitto`, a topic-based publish-subscribe framework for IoT. It allows brokers and the clients to leverage the TrustZone TEE, by encrypting the messages sent on the network to prevent the broker from being able to read them, while maintaining the publish-subscribe pattern. Similarly it allows full decoupling between publishers and subscribers, shielding the subscriptions inside the TEE.

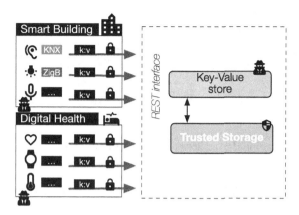

Fig. 2. Two possible application scenarios where a trusted key/value storage system is valuable. Clients (on the left-side) issue requests to store key-value pairs into the key-value store, which stores those into a trusted storage.

3 Motivating Scenarios

In this section, we describe our two main real-world scenarios behind KEVLAR-TZ, also depicted in Fig. 2. The use-cases originate from two ongoing EU H2020 projects, in collaboration with industry-leading companies, which we details next.

3.1 Digital Health

The first scenario stems from the H2020 project MOORE4MEDICAL.[1] One of its objectives is to use wearable sensors and remote sensing technologies to reduce hospitalization, resulting in more comfort for the patient and less costly clinical trials in drug development. In this context, the monitoring of vital signs is increasingly off-loaded and out-sourced to third-party untrusted data centers. The main reason for such off-load is to exploit the economy of scale that comes with cloud computing. The flow of data is mainly generated from smart medical devices and sensors and it is composed of a mix of physiological signals (*e.g.*, electrocardiograms, photopletymograms) and vital signs (*e.g.*, heart rare, respiration rate, stress levels). The data streams are highly heterogeneous, since the physiological signals can reach high sampling rates (*e.g.*, Holter operate at 1 kHz) and the vital signs have typically much lower sampling rates ($\sim$1 Hz).

3.2 Smart Building Management

The second scenario stems from TABEDE[2], an EU H2020 project with the aim to integrate energy grid demand-response schemes into buildings through low-cost extenders for Building Management Systems or as a standalone system, which is independent

---

[1] https://moore4medical.eu/.

[2] http://www.tabede.eu/.

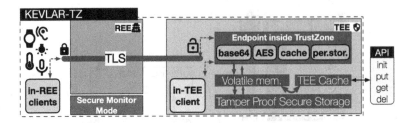

Fig. 3. Architecture of the KEVLAR-TZ TA.

from communication standards and integrates innovative flexibility algorithms. The flow of information relies on MQTT brokers deployed at the edge to minimize latency and limits the physical access from untrusted entities. However, it directly raises several privacy and security concerns. The flow of data is mainly generated from home appliances and sensors and it is composed of physical magnitudes such as electric current, temperature, or humidity. The data streams are generated at a slow frequency (<1 Hz) and are transferred via a large variety of communication protocols (*e.g.*, EnOcean [33], KNX [32], Zigbee [20]).

4   Architecture

KEVLAR-TZ implements a secure key-value storage with non-volatile entries (*i.e.*, available across reboots). To do so, we leverage OP-TEE's Trusted Storage API [8] to store keys to a secure persistent storage, while implementing a cache in volatile memory to minimize the number of requests made to the persistent storage. The key idea is to limit as much as possible operations (*i.e.*, read/write) involving the persistent storage, as they are considerably slower (see our evaluation in Sect. 6).

The architecture of KEVLAR-TZ is depicted in Fig. 3. In the remainder of this section, we describe the designing principles behind its various components as well as their interaction. Finally, we detail the typical workflow of a single write operation, a keystone operation of KEVLAR-TZ.

Secure Persistent Storage. The persistent storage area is a dedicated hardware component that guarantees data durability, confidentiality and integrity. OP-TEE supports two modes for secure storage: *(1)* using the REE file-system (the default option), or *(2)* relying on a Replay Protected Memory Block (RPMB) partition of an eMMC device [38]. KEVLAR-TZ uses the REE file-system.

KEVLAR-TZ implements a wrapper around the Trusted Storage API to access directly to writing and reading operations, which otherwise requires the management of several internal OP-TEE components (omitted from the Fig. 3 for the sake of clarity).

This wrapper exposes two functions:

- read_ss(const char *key, char *value, uint32_t *value_sz): reads the data mapped to a given key, which is bound to the array pointed by value;

- `write_ss(const char *key, const char *value, uint32_t value_sz)`: writes the data in `value` mapped to the `key` into persistent storage.

Finally, we note that the available storage memory dedicated to this component is only limited by the underlying hardware.

Volatile Memory – Cache. This component is the secure caching component of KEVLAR-TZ. Our design supports a few cache eviction policies (currently limited to Least Recently Used LRU and FIFO). The implementation uses structs inserted in a queue and a hash table. These are used to handle the key and value of each entry. The queue is used to remember the order of deletion of entries when new entries are to be added to a full cache; the hash table is used to access entries in average constant time. The cache is `write-through` [29], so that if the trusted application is stopped unexpectedly, no data is lost.

API for Trusted Applications. KEVLAR-TZ provides a very simple API for applications running inside the TEE with four operations:

- Initialize a cache with a given configuration consisting of cache size, hash output size and eviction policy;
- Delete a cache, freeing all space used in volatile memory. Objects in persistent storage are left untouched.
- Query a cache, to fetch the value associated to a given key. For instance, when using MQT-TZ [40], for a given ID, the cache will return the corresponding encryption key.
- Save a new key/value pair in volatile and persistent memory.

TCP Interface for Applications of REE. The TEE and REE are two different systems and, as such, programs can't communicate (*i.e.*, share data) between each other as if they where running on the same machine. However, KEVLAR-TZ can be useful as a secure cache service to an application running in the *normal world* (*e.g.*, in the MQT-TZ broker scenario [40]). To expose KEVLAR-TZ to the *normal world*, we designed and implemented a TCP interface, protected by TRUSTZONE, that allows to communicate KEVLAR-TZ with any other application reachable on the network.

The establishment of the TCP connection works as follows. First, an application in the REE opens a server TCP socket. Secondly, KEVLAR-TZ connects to such socket and waits (*i.e.*, blocks) for new messages. Once a new message is received, KEVLAR-TZ will execute the requested operation and return the desired value.

The Workflow of a Write. To conclude the description of the architecture, we take a step-by-step walkthrough for a `write` operation to insert a new key/value pair into KEVLAR-TZ. When an REE-based application needs to store a new key/value, it must first connect to KEVLAR-TZ via TCP, and pass over the content of the key/value pair. For the sake of simplicity, we assume those to be encoded using `base64`. Once received by the KEVLAR-TZ TA, they get base64-decoded, and saved to the persistent storage. The architecture allows to attach additional application-specific processing operations to the inserted key/value pairs, both before or after the value is retrieved. For instance, one might send a cipher that will be decrypted with one value and encrypted with another [40], securely changing the encryption key of a cipher without the REE ever getting ahold of any of them. This post-retrieve operations can be changed to any operation needed for the application that is using KEVLAR-TZ.

If an application in the *secure world* uses KEVLAR-TZ to store a new key, it can directly leverage the functions exposed by the KEVLAR-TZ API (`cache_save_object(Cache *cache, char *id, char *data)`), which takes the binary values and stores them to the persistent storage.

5   Implementation

This section describes some of the internal details and implementation choices of KEVLAR-TZ. The system itself is implemented in C, and consists of 791 LoC, released as open-source from https://github.com/mqttz/kevlar-tz/. We note that applications implemented using the OP-TEE framework are basically organized as two distinct components: the Host Application (HA) and the corresponding Trusted Application (TA). The host application runs on the *normal world* and initializes and finalizes the TEE context using the TEE Client API. Moreover, the HA is in charge of invoking functions over the Trusted Application, and can do so multiple times, dividing the work between the *normal* and *secure world*. However, the TEE's volatile memory is lost between calls, hence KEVLAR-TZ's Host Application only invokes the TA once. The TA acts as a daemon that receives queries. We detail the TA components next.

5.1   KEVLAR-TZ Trusted Application

The KEVLAR-TZ trusted application is split into several modules. The implementation of a particular module is independent of the rest, to facilitate future evolutions of the code in a loosely coupled manner (*e.g.*, you can change the communication module to work with UDP instead of TCP, different symmetric encryption algorithm, *etc.*). The KEVLAR-TZ TA is composed of the following modules, which we evaluate individually and as a part of micro-benchmarks in Sect. 6.

Persistent Storage Module. This module implements the functions `read_ss` and `write_ss`, which read and write persistent storage, respectively. Our implementation follows the guidelines from the Linaro Security Working Group.[3]

Cache Module. The KEVLAR-TZ cache module directly implements the proper cache API, namely: `init_cache`, `free_cache`, `cache_query`, and `cache_save_object`. In our implementation, the cache is made of nodes that are part of both a queue and a hash table, which enables accessing objects in constant time (on average). The cache module also interacts with the persistent storage (using the pertinent module). Any access to the key-value storage can be done through the cache, whether the value was stored on volatile memory or not.

AES Module. Our prototype includes a symmetric cipher module on top of AES. It directly exposes two functions: `encrypt`, which encrypts data with a given key, and

---

[3] https://github.com/linaro-swg/optee_examples/tree/master/secure_storage.

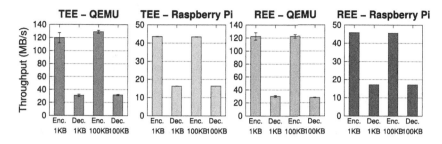

Fig. 4. Base64 encoding and decoding throughput for randomly generated data.

reencrypt, which given two keys and a cipher, decrypts it with one key and encrypts it with the other. Our implementation uses the Cryptographic Operation API implemented by OP-TEE to encrypt and decrypt the data. We extended it to support PCKS padding, *i.e.*, the default padding used by OpenSSL and MQT-TZ.

Base64 Module. This module implements standard Base64 encoding/decoding operations (*i.e.*, base64_encode, base64_decode), as well as auxilary ones (*i.e.*, base64_decode_length to return the length an encoded string after the decoding). The encoding and decoding implementations leverage an open-source library.[4] This module is used to encode and decode data transmitted to other applications over the network layer to simplify the parsing of data, in particular when dealing with multipart binary messages.

Trusted TCP Module. KEVLAR-TZ uses TCP to communicate with untrusted applications. It exposes functions to initialize and close a connection (*i.e.*, net_connect and net_disconnect) as well as send and receive packets (*i.e.*, net_send and net_receive). The implementation uses the socket library that OP-TEE exposes, and while we use TCP, the code can easily be adapted to use other protocols without any changes on any other part of the application.

6 Evaluation

This section presents our experimental evaluation of KEVLAR-TZ using both micro- and macro-benchmarks. Our goal is to define the overheads of running KEVLAR-TZ to further assess whether the trade-offs to have a secure storage system are reasonable for a real-world scenario.

Evaluation Settings. We deploy KEVLAR-TZ on a Raspberry Pi 3 Model B+ as well as on an emulated environment using QEMU version 8[5] to test the application. QEMU is a tool that has been proven useful, despite its limitations, in validating design and implementation in ARM processors without having to deploy large (and potentially) expensive testbeds. The QEMU runtime is deployed on a Lenovo ThinkPad with Intel® Core™ i7-5600U CPU @ 2.60 GHz. We rely on OP-TEE version 3.11.0.

---

[4] https://web.mit.edu/freebsd/head/contrib/wpa/src/utils/base64.c.

[5] https://www.qemu.org.

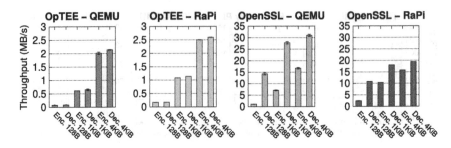

Fig. 5. Encryption and decryption throughput. We compare the built-in OP-TEE library for cryptographic operations against OpenSSL. For both cases we deploy them in TEE, and compare the throughput to encode and decode randomly generated data.

6.1 Micro-benchmarks

We begin by micro-benchmarking two of the subcomponents of the KEVLAR-TZ TA, namely the Base64 encoder and the one in charge of cryptographic operations.

Base64 Encoding and Decoding. We measure the throughput of the base64 encoding and decoding operations. The measurements have been done by measuring the encoding and decoding of randomly generated data of 1KB and 100KB, both for the hardware deployment as well as under emulation. In both cases, the component is deployed in the TEE. We show average and standard deviation for each configuration, which is executed 200 times. Our results are shown in Fig. 4. First, we observe the size of the data payload does not negatively affect the observed throughput, whereas we do observe differences between the emulated and hardware environment. For instance, encoding 100KB of data reaches 43 MB/s, while the QEMU is approximately 4× faster, reaching 130 MB/s. Similar differences can be observed for smaller data and decoding. We also report the results obtained when executing the same operations in the REE. As we see, encoding and decoding throughputs are similar, due to the operations being GPU-intense, instead of memory-intense.

Cryptographic Operations. Next, we measure the throughput of the cryptographic operations run by KEVLAR-TZ, *i.e.*, symmetric encryption and decryption. We generate random data of different sizes: 128 B, 1 kB and 4 kB. Figure 5 depicts our results. We observe that encryption and decryption achieve similar encoding and decoding throughputs in each of the two environments (QEMU and the Raspberry Pi). For instance, we observe an average of 2 MB/s encrypting a payload of 4kB in QEMU, and a 25% improvement for the same test in hardware. Expectedly, decryption operations are slightly faster (by 6% on average). We compare our results with OpenSSL version 1.1.1f, running on the REE of both QEMU and Raspberry Pi. We observe that OpenSSL in the REE is much faster, especially for decryption operations which can be parallelized: this is expected, as OpenSSL optimizes the compiled binary for the underlying hardware. We leave as future work further investigation and porting of a (subset of) OpenSSL to run in the TEE.

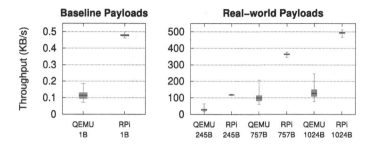

Fig. 6. Trusted TCP server: incoming throughput.

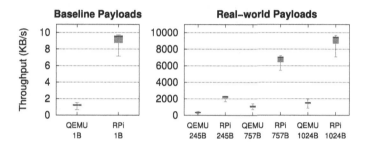

Fig. 7. TCP throughput REE to REE

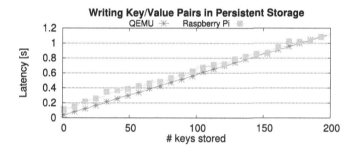

Fig. 8. Time to store a 32 B encryption key (value) with a 12 B ID (key) to persistent storage.

TCP Communication. The TPC sockets handle the communication between KEVLAR-TZ and untrusted applications. In this benchmark, we measure the throughput of our trusted TCP channels, whose endpoints terminate into the TRUSTZONE area. We measure the throughput for messages of different sizes: 1B, 245B (*i.e.*, 128B once encrypted and encoded in base64), and 757B (*i.e.*, 512B plus AES encryption and base64 encoding), and 1024B. We use these values since they represent a reasonable range of values found in real-world deployments. Figure 7 reports our results for the two testing environments. We observe that the throughput is significantly higher for larger amounts of data. Concerning the system used, we see that the Raspberry Pi is much faster than the emulated environment (Fig. 6 and Fig. 7).

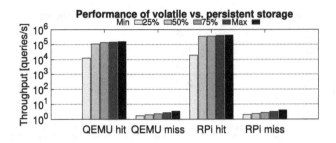

Fig. 9. Throughput of queries. We compare the difference between volatile memory (cache hits) and persistent storage (cache miss) on both hardware (Raspberry Pi) and emulated (QEMU) environments. The percentiles of the distribution are represented with shades of gray. From the brightest to the darkest: minimum, 25th, the 50th (median), the 75th and the maximum percentile.

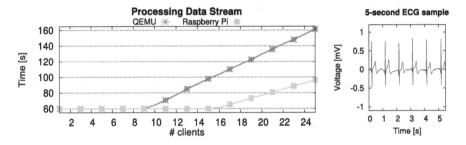

Fig. 10. Time to process a 60-second data stream from ECG sensors.

Cache Module. The last in our series of micro-benchmarks focus on the throughput of the cache module itself. First, we fill up the persistent storage with 200 keys, using a payload of 32 B. Figure 8 indicates that as the number of keys increase, there is a corresponding increase in the time to insert the key and value in the persistent storage.

Finally, we query the previously stored keys by issuing request queries for random keys to the cache module. Each cache request can result in a *hit* or *miss*. These results are shown in Fig. 9. We can observe 5 orders of magnitude between the hits and miss throughputs, both in the case of emulated as well as hardware deployments.

6.2 Macro-benchmark: Digital Health

We conclude our evaluation by demonstrating the overall performance of KEVLAR-TZ. We setup the Digital Health scenario (Sect. 3.1), where heart-rate monitoring data streams are pushed toward KEVLAR-TZ, leaving the Smart Building use-case to future work. For the considered workload, we use a database obtained from CSEM's proprietary wrist-located sensors and chest-located dry electrodes [15]. In particular, cardiac data is obtained following a standardized protocol in which they perform a range of physical activities from sedentary to vigorous [18]. A 5-second sample of the ECG used is shown on Fig. 10. In this scenario, the sensors inject 10 electrocardiogram data points every 93.4 ms. Each data point embeds the following information: the time when it was taken and the voltage measured. Figure 10 compares the time taken to process 60 s of such streaming for different amounts of clients. We conclude that the Raspberry Pi takes approximately 0.064 s to process 1 s of streaming of 1 client, while the emulated environment takes 0.107 s for the same amount of data.

7   Related Work

The problem of executing software inside TEEs in general, and TRUSTZONE in particular, has attracted several research groups. CaSE [44] is a cache-assisted secure execution framework for the TRUSTZONE to defend against multiple attacks. Others [28, 36, 41] have implemented frameworks for TEEs to securely process data streams that could benefit from KEVLAR-TZ. However, while such projects have implemented full-fledged frameworks, KEVLAR-TZ provides a lean and resource-efficient cache with an easy-to-use API for applications that need fast access to persistent data.

A service like KEVLAR-TZ is available within MQT-TZ [40], a publish-subscribe framework optimized for IoT and TRUSTZONE deployments and backward compatible with mosquitto, a well-known MQTT messaging framework supporting TLS. In that context, a secure cache like the one developed in KEVLAR-TZ protects data against eavesdroppers or untrusted brokers. KEVLAR-TZ offers a more generic approach, including an API to use it from inside the TEE and a modular design to choose a specific cache eviction policy or some of its internal subcomponents. Recently [39, 43], authors tried to hardening TEE applications against a broad set of attacks, including side-channels or against known weaknesses of the implementation language. While some of the countermeasures developed there could be beneficial for KEVLAR-TZ, we consider those out of scope. In [22], authors implement a cache to speed up operations on a secure Bitcoin wallet, while using the TRUSTZONE's persistent storage. While the focus is on the security of the private keys used to unlock the cryptocurrency wallet, the approach is similar to KEVLAR-TZ.

To the best of our knowledge, KEVLAR-TZ is the first application specifically designed to run on a TRUSTZONE and provide a lightweight cache to leverage the TRUSTZONE's persistent storage while maintaining a minimal read/write latency. KEVLAR-TZ implements a generic cache that can be easily embedded into other Trusted Applications or used as a secure storage for an untrusted application in the *normal world* without significantly increasing the trusted computing base.

8   Conclusion and Future Work

Motivated by the increasing attack surface of today's edge devices, KEVLAR-TZ addresses an integral part for storing and performing computations over the collected/transmitted data in a privacy-preserving fashion. This becomes critical when the data is highly sensitive and personal, which is the case for nowadays medical implantables, wearables, and nearables. For instance, in scenarios where such IoT devices interact by means of publish/subscribe frameworks, as is typical in real-world deployments, protecting the brokers with a minimal increase in power consumption is necessary in order to preserve the ubiquity of such network of sensing devices.

We intend to extend KEVLAR-TZ along the following lines. First, we intend to extend the API exposed to the Trusted Application so that it is easier to implement new functions (similar to the already implemented reencryption. Second, standardizing the length of the messages going through TCP when communicating with untrusted applications, so that binary data can be sent and easily parsed, this will reduce the amount of bytes sent as well as eliminate the base64 dependency. Finally, we intend to compare KEVLAR-TZ to other TRUSTZONE cache implementations.

Acknowledgements. This work is supported in part by Moore4Medical, which has received funding within the Electronic Components and Systems for European Leadership Joint Undertaking (ECSEL JU) in collaboration with the European Union's H2020 framework Programme (H2020/2014-2020) and National Authorities, under grant agreement H2020-ECSEL-2019-IA-876190. Moreover, this project has received funding from the European Union's Horizon 2020 research and innovation programme under grant agreement No 766733.

References

1. ARM TrustZone Developer. https://developer.arm.com/technologies/trustzone. Accessed 15 Feb 2021
2. TEE Client API Specification v1.0 (GPD_SPE_007). https://globalplatform.org/specs-library/tee-client-api-specification/. Accessed 15 Feb 2021
3. TEE Internal Core API Specification v1.2.1 (GPD_SPE_010). https://globalplatform.wpengine.com/specs-library/tee-internal-core-api-specification-v1-2/. Accessed 15 Feb 2021
4. Digital impact how technology is accelerating global problem solving (2018). https://www.cisco.com/c/dam/assets/csr/pdf/Digital-Impact-Playbook.pdf
5. AWS Nitro Enclaves (2021). https://aws.amazon.com/ec2/nitro/nitro-enclaves/
6. Confidential VM and Compute Engine (2021). https://cloud.google.com/compute/confidential-vm/docs/about-cvm
7. Global platform (2021). http://www.globalplatform.org
8. OP-TEE Secure Storage API (2021). https://optee.readthedocs.io/en/latest/architecture/secure_storage.html
9. Wearable computing devices market - growth, trends, COVID-19 impact, and forecasts (2021–2026) (2021). https://www.researchandmarkets.com/reports/4787502/wearable-computing-devices-market-growth
10. Alves, T., Felton, D.: TrustZone: integrated hardware and software security. ARM Inf. Q. **3**(4), 18–24 (2004)
11. Amacher, J., Schiavoni, V.: On the performance of ARM TrustZone. In: Pereira, J., Ricci, L. (eds.) DAIS 2019. LNCS, vol. 11534, pp. 133–151. Springer, Cham (2019). https://doi.org/10.1007/978-3-030-22496-7_9
12. Bennett, T.R., Wu, J., Kehtarnavaz, N., Jafari, R.: Inertial measurement unit-based wearable computers for assisted living applications: a signal processing perspective. IEEE Sig. Process. Mag. **33**(2), 28–35 (2016)
13. Cao, Z., Dong, S., Vemuri, S., Du, D.H.C.: Characterizing, modeling, and benchmarking RocksDB key-value workloads at Facebook. In: Proceedings of USENIX FAST 20, pp. 209–223. USENIX Association (2020)
14. Chaudhuri, S., Pawar, T.D., Duttagupta, S.: Ambulation Analysis in Wearable ECG. Springer, Heidelberg (2009). https://doi.org/10.1007/978-1-4419-0724-0

15. Chételat, O., et al.: Clinical validation of LTMS-S: a wearable system for vital signs monitoring. In: Proceedings of IEEE EMBC 2015, pp. 3125–3128 (2015)
16. Costan, V., Devadas, S.: IntelSGX explained. IACR Cryptol. ePrint Arch. **2016**(86), 1–118 (2016)
17. Coyle, S., Curto, V.F., Benito-Lopez, F., Florea, L., Diamond, D.: Wearable bio and chemical sensors. In: Wearable Sensors, pp. 65–83. Elsevier (2014)
18. Delgado-Gonzalo, R., et al.: Human energy expenditure models: beyond state-of-the-art commercialized embedded algorithms. In: Duffy, V.G. (ed.) DHM 2014. LNCS, vol. 8529, pp. 3–14. Springer, Cham (2014). https://doi.org/10.1007/978-3-319-07725-3_1
19. Delgado-Gonzalo, R., et al.: Physical activity. In: Tamura, T., Chen, W. (eds.) Seamless Healthcare Monitoring, pp. 413–455. Springer, Cham (2018). https://doi.org/10.1007/978-3-319-69362-0_14
20. Farahani, S.: ZigBee Wireless Networks and Transceivers. Newnes, Oxford (2011)
21. Faraone, A., Delgado-Gonzalo, R.: Convolutional-recurrent neural networks on low-power wearable platforms for cardiac arrhythmia detection. In: Proceedings of IEEE AICAS 2020, pp. 153–157 (2020)
22. Gentilal, M., Martins, P., Sousa, L.: TrustZone-backed bitcoin wallet. In: Proceedings of CS2 2017, pp. 25–28 (2017)
23. Gentry, C., et al.: A Fully Homomorphic Encryption Scheme, vol. 20. Stanford University, Stanford (2009)
24. Gokhale, S., Agrawal, N., Noonan, S., Ungureanu, C.: KVZone and the search for a write-optimized key-value store. In: HotStorage (2010)
25. Göttel, C., et al.: Security, performance and energy trade-offs of hardware-assisted memory protection mechanisms. In: Proceedings of SRDS 2018, pp. 133–142. IEEE (2018)
26. Halevi, S., Shoup, V.: Design and implementation of a homomorphic-encryption library. IBM Res. (Manuscr.) **6**(12–15), 8–36 (2013)
27. Han, J., Haihong, E., Le, G., Du, J.: Survey on NoSQL database. In: Proceedings of PerCom 2011, pp. 363–366. IEEE (2011)
28. Havet, A., Pires, R., Felber, P., Pasin, M., Rouvoy, R., Schiavoni, V.: SecureStreams: a reactive middleware framework for secure data stream processing. In: Proceedings of ACM DEBS 2017, DEBS '17, pp. 124–133. Association for Computing Machinery (2017)
29. Jouppi, N.P.: Cache write policies and performance. ACM SIGARCH Comput. Archit. News **21**(2), 191–201 (1993)
30. Kaplan, D., Powell, J., Woller, T.: AMD memory encryption. White paper (2016)
31. Lee, D., Kohlbrenner, D., Shinde, S., Asanović, K., Song, D.: Keystone: an open framework for architecting trusted execution environments. In: Proceedings of EuroSys 2020, pp. 1–16 (2020)
32. Lee, W.S., Hong, S.H.: Implementation of a KNX-ZigBee gateway for home automation. In: Proceedings of IEEE ICCE 2009, ISCE'09, pp. 545–549. IEEE (2009)
33. Li, Y., Hong, S.H.: BACnet-EnOcean smart grid gateway and its application to demand response in buildings. Energy Build. **78**, 183–191 (2014)
34. Lin, H., Bergmann, N.W.: IoT privacy and security challenges for smart home environments. Information **7**(3), 44 (2016)
35. Padalalu, P., Mahajan, S., Dabir, K., Mitkar, S., Javale, D.: Smart water dripping system for agriculture/farming. In: Proceedings of I2CT 2017, pp. 659–662. IEEE (2017)
36. Park, H., Zhai, S., Lu, L., Lin, F.X.: StreamBox-TZ: secure stream analytics at the edge with TrustZone. In: Proceedings of USENIX ATC 2019, pp. 537–554. USENIX Association (2019)
37. Pinto, S., Santos, N.: Demystifying arm TrustZone: a comprehensive survey. ACM Comput. Surv. (CSUR) **51**(6), 1–36 (2019)

38. Reddy, A.K., Paramasivam, P., Vemula, P.B.: Mobile secure data protection using eMMC RPMB partition. In: Proceedings of CoCoNet 2015, pp. 946–950. IEEE (2015)
39. Sasaki, T., Tomita, K., Hayaki, Y., Liew, S.P., Yamagaki, N.: Secure IoT device architecture using TrustZone. In: Proceedings of IEEE SECON 2020, pp. 1–6 (2020)
40. Segarra, C., Delgado-Gonzalo, R., Schiavoni, V.: MQT-TZ: hardening IoT brokers using ARM TrustZone. In: Proceedings of SRDS 2020 (2020)
41. Segarra, C., Delgado-Gonzalo, R., Lemay, M., Aublin, P.-L., Pietzuch, P., Schiavoni, V.: Using trusted execution environments for secure stream processing of medical data. In: Pereira, J., Ricci, L. (eds.) DAIS 2019. LNCS, vol. 11534, pp. 91–107. Springer, Cham (2019). https://doi.org/10.1007/978-3-030-22496-7_6
42. Tamura, T., Maeda, Y., Sekine, M., Yoshida, M.: Wearable photoplethysmographic sensors–past and present. Electronics 3(2), 282–302 (2014)
43. Wan, S., Sun, M., Sun, K., Zhang, N., He, X.: RusTEE: developing memory-safe ARM Trust-Zone applications. In: Proceedings of ACSAC 2020, ACSAC '20, pp. 442–453. Association for Computing Machinery (2020)
44. Zhang, N., Sun, K., Lou, W., Hou, Y.T.: CaSE: cache-assisted secure execution on ARM processors. In: Proceedings of IEEE SP 2016, pp. 72–90 (2016)

Analysis and Improvement of Heterogeneous Hardware Support in Docker Images

Panagiotis Gkikopoulos[1] , Valerio Schiavoni[2(✉)] , and Josef Spillner[1]

[1] Zurich University of Applied Sciences, Winterthur, Switzerland
{pang,spio}@zhaw.ch
[2] University of Neuchâtel, Neuchâtel, Switzerland
valerio.schiavoni@unine.ch

Abstract. Docker images are used to distribute and deploy cloud-native applications in containerised form. A container engine runs them with separated privileges according to namespaces. Recent studies have investigated security vulnerabilities and runtime characteristics of Docker images. In contrast, little is known about the extent of hardware-dependent features in them such as processor-specific trusted execution environments, graphics acceleration or extension boards. This problem can be generalised to missing knowledge about the extent of any hardware-bound instructions within the images that may require elevated privileges. We first conduct a systematic one-year evolution analysis of a sample of Docker images concerning their use of hardware-specific features. To improve the state of technology, we contribute novel tools to manage such images. Our heuristic hardware dependency detector and a hardware-aware Docker executor *hdocker* give early warnings upon missing dependencies instead of leading to silent or untimely failures. Our dataset and tools are released to the research community.

Keywords: Docker · Containers · Trusted execution · Hardware dependencies

1 Introduction

Portability is a desirable property in cloud computing [20,27]. Virtual machine images, container images and other executable artefacts ought to be flexibly deployed across clouds [11], migrate from the cloud to the edge [15], or be confined within differentiated cloud security zones [31]. Nevertheless, limitations to portability arise from the differences in the underlying heterogeneous hardware. Apart from targeting the basic processor architecture, new cloud service paradigms such as accelerated computing or secure computing demand support for further hardware extensions abstracted as shared resources [37]. Any hardware thus requires support in the boot process (BIOS/EFI), operating system,

© IFIP International Federation for Information Processing 2021
Published by Springer Nature Switzerland AG 2021
M. Matos and F. Greve (Eds.): DAIS 2021, LNCS 12718, pp. 125–142, 2021.
https://doi.org/10.1007/978-3-030-78198-9_9

virtualisation layers and application execution stacks, as well as in the applications and their constituent artefacts (*e.g.,* images). Among the hardware features of interest to cloud application engineers are FPGAs, GPUs and nested virtualisation [30,32,34], as well as security-increasing hardware.

Secure (confidential) cloud computing is one of the emerging concepts affected by reduced portability: tenants offload computation to third-party untrusted providers without having to worry about security issues typically associated with cloud offloading [22]. Over the years, this concept has been mapped to concrete secure architectures involving monitoring and intrusion detection [26], algorithmic proofs on data, trusted boot [23], physical security including hardware security tokens and modules [18] and policy languages. Recently, hardware-based trusted execution environments (TEEs) enabled outsourcing the processing of confidential data with high privacy requirements [12] towards untrusted clouds.

Mapping this concept to hardware requires support for special CPU instructions as well as appropriate configuration of hypervisors and other execution parts. Several vendor-specific instruction sets exist nowadays in processors available in the consumer market, as well as those offered by cloud providers [2,5]. Specifically, we mention Intel Software Guard Extensions (SGX) [19], AMD Secure Enhanced Virtualisation (SEV) [24], or ARM TrustZone [8,28].

In most cloud environments, Docker containers become the standard *de facto*, as application developers migrate towards integrated platform services, *e.g.,* IBM Code Engine, Amazon ECS, Azure Container Service and Google Container Engine. Research on heterogeneous hardware support for container execution has been limited to few aspects, and in particular has not covered TEEs. For highly security- and privacy-sensitive software applications, such as those in the domains of e-health, banks or smart metering, the use of TEEs offers many benefits. To drive their adoption, it is necessary to encapsulate the use in containerised form. Yet container runtime support for heterogeneous hardware in public clouds is still lacking, in particular for secure execution. This is surprising given that certain features are today available to providers of cloud infrastructure-as-a-service. For instance, all major cloud providers offer instances with SGX-/SEV-capable CPUs, nevertheless access to consumers is either limited or disabled. More specifically, Azure offers SGX/SEV capabilities with their Confidential Compute instances, while IBM or Alibaba have them enabled only for their bare metal instances. AWS and Google do not provide SGX-enabled instances, as the feature is disabled in their systems' BIOS.[1] In general, no cloud provider natively supports a container runtime that makes use of SGX. We believe this situation is going to fundamentally change over the next few years, and in that perspective, the research focus will shift to provide efficient support in the application stacks and artefact management tools, nowadays largely container-based.

To allow a Docker container to utilise a hardware-specific feature of the host system, the relevant device driver or kernel module needs to be explicitly mounted to the container at runtime. Some features, such as SGX, can be con-

---

[1] Google just recently announced SEV-enabled instances [5], while AWS is introducing Nitro Enclaves, heavily inspired by Intel SGX [1].

figured to run in simulation mode in the absence of supporting hardware. Base images that offer the relevant development tools for these features are sometimes provided by the hardware vendors themselves (*e.g.*, Nvidia Docker [6]), other companies (*e.g.*, SCONE [7,9]) or by members of the developer or research community. For the SGX use-case, the Graphene Secure Container Environment (GSCE) [3] aims to wrap the standard Docker engine to allow standard images to run their applications within SGX enclaves, although this is in preliminary stages of development.

While our analysis shows that only few Docker images require specialised hardware at the time of writing, this is expected to change in the future. Already now, the discoverability of hardware in the form of CPU architectures per tag is limited, leading to issues in mixed environments. Making conscious use of the hardware features requires knowledge about them, which is presently absent from container images and handling tools and motivates our research. By consciously leveraging specific hardware types, augmented images can be invaluable to certain sectors, *e.g.*, Highly Information Sensitive Computing (HISC), High Performance Computing (HPC) and FPGA-hosted blockchain-as-a-service [16,21], enabling the integration of containers to their niche workloads.

The contributions of this paper are fourfold. We introduce a *systematic analysis* of the content of Docker images with emphasis on heterogeneous hardware, especially on TEEs for security and GPUs for acceleration. In contrast to existing empirical works, our analysis follows a three-staged process: automated monitoring for metadata inspection, static image inspection, and manual runtime inspection. We also contribute *augmented metadata* that reflects the analysis results, and an improved *hardware-aware Docker executor* `hdocker` that parses the metadata to increase upfront assessment about the likelihood of hardware-dependent execution failure. We follow an *open science* approach. Our tools and datasets are released and available from https://doi.org/10.5281/zenodo.4531794.

Roadmap. This paper is organized as follows. In Sect. 2, we provide a more comprehensive background on processor architectures and Docker container images. Section 3 describes our three-step methodology. We present our evaluation strategy and experimental results in Sect. 4. In Sect. 5, we present our proposed extensions. We cover related work in Sect. 6. Finally, we conclude and present future work in Sect. 7.

2   Background

2.1   Processors and Hardware Heterogeneity

At the most fundamental level, hardware support means the ability to execute on a given processor architecture. Public clouds typically include `amd64` (x86-64) and `arm64`, with minority occurrences of `i386`, `ppc64el` (IBM) or `mipsel` (Loongson). However, discussions of heterogeneous hardware refer to a broader set of features, such as specific instruction sets. When supported by

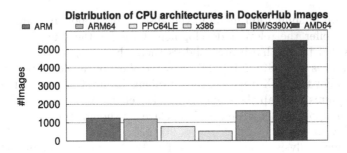

Fig. 1. Distribution of images types in an ∼11'000 images non-random sample collected as of February 4th, 2021. X-axis: processor architecture.

BIOS/EFI, hypervisor and operating system, applications can typically rely on more than 100 unique CPU flags, *e.g.*, sse3 for streaming operations or avx for vectoring. This also includes hardware-assisted TEEs, *i.e.*, Intel SGX and AMD SEV or hardware-assisted virtualisation technology (*i.e.*, Intel VT-x, AMD-V, HVM, *etc.*). Similarly, another group captures support for expansion devices or cards. This became increasingly relevant in recent years, by the usage of GPUs for high-performance computing, machine learning and simulations. We include in this group support for fast/low-latency disks (*e.g.*, NVMe non-volatile memories) and network links (*e.g.*, InfiniBand).

2.2   Docker Images

Since its introduction in 2013, Docker emerged as one the most popular cloud-native software artefacts and as such an integral part of modern DevOps operations Several frameworks and development environments are now available as drop-in solutions using Docker, significantly reducing the overhead of both setting them up and orchestrating them.

Images can be distributed in two ways. The first largely adopted method is using a container registry, the largest one being DockerHub.[2] There are private registries, curated by specific vendors[3], which incorporate stricter standards, *i.e.*, built-in security scanning of all images motivated by several security issues found on public registries [33]. The second distribution method is to include the Dockerfile in a publicly accessible code repository (*e.g.*, GitHub), for users to build the image themselves [17].

Docker has support for multiple CPU architectures, namely x86, x86-64, ARM, ARM64, PowerPC 64 LE and IBM's POWER and Z architectures. We fetched and analyze a sample of the publicly accessible Docker images on DockerHub, constituted by approximately 11'000 images (as we detail later in Sect. 3). We report these results in Fig. 1 (also released to the research community, see "Data and Code" section at end of paper). Unsurprisingly, x86-64 leads by a large

---

[2] Docker Hub: https://hub.docker.com/.

[3] Red Hat Registry: http://quay.io, Tenable: http://tenable.io.

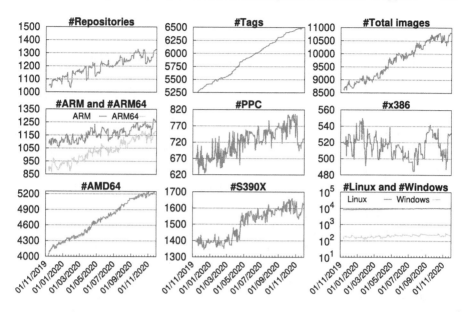

Fig. 2. Monitoring metrics for Nov 11, 2019 to Feb 4, 2021

margin with ~48% of the images. Interestingly, IBM Z (S390X in Fig. 1) is second most popular (with ~15%). We observe that ARM64 is the fastest trending image type, after x86-64, showing a 1.7% monthly increase (Fig. 2). Docker has recently introduced an experimental multi-architecture builder in which several versions of an image, compatible with multiple processor architectures are built simultaneously, thus speeding up the process of introducing compatibility for different architectures.

Metadata available from the official registry provides basic overview metrics, such as supported architectures and OS versions, as well as the number of images and tags within a repository. However, global statistics cannot currently be obtained from DockerHub, as the API endpoint for the global catalog metadata is disabled. Utilization of Docker images in contexts that require specialized hardware is now an emergent use-case, varying from Nvidia GPUs to Intel SGX-compatible CPUs, though adoption appers to be at an early stage, judging from the number of repositories and their omission from the list of official images. They require the host to have the correct hardware and driver support installed, and are thus limited in their reach to end users, but provide the ability to leverage Docker's advantages for applications that require specialized hardware features, such as secure execution and GPU-accelerated HPC. Still, metadata does not reflect hardware dependencies, and that makes such repositories difficult to detect with automated means, which is why we searched by specific vendors (namely Nvidia and Intel) and hardware features (CUDA and SGX) heuristically to create the sample for the evaluation of hardware support.

3   Methodology

The methodology followed to assess the hardware support in Docker images is divided into three steps. The first one (Fig. 3-❶) consists of automatic monitoring of the main DockerHub repository to retrieve a representative sample of the most used images. The metadata from the sample images is then stored and analysed for information on any specific hardware they support or require. The second step (Fig. 3-❷) dives deeper into the images and attempts to find any traces of hardware-specific binaries or configuration files. Finally, the third one (Fig. 3-❸) performs basic manual runtime testing of a targeted selection of Docker images from DockerHub that use specific hardware features, to assess their quality and maturity.

The automated sampling of DockerHub metadata uses a two-tier approach. The search starts with the official Docker images, collected in a private *library* repository. The metadata from this repository is collected and added to the dataset. For each entry in the resulting data, we assume each image to correspond to an organisation, which maintains its own repository. For example, the image `nginx` is controlled and maintained by a corresponding `nginx` organization. We thus repeat the search for each of these possible organisations, adding the data returned (if any) to the dataset. This process essentially creates a shallow family tree of two levels, stemming from the official images. This serves to effectively increase the sample size by an order of magnitude, granting us a higher number of images to investigate. This selection process is scripted and both it and the metadata analysis runs nightly on a scheduled monitoring setup.

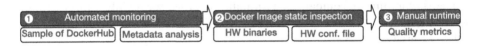

Fig. 3. Our methodology to gather and validate DockerHub's image data/metadata.

Compared to typical random sampling, this method has the advantage of specifically targeting repositories within DockerHub that are considered of high-quality/high-profile, as their maintainers are either verified or certified publishers. It should be noted that the goal of this sampling is to feed the next steps with potential targets, not to obtain global metadata statistics for Docker Hub as a whole. As such, the statistics are meant as an indication of hardware support in the official and related repositories and do not represent a study of Docker Hub as an ecosystem.

Currently, the metadata provided by DockerHub's API does not provide any insight on whether or not an image requires specific hardware to be present on the host in order to function. A possible *hardware features* field could rectify this. In the present state of the metadata, the only way to select images with specific hardware requirements beyond CPU architecture is to rely on the web front-end's text search function, a rather cumbersome and unreliable approach.

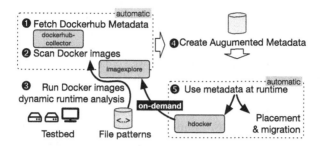

Fig. 4. Data-driven process: from experiment (steps ❶,❷,❸) to augmented metadata usage (❹,❺); `dockerhub-collector`, `imagexplore`, and `hdocker` are open-source.

For example, a search of the keyword 'SGX' with the intention of discovering images that utilise Intel SGX, will also yield images submitted by users with the characters 'sgx' in their username. Naturally, such a search will exclude any images that use the hardware but don't include it in their name or description.

However, due to the relatively small number of images using targeted hardware technology, it is still possible to hand-pick a sample and assess them heuristically for typical quality metrics, such as compatibility, documentation and best practices. For the sake of illustration, we restrict the choice of the target technologies to: *(1)* Intel SGX, as a secondary processor architecture feature with high significance for security-conscious use cases, and *(2)* support for Nvidia GPUs, arguably the most common example of heterogeneous computing power. For the former, adoption is still rather limited. We believe this to change as SGX drivers have just been up-streamed into the mainline Linux kernel[4]. For the latter, adoption is more wide-spread, with many individual user-contributed repositories, so the search is narrowed down to the images contributed by the hardware vendor themselves, and restricted to static analysis.

4   Evaluation

We ran three separate experiments, one for each of the aforementioned methodic steps. Figure 4 gives an overview about the experiments, the resulting augmented metadata and its use in specific container and cloud management tools.

Automated Monitoring. We setup automated long-term monitoring and tracking of Docker container images via the global Microservices Artefact Observatory.[5] The observatory creates execution schedules for each registered monitoring tool, and shares these tools with other nodes within a federated cluster architecture for highly reliable observation and metadata retrieval. The `dockerhub-collector` tool periodically requests DockerHub's public API to retrieve metadata on the 'library' repository. This repository is unique: it is

---

[4] 42nd rev https://lore.kernel.org/lkml/20201214114200.GD26358@zn.tnic/.
[5] MAO: https://mao-mao-research.github.io/.

curated by DockerHub itself and contains 'official images', *i.e.,* the most useful, popular and high-quality images available. Using this data as a starting point, we identify 'sister repositories', *i.e.,* attempt to see if the developer of each image maintains their own repository, for which we request metadata. This selection process is integrated into the tool and automated. It increases the sample from the 164 repositories of the official set to ∼1200 repositories.

The continuous metadata collection has been running on each machine in the cluster daily, starting on November 11, 2019. The data snapshots obtained by each machine are compared for inconsistencies and then aggregated into a single dataset to analyse the hardware trends. The images with SGX and Nvidia support are selected manually in irregular intervals, based on a search of the repository for the specific hardware feature as explained before. The final lists describing the samples, after filtering out duplicates, images without any version and irrelevant repositories, are included in the dataset to ease reproducibility. Thus, we curated multiple lists of images as February 2021 snapshot for the evaluation: full library and associated images (∼11'000), strict library subset (164), SGX (67) and Nvidia (36). We applied static scanning to the last two, and dynamic assessment to the last.

Static Image Inspection. To gain further insights into the hardware-related aspects of container images, we developed `imagexplore`, a tool to uncompresses all layers of an image and recursively search for the occurrence of certain files, directory and content patterns. These come from a knowledge base created with file glob patterns as well as text and binary symbols hinting at the presence of hardware-specific features. Matches result from the installation of the SGX toolkits, Nvidia device drivers, USB devices or other hardware-related software leaving traces in the system. For example, an SGX base image needs to contain the SGX SDK. Thus, toolkit files can be detected in a predictable manner to confirm the presence of the SDK. Extending the knowledge base with additional patterns for different hardware devices enables the detection of images that utilize them, giving information on potential deployment issues due to hardware incompatibility. Evidently, this experiment leads to suspicions but not always to verified cases due to false positives. Hence, our method encompasses the manual verification of any edge cases. Furthermore, the scanning encompasses all files in the `/dev` file system, as those are not supposed to be part of any container image but their accidental addition may reveal further insights. This scanning phase is performed for all the automatically retrieved library and SGX images.

Manual Runtime Inspection. Beyond the static testing, we conduct dynamic runtime invocation on the SGX images to find out the actual use of any TEE-related operation. This test is run on an SGX machine using an Intel Core i7-8650U. We categorised the SGX images into *(1)* base images and *(2)* those for applications or tools. We assessed them on the presence of documentation, instructions and the ability to initialise on an SGX-compatible machine. It is important at this stage to define what 'initialise' means in this context. For an application or tool, this is trivial: we expect some program output or the successful initialisation of a service. For a base image, we expect to setup a functional

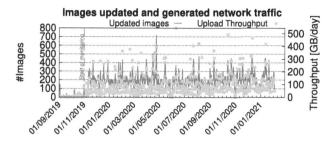

Fig. 5. Images updated and data uploaded from Sept'19 until Feb'21; y2axis (right side): inbound network traffic originated by updates of the images on the y1axis.

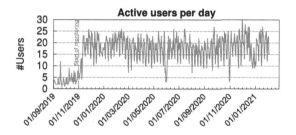

Fig. 6. Active users by day from Sept'19 until Feb'21.

development environment when we run the image in interactive mode. This was achieved by inspecting the image to ensure the SDK and relevant dependencies are present. In the case of curated images, code samples are provided in the documentation that can be used to test the image. Due to the small number of SGX images, we allowed a minimal troubleshooting, which we define being able to run the images by just following the instructions (if any). In case of errors, we see if it is straightforward to resolve, *e.g.,* mounting a file in a volume or specifying a command-line argument. If not, the image is deemed as not working, although its usability mainly depends on incomplete (or lack of) documentation. The minimal configuration possible for an image without instructions or other forms of documentation is to run it with no options besides mounting the SGX-related virtual devices from the host (*i.e.,* /dev/isgx and /dev/mei0). For base images, this proved sufficient on the majority of occasions, as the images contained all the development tools they needed except for the hardware driver component.

4.1 Results

Automated Monitoring Results. The automated monitoring of Docker Hub's public metadata gives the basic overview of processor architecture and operating system support discussed above. While not novel in itself, we further consider the amount of activity on the chosen sample during the same time period. Figure 5 and Fig. 6 present respectively the amount of image updates

Table 1. Automated static analysis of the SGX, Nvidia and library container samples.

	SGX images	Nvidia images	Library images
Count	67	36	164
Successfully retrieved	62 (93%)	14 (39%)	156 (95%)
Cumulative disk size	61 GB	15 GB	75 GB
Hardware dep detection correctness	58 (94%)	10 (71%)	152 (98%)
Detection time	1876.7 s	211.0 s	1080.4 s
Exceptions	False pos.	False pos.	False neg.
Excepted images	sgx-django, sgx-bootstrap, sgx-cosmos, payload-ethash	egx-*, eac	odoo, crux, sourcemage

Table 2. Device files in the SGX and library container samples.

	SGX images	Nvidia images	Library images
Average /dev layers	2.1	1.0	1.0
Multiple /dev layers	10 (15%)	0 (0%)	8 (5%)
Shadow /dev files	27..36 (53%)	1..2 (14%)	6..11 (7%)
Further /dev files	27 (40%)	1 (7%)	3..8 (5%)

and total data volume per day, as well as the number of unique usernames that appeared in each day's data, extracted from the same dataset. The goal of this observation is to ensure that our sample does not come from an inactive subset of Docker Hub, and thus reflects recent trends. In the observed period, the total amount of data pushed to these repositories was ~23TB.

Static Image Inspection Results. We run the `imagexplore` tool on three sets of container images: *(1)* 67 SGX candidates, *(2)* 36 Nvidia candidates, and *(3)* 164 official library images as subset of the sample whose metadata we continuously retrieved over multiple months. Due to the absence of a `:latest` tag or non-public images, not all pulls succeed, thus these numbers are slightly reduced especially for less maintained non-official images for which non-default tags have therefore been recorded. All layers of all images are unpacked on disk for the analysis. We expect the tool to indicate 100% SGX and Nvidia dependencies in the first two sets (minus false positives), and 0% any hardware dependency in the third set (minus false negatives). Table 1 compares the results. Among the SGX candidates, four use the name coincidentally but do not contain any SGX-related code. Similarly, among the suspected Nvidia images, four contain code to run the Kubernetes-based EGX AI platform that is offered by Nvidia but do not contain any hardware-related code themselves. Among the library images, three are operating system distributions with support for USB devices that are successfully detected, whereas the vast remainder are pure application containers. The average scanning time per image already present locally is 7.0 s for library images, 15.1 s for Nvidia images and 30.3 s for SGX images on a server with Xeon E3-1270 CPU @ 3.80 GHz. The main contributor to the significant difference is that most library images are rather tidy base images whereas especially the SGX images contain many layers with thousands of added files.

Concerning the /dev file system, the official images show better quality compared to the SGX images. However, in both sets, a lot of superfluous files were found. The Nvidia images are quality-wise in between with still a few of such files. Most of them mirror the standard device files added automatically by Docker, whereas almost as many consist of various other files to access audio devices, RAM disks, shared memory and other hardware. We suspect careless creation of images by snapshotting running container instances without proper post-execution cleanup of device files is the main reason. This hypothesis is supported by the occasional leftover of temporary files (/tmp, /var/tmp) in both sets of images. Table 2 compares the device file findings, with the optimal metric being 0 in all rows.

Manual Runtime Inspection Results. The mentioned categories yield 33 base images (49.25% of total), 29 apps/tools (43.28%) and 5 images (7.46%) whose functionality could not be determined due to lack of documentation. The latter ones are excluded from the percentage calculations that follow. As for quality metrics, 47 of the images (75.81%) initialised successfully when tested and only 14 of them (22.58%) had any documentation or instructions.

Considering Docker Hub's limitations on making images private, the bulk of the undocumented images are likely experiments that were not meant to be shared. Even within these 67 images, a certain degree of deduplication was possible. Upon manual inspection 28 of the images were derivatives of others in the same set, of which 18, based on their functionality, were duplicated of earlier versions of other images. Examples include several variations of the SGX base image, which provides the SGX SDK and Platform Software (PSW) and an example 'hello world' application, cementing the observation that many images available were simply the results of users experimenting with the technology, or following tutorials. The lack of documentation and the amount of 'hello world' duplicates in the sample is a clear indication that the majority of images that use the SGX technology are experimental, and thus adoption of the technology is in its infancy on the Docker ecosystem.

In terms of observed errors among the 15 failures, there were image initialisation errors for 4 images and an enclave initialisation for 1. Others were application-specific errors. It is important to mention that as with any heuristic evaluation, the testing methodology can affect the final result and as such, the 15 failures have to be treated as an upper bound. As a secondary experiment, we attempted to run the tools that ran successfully, but without mounting the SGX devices. For them, 8 out of 15 ran successfully in simulation mode, with only two 'hello world' applications and an SGX-specific stress testing tool failing due to enclave initialisation errors. The 4 remaining failures were instances where the output of the program made it difficult to understand if initialisation was successful, *i.e.*, possibly false-negatives.

The high success rate of the base images, even those with no documentation, also has a simple explanation. These images usually only include the SGX dependencies (the SDK and PSW) and typically some language specific dependencies for development. Thus, generically running them interactively by simply mounting the SGX device drivers is expected to yield a high degree of success. The spreadsheet used to track this heuristic evaluation is available in the publicly released dataset.

Images with support for Nvidia GPUs are far more numerous, potentially up to 1411 image repositories in our latest snapshot. We note that the company maintains 2 distinct organisation accounts (`nvidia` and `nvidiak8s`, respectively with 22 and 12 repositories), the latter focused on Kubernetes-related images. A common characteristic of both is the almost complete absence of documentation within Docker Hub itself. Instead, all relevant documentation is available in Nvidia's Github repositories, where the source code for these images can also be found. The absence of links from the Docker Hub repositories to the ones in Github however, means that the only reliable source of information on these images and their usage is Nvidia's Github. This is by no means an oddity, as typically Docker Hub is used to store images for public distribution and serves as a medium for users that wish to use a specific tool without building from source code manually, one of the main advantages of Docker. In that context, only having minimal documentation on Docker Hub (usually related to differences in using the image compared to running a tool natively) makes sense, as the main source code repo is responsible for housing the full documentation.

Listing 1.1. Hardware features extensions.

```
1 {
2   "platform": {
3     "architecture": "amd64",
4     "os": "linux",
5     "features": [
6       "sse4"
7     ]}}
```

Listing 1.2. Support for heterogeneous hardware sources.

```
1 {
2   "platform": {
3     "cpu": {
4       "architecture": "amd64",
5       "features": {
6         "SGX": "supported",
7         "sse4": "required"
8       }
9     },
10     "hardware": {
11       "GPU": "nVidia"
12     },
13     "os": "linux"
14   }}
```

4.2   Augmented Metadata

As mentioned earlier, Docker images built to utilize specialized hardware can benefit from augmented metadata to include hardware requirements. Such images are still a relatively small niche within the ecosystem. However, additional metadata can benefit users attempting to deploy them, as a clearer picture can be obtained by the Docker client on whether the image can be expected to function in the target system. To this end, we propose hardware-specific fields be added to the metadata of Docker registry entries. Furthermore, with Docker Hub's new rate-limiting policy (*i.e.,* 100 image pulls every 6 h), pulling an image simply for the sake of inspecting is problematic for free-tier users: with better metadata, operators can make informed decisions about image pulls ahead of time. Note that part of the additional information we propose to include is contained in the experimental image manifest v2, schema 2 of the Docker registry API specification [4] (see Listing 1.1, `features` element). Evidently, this implementation has some limitations. First and foremost, the image manifests are not available via the public API. As a consequence, one must pull the image and inspect it manually, a process that is hard to automate and requires storage space and network bandwidth for then potentially non-executable images. For instance, `docker run` will currently pull an AMD64 image on ARM before complaining about incompatible binary formats. Secondly, in terms of hardware, only CPU architectures and instruction sets are considered. Consequently, one cannot identify if an image uses GPUs or FPGAs from its manifest alone. Finally, CPU architecture variants and features are written to the manifest manually but cannot be verified during validation. This leaves the inclusion of this information at the discretion of the developer and the validation up to the end user.

Thus, we propose an extension of the platform information that distinguishes CPU architecture and features, as well as other hardware devices supported. Listing 1.2 shows an example in augmented JSON format that serves as downward-compatible replacement for the current Docker registry metadata. We argue that it is important to distinguish a hardware feature as `supported`, *e.g.,* its functionality can be emulated/simulated if the hardware component is missing), or `required`, *e.g.,* the container will fail without it.

Moreover, specific hardware support from the host needs to be passed through to the running container. Hence, rather than replicating pass-through parameters in all scripts and composition documents (Listing 1.3), we argue for tightly binding them with the container metadata. Similar to how permissions are confirmed by users of mobile phone applications, administrators can interactively approve applications based on displayed host device access permissions. In addition, some containers require volumes to be mounted, or access to the Docker daemon socket, to be indicated in the extended metadata structure.

Listing 1.3. Pass-through support.

```
1  {
2    "platform" as defined above
3    ...
4    "passthru-devices": [
5      "/dev/kvm", "/dev/net/tun", "/dev/bus"
6    ],
7    "volumes": [
8      "/run/secrets", "/var/run/docker.sock"
9    ]}
```

4.3 Improved Container Image Tooling

Finally, we introduce hdocker, a hardware-aware wrapper around the docker run command, to perform several tasks that streamline the use of Docker containers across heterogeneous hardware architectures. Specifically, hdocker can:

- Report on the availability of tags per architecture and architectures per tag.
- Check whether CPU flags and hardware devices are present and activated, beyond the standard CPU architecture and operating system.
- Check whether device files and volumes are appropriately declared to be mounted in the invocation parameters.
- Inform the user with clear actionable advice in case of unsupported features.
- Automate the analysis (using imagexplore) and decisions if asked to do so and if possible.

The hdocker tool is metadata-driven, as it parses the augmented metadata curated from our experiments. Unless cached locally, it downloads all container image layers, runs imagexplore over all images, and store the resulting JSON metadata files. If the registry uses our augmented schema to retain this information, end users would not have to perform the image pull and analytics to obtain the hardware requirements of the image and hdocker could configure the hardware pass-through automatically.

Beyond the designed and implemented hdocker CLI, we also envision further tools to assess the metadata in a similar way. Among them are autonomous container migration tools that work as target node filters in heterogenous computing continuums (*i.e.*, cloud/edge/fog/IoT or osmotic settings [36]).

5 Discussion

While Docker images that support or require specialised hardware still comprise a very small share of the total available images, we argue that their significance to industries that make use of heterogeneous or specialised hardware justifies communicating support for such features in an image's public metadata.

Our proposed support is nevertheless not a simple addition to the metadata schema. There are certain requirements for making its adoption meaningful.

Docker CLI Support. The hardware features would have to be specified by the user through the Docker CLI during a build, or detected by the Docker builder. The latter is harder to implement, but would enforce the hardware specification, whereas developers would neglect specifying the hardware requirements.

Dockerd Support. When attempting to run an image with specific hardware requirements that are not met, the Docker daemon would need to alert the user of the issue, rather than `hdocker`.

Docker Registry Support. The hardware-related metadata would have to be part of the public Docker registry API, so that end-users can make informed decisions on the images they deploy ahead of time. The need for this is accentuated by the rate limit introduced by Docker Hub recently, forcing operators to be mindful of image pulls they make.

6   Related Work

Analyzing and understanding large container datasets offers substantial insights on current trends among practitioners and DevOps engineers' best practices. In [38], authors produce a large-scale dataset of more than 450'000 Docker images by crawling Docker Hub, downloading and decompressing images and analysing their contents. The dataset is populated with file-level metrics such as compression ratios, file types and sizes, and content-level metrics, *i.e.*, programming languages, compressed files and database systems. Despite rich metadata including deduplication metrics, the underlying OS or architecture features are ignored. Moreover, the dataset is not made available, forcing the research community and ourselves to implement, deploy and run our own crawler to get complementary insights. While our automated monitoring is on a smaller scale, we produce and release a curated dataset that provides historical metrics by monitoring at regular intervals over a longer period of time. Our dataset also serves as an example of the type of insights that could be obtained by applying our methods to other repositories, such as those maintained by specific organisations.

Approximate Concrete Execution [14] applies binary analysis to container images used in serverless platforms such as Google Cloud Run and AWS Fargate. It uses function-level fingerprinting to identify security problems in an early stage, based on a database associating fingerprints to such issues. The same technique could be used to fingerprint hardware dependencies. For simplicity, we look at container images at a coarse-grained level – if any script or application therein depends on a specific hardware feature, no matter if this is run on startup or just placed accidentally in the image, we consider the dependency to exist.

Several container orchestration tools have been recently proposed specifically for heterogeneous hardware clusters. However, they lack the necessary detection and expression of hardware dependencies within the container images or composed applications. DRAPS [25] focuses on resource allocation, and thus in quantitative differences in CPU performance, amount of RAM and network/block device I/O latency, whereas our work investigates hardware differences at a deeper and qualitative level. Our work is complementary and necessary to further improve heterogeneous cloud application orchestration with upfront predictability about the likelihood of failure.

Dockemu extends the network simulator NS-3 with portable containers to cover IoT scenarios [29]. It supports heterogeneity in nodes and links between them, but does not cover hardware differences in detail. We anticipate the use of our results for building better heterogeneous cloud simulators and emulators.

The metadata expressivity limitation of Docker Hub and privately deployed container image registries have been widely covered by researchers. ConHub [35] is an extended metadata management system for Docker images on top of a relational database. It supports CQL queries and user-defined metadata, letting users manage hardware-dependent images when importing augmented metadata, similar to the ones we propose. Similarly, Docker2RDF [10] and DockerFinder [13] offer queryable endpoints that will benefit from richer descriptions including on hardware restrictions at pull time. While we focus on hardware features, studies exist [17] to analyse image content in terms of programming languages, runtimes, security vulnerabilities and reproducible builds, leading to further metadata.

7   Conclusion and Future Work

Our multi-method analysis on Docker container images identified limitations on the handling of heterogeneous hardware, an increasingly relevant matter in typical container environments such as differentiated cloud services. We released a new DockerHub dataset on the metadata of ~11'000 Docker images over the period of more than one year. We offer insights on available and used hardware features, e.g., related to security (SGX) and machine learning (Nvidia). We validated initial search findings with static analysis, and cross-validated those with runtime testing. Further, we contributed new proposals to augment the container image metadata with hardware, device and volume information as well as tools to exploit the knowledge at runtime for more user-friendly application handling. Overall, we observed a solid growth of images and tags across architectures, with the exception of x386, whilst a low number of non-toy, non-base images exploiting specific hardware beyond the basic CPU architecture. As future work, we aim at extending container image quality benchmarks with hardware details, and look further into enclaved and isolated application execution in the cloud.

Data and Code
Metadata, analysis data, tools and code for reproducibility are made publicly available at https://doi.org/10.5281/zenodo.4531794.

References

1. AWS Nitro Enclaves. https://aws.amazon.com/ec2/nitro/nitro-enclaves/
2. Confidential computing on Azure. https://docs.microsoft.com/en-us/azure/confidential-computing/overview

3. Graphene Secure Container Environment. https://github.com/oscarlab/graphene/tree/master/Tools
4. Image Manifest Version 2, Schema 2. https://docs.docker.com/registry/spec/manifest-v2-2/
5. Introducing Google Cloud Confidential Computing with Confidential VMs. https://cloud.google.com/blog/products/identity-security/introducing-google-cloud-confidential-computing-with-confidential-vms
6. NVIDIA Docker: GPU Server Application Deployment Made Easy. https://developer.nvidia.com/blog/nvidia-docker-gpu-server-application-deployment-made-easy/
7. SCONTAIN Homepage. https://scontain.com/
8. Amacher, J., Schiavoni, V.: On the performance of ARM TrustZone. In: Pereira, J., Ricci, L. (eds.) DAIS 2019. LNCS, vol. 11534, pp. 133–151. Springer, Cham (2019). https://doi.org/10.1007/978-3-030-22496-7_9
9. Arnautov, S., et al.: SCONE: secure linux containers with intel SGX. In: 12th USENIX Conference on OSDI, pp. 689–703 (2016)
10. Ayed, A.B., Subercaze, J., Laforest, F., Chaari, T., Louati, W., Kacem, A.H.: Docker2rdf: lifting the docker registry hub into RDF. In: 2017 IEEE World Congress on Services (SERVICES), pp. 36–39. IEEE (2017)
11. Binz, T., Breitenbücher, U., Kopp, O., Leymann, F.: TOSCA: portable automated deployment and management of cloud applications. In: Advanced Web Services, pp. 527–549. Springer (2014). https://doi.org/10.1007/978-0-8176-4540-3
12. Felber, P., et al.: Secure end-to-end processing of smart metering data. J. Cloud Comput. **8**(1), 19 (2019)
13. Brogi, A., Neri, D., Soldani, J.: DockerFinder: multi-attribute search of docker images. In: IEEE International Conference on Cloud Engineering (IC2E) (2017)
14. Byrne, A., Nadgowda, S., Coskun, A.: ACE: just-in-time serverless software component discovery through approximate concrete execution. In: Proceedings of Middleware Workshops/Sixth International Workshop on Serverless Computing (WoSC6) (2020)
15. Carrasco, J., Durán, F., Pimentel, E.: Live migration of trans-cloud applications. Comput. Stand. Interfaces **69**, 103392 (2020)
16. Cho, K., Lee, H., Bang, K., Kim, S.: Possibility of HPC application on cloud infrastructure by container cluster. In: IEEE International Conference on CSE and Computational Science and IEEE International Conference on EUC, pp. 266–271 (2019)
17. Cito, J., Schermann, G., Wittern, J.E., Leitner, P., Zumberi, S., Gall, H.C.: An empirical analysis of the docker container ecosystem on github. In: IEEE/ACM 14th International Conference on Mining Software Repositories (MSR), pp. 323–333 (2017)
18. Coppolino, L., D'Antonio, S., Mazzeo, G., Romano, L.: A comprehensive survey of hardware-assisted security: from the edge to the cloud. Internet Things **6**, 100055 (2019)
19. Costan, V., Devadas, S.: Intel SGX explained. IACR Cryptol. ePrint Arch. **2016**(86), 1–118 (2016)
20. Di Martino, B.: Applications portability and services interoperability among multiple clouds. IEEE Cloud Comput. **1**(1), 74–77 (2014)
21. Florin, R., Ionut, R.: FPGA based architecture for securing IoT with blockchain. In: International Conference on Speech Technology and Human-Computer Dialogue, SpeD 2019, pp. 1–8. IEEE (2019)

22. Herardian, R.: The soft underbelly of cloud security. IEEE Secur. Privacy **17**(3), 90–93 (2019)
23. Johnson, S., Rizzo, D., Ranganathan, P., McCune, J., Ho, R.: Titan: enabling a transparent silicon root of trust for cloud. In: Hot Chips: a Symposium on High Performance Chips (2018)
24. Kaplan, D., Powell, J., Woller, T.: AMD memory encryption. White paper (2016)
25. Mao, Y., Oak, J., Pompili, A., Beer, D., Han, T., Hu, P.: DRAPS: Dynamic and Resource-Aware Placement Scheme for Docker Containers in a Heterogeneous Cluster. CoRR abs/1805.08598 (2018). http://arxiv.org/abs/1805.08598
26. Modi, C., Patel, D., Borisaniya, B., Patel, H., Patel, A., Rajarajan, M.: A survey of intrusion detection techniques in cloud. J. Netw. Comput. Appl. **36**(1), 42–57 (2013)
27. Petcu, D.: Portability and interoperability between clouds: challenges and case study. In: Abramowicz, W., Llorente, I.M., Surridge, M., Zisman, A., Vayssière, J. (eds.) ServiceWave 2011. LNCS, vol. 6994, pp. 62–74. Springer, Heidelberg (2011). https://doi.org/10.1007/978-3-642-24755-2_6
28. Pinto, S., Santos, N.: Demystifying ARM TrustZone: a comprehensive survey. ACM Comput. Surv. (CSUR) **51**(6), 1–36 (2019)
29. Portabales, A.R., Nores, M.L.: Dockemu: extension of a scalable network simulation framework based on docker and NS3 to cover IoT Scenarios. In: Proceedings 8th International Conference on Simulation and Modeling Methodologies, Technologies and Applications, SIMULTECH 2018, pp. 175–182. SciTePress (2018)
30. Ren, J., Qi, Y., Dai, Y., Yu, X., Shi, Y.: Nosv: a lightweight nested-virtualization VMM for hosting high performance computing on cloud. J. Syst. Softw. **124**, 137–152 (2017)
31. Schinianakis, D., Trapero, R., Michalopoulos, D.S., Crespo, B.G.: Security considerations in 5G networks: a slice-aware trust zone approach. In: IEEE WCNC, pp. 1–8 (2019)
32. Shepovalov, M., Akella, V.: FPGA and GPU-based acceleration of ML workloads on Amazon cloud - a case study using gradient boosted decision tree library. Integration **70**, 1–9 (2020)
33. Shu, R., Gu, X., Enck, W.: A study of security vulnerabilities on docker hub. In: Proceedings of 7th ACM CODASPY, pp. 269–280 (2017)
34. Tarafdar, N., Eskandari, N., Lin, T., Chow, P.: Designing for FPGAs in the cloud. IEEE Des. Test **35**(1), 23–29 (2018)
35. Tian, C.X., Pan, A., Tay, Y.C.: ConHub: a metadata management system for docker containers. In: Proceedings of 25th ACM International Conference on Information and Knowledge Management, CIKM 2016, pp. 2453–2455 (2016)
36. Villari, M., Fazio, M., Dustdar, S., Rana, O., Jha, D.N., Ranjan, R.: Osmosis: the osmotic computing platform for microelements in the cloud, edge, and Internet of Things. IEEE Comput. **52**(8), 14–26 (2019)
37. Yeh, T., Chen, H., Chou, J.: KubeShare: a framework to manage GPUs as first-class and shared resources in container cloud. In: 29th International Symposium High-Performance Parallel and Distributed Computing, pp. 173–184. ACM (2020)
38. Zhao, N., et al.: Large-scale analysis of the docker hub dataset. In: 2019 IEEE International Conference on Cluster Computing, Cluster, pp. 1–10 (2019)

Invited Paper

Simulation of Large Scale Computational Ecosystems with Alchemist: A Tutorial

Danilo Pianini[(✉)][iD]

Dipartimento di Informatica, Scienza e Ingegneria, Alma Mater
Studiorum—Università di Bologna, 47522 Cesena, FC, Italy
danilo.pianini@unibo.it

Abstract. Many interesting systems in several disciplines can be modeled as networks of nodes that can store and exchange data: pervasive systems, edge computing scenarios, and even biological and bio-inspired systems. These systems feature inherent complexity, and often simulation is the preferred (and sometimes the only) way of investigating their behavior; this is true both in the design phase and in the verification and testing phase. In this tutorial paper, we provide a guide to the simulation of such systems by leveraging Alchemist, an existing research tool used in several works in the literature. We introduce its meta-model and its extensible architecture; we discuss reference examples of increasing complexity; and we finally show how to configure the tool to automatically execute multiple repetitions of simulations with different controlled variables, achieving reliable and reproducible results.

Keywords: Simulation · Pervasive computing · Self-organization

1 Introduction

The growing complexity of modern coordinated systems, fostered by trends such as cyber-physical systems (CPSs) and the Internet of Things, is a driving force behind novel development languages and methods. Techniques commonly used in classic centralized software development fall short when the system at hand features distribution, heterogeneity, and asynchronous communication. One relevant issue when developing software for distributed systems is testing: local execution of tests, the most common way of verifying system behavior before deployment, gets much harder when multiple distributed components are under test. Even worse, many such systems are (self-)adaptive, and feature autonomic behavior in face of unpredictable events, such as mobility, communication failures, or devices entering and leaving the system. In this context, simulation is key: by capturing the appropriate level of abstraction, simulators can provide insights into the coordinated system behavior without resorting to complex deployments. Moreover, they allow for experimenting with extreme situations, unlikely or even plain impossible, and explore the behavior of the system under test when subject to such extreme events.

© IFIP International Federation for Information Processing 2021
Published by Springer Nature Switzerland AG 2021
M. Matos and F. Greve (Eds.): DAIS 2021, LNCS 12718, pp. 145–161, 2021.
https://doi.org/10.1007/978-3-030-78198-9_10

In this paper, we provide a tutorial introduction to Alchemist[1] [21], a simulation platform that has been successfully leveraged in the literature for a variety of different scenarios; including crowd tracking and steering, distributed algorithms evaluation, resource management, and even morphogenesis of multicellular organisms. The paper is organized as follows: Sect. 2 introduces the meta-model of the simulator and its extension system; Sect. 3 provides a sequence of increasingly richer examples, guiding the reader to an operative understanding of the simulator; Sect. 4 discusses how the simulator can be leveraged to extract data from multiple repetitions of simulations, and how specific executions can be reproduced exactly, thus allowing to debug and explore the system behavior in case rare anomalies are discovered; finally, Sect. 5 concludes the work.

2   A Meta-model of Computational Ecosystems

When designing a simulator, the most important decision to take is *what* the simulator should simulate, namely, what is its domain model. The decision is rather thorny, as decisions on the model are critical for optimization: the simpler the model, the larger the number of assumptions that can be made, the larger space for the designer to write specific optimization. The usual engineering process behind the creation of a simulator involves a selection of the model features, the decision of the time model (usually, the choice is between time-driven and event-driven), and finally the design of an engine that can support the execution in time of the model. Alchemist is atypical in this sense: since at the time of its conception performance was a major issue, it was conceived as an experimental tool meant to understand whether existing (and proven to be fast) engines could be extended to support the desired model without losing too much performance.

Alchemist is a by-product of the SAPERE European Project [33], where the goal was to coordinate pervasive software ecosystems with a biochemical and ecological metaphor. The idea behind the simulator was to extend existing high-performance stochastic chemistry simulation algorithms, adding support for:

- multiple interconnected "compartments" (containers of molecules),
- complex data types,
- non-exponentially distributed events,
- richer environment manipulation (chemical reactions are rather simple),
- different rules (reactions) in different compartments.

The latter requirement, in particular, restricted the choice of possible engine algorithms, ruling out the one identified by Slepoy et al. [25], thus orienting the choice towards the Gibson-Bruck algorithm [11]. Adaptation to the new model required important changes to the engine optimization structure, but it succeeded in preserving most of the performance [21]. Details on the internals of the simulator are out of the scope of this work and are documented in [21].

---

[1] https://alchemistsimulator.github.io.

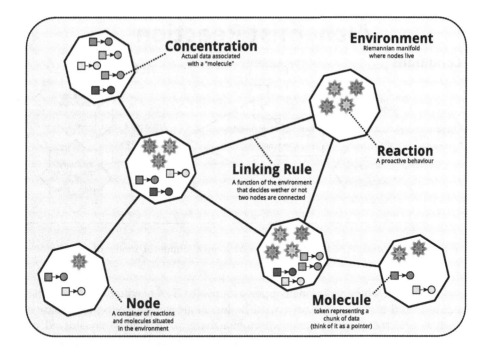

Fig. 1. A pictorial representation of the Alchemist simulator meta-model.

2.1 Abstract Meta-model

The abstract meta-model of Alchemist is hence influenced by its chemical origin. A pictorial view of such meta-model is presented in Fig. 1; the meta-model has the following entities:

- **Environment:** a Riemannian manifold modeling space, containing nodes and mapping them to positions;
- **Position:** a coordinate in the environment;
- **Node:** A container of molecules and reactions, living inside the environment;
- **Molecule:** the name of a data item;
- **Concentration:** the value associated with a particular molecule;
- **Linking rule:** a function associating each node to a neighborhood;
- **Neighborhood:** a structure composed of one central node and a set of other nodes considered its neighbors;
- **Reaction:** an event changing the status of the environment, made of a (possibly empty) set of conditions, a time distribution, a rate equation, and at least one action;
- **Condition:** a function of environment outputting a positive real number (usually but not necessarily interpreted as a boolean);
- **Action**: a change in the environment.

In this model, the sole source of changes in the environment is the execution of reactions, whose structure is depicted in Fig. 2. Alchemist is indeed a discrete

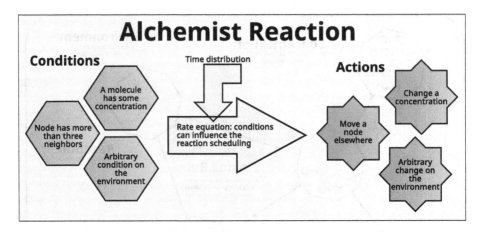

Fig. 2. A pictorial representation of the Alchemist simulator model of reaction.

event simulator, where reactions happen atomically. The peculiar structure with conditions and actions associated with nodes, along with a concept of context (which is omitted from the main discussion here, as it can be considered an implementation detail from the point of view of the user), allow Alchemist to build and maintain a dependency graph, speeding up significantly the scheduling of events [25].

2.2 Executable Models: Incarnations

In the previous discussion, we did not describe precisely what concentration is. Indeed, all Alchemist entities abstract from the type associated with the concentration; which has been purposely designed as abstract to allow extensibility. An Alchemist component fixing the concentration type is called an *incarnation*. Incarnations usually come not just with a well-defined type of concentration, but with complementary conditions, actions, reactions, and, possibly, means to create them from strings with custom syntax. Currently, the simulator features four incarnations: biochemistry, sapere, protelis, and scafi.

The *biochemistry* incarnation models concentration as a floating-point number. It provides a way to write specifications in a custom language derivative of chemical reactions, as well as custom nodes modeling the behavior of cells (for instance, supporting chemotaxis via polarization [7]). This incarnation has been used in the literature, for instance, to run stochastic simulations of the morphogenesis of Drosophila Melanogaster starting from a single cell [15].

The *sapere* incarnation is the oldest incarnation of the simulator and is meant to provide support for designing self-organizing mechanisms with the SAPERE [33] metaphor. In this incarnation, the concentration is a set of ground Linda-like tuples [10] matching a template (represented by a molecule); reactions are chemical-like rewriting rules, and nodes thus become programmable tuple spaces. This incarnation has been used in the literature for simulating, for instance, crowd evacuation [16] and steering[2], anticipatory adaptation [14], and resource discovery [27].

In the *protelis* incarnation, concentration is defined as Java `Object`; in fact, this incarnation is meant to let nodes execute specifications written in the Protelis aggregate programming language [22], which can manipulate arbitrary data structures. This is likely the incarnation most commonly used in the literature, featuring dozens of examples including crowd tracking [3] and dispersal [30][3], target counting [20][4], drone coordination [5], and several distributed algorithms [1, 2, 29] and patterns [19].

Finally, the *scafi* incarnation provides support for the Scafi Scala DSL for aggregate programming [31]. Similar to Protelis, Scafi can manipulate arbitrary data types, hence the incarnation defines `Any` as concentration type. In the literature, Scafi has been exercised, for instance, in distributed peer-to-peer chats [5] and situated problem-solving [4].

3   Guided Examples

In this section, we will introduce a sequence of increasingly rich scenarios, showcasing the tool's capabilities and providing a path for learning the basics. The reader might experiment with the tool while reading this paper: the simulator comes with minimal requirements (a Java Virtual Machine 11 or newer), and a repository[5] [18] containing all examples and instructions is provided. In this paper, we will not go through all the technical details related to the environment setup (also, these details might change in the future with new versions of the tool); rather, we recommend checking out the simulator website and online manual[6]. All the code snippets presented here refer to the simulator at version 11.0.0.

3.1   The YAML-Based Simulation Specification Language

The extensible incarnation-based architecture of the simulator provides flexibility on the one hand, but it inevitably complicates the environment configuration, as it opens a potentially limitless range of options. On the one hand, the user must be able to write and use their custom extensions, but on the other hand, the simulation specifications should be as declarative, succinct, and human-readable as possible. Alchemist found a sweet spot between these requirements by relying on the YAML data serialization standard[7], a superset of JSON [6]. For the sake of self-containedness, we here introduce a few features of YAML which will be largely used in the remainder of the paper.

---

[2] A video is available at https://www.youtube.com/watch?v=QkWDynuELuo.

[3] A video is available at https://www.youtube.com/watch?v=606ObQwQuaE.

[4] A video is available at https://www.youtube.com/watch?v=MOwS6vQnubY.

[5] https://github.com/DanySK/DisCoTec-2021-Tutorial.

[6] https://alchemistsimulator.github.io/.

[7] https://yaml.org/spec/1.2/spec.html.

A YAML Primer. YAML scalars can be integers (e.g., 42), floating-point numbers (e.g., `4.1` or `6.022e+23`), null values (`null`, `~`), booleans (`true`, `false`), or strings. Strings in YAML do not need to be quoted, although they can be if disambiguation is needed (for instance, `"42"` and `"42"` evaluate to strings rather than integers). Comments are prefixed by `#`. YAML mappings are key-value pairs (similar to dictionaries or hashes in other languages). They can be written by using a JSON-like syntax:

```
{one: 1, two: 2}
```

but they are usually expressed in a more human-readable form:

```
one: 1
two: 2
```

Mappings can be nested, and the two styles can be freely mixed. Nested mappings in human-readable form rely on semantic indentation to determine hierarchies:

```
integers:
  the_answer: 42
  the_beast: 666
floats: { avogadro: 6.022e+23, gravitational: 6.67408e-11 }
```

In case keys are repeated multiple times, the syntax is considered valid but only the latter entry is considered. YAML sequences are ordered collections of possibly equal elements, similar to arrays or lists in other languages. Similar to mappings, they feature two forms: a JSON-like syntax where elements are comma-separated and surrounded by square brackets, and a semantic-indented form:

```
- this is an element of the lists
- the following element is a nested list
- [one element of the nested list, another element of the nested list]
- the following elements are a nested list as well
  - one element of the nested list
  - another element of the nested list
```

Besides readability, one key reason to pick YAML over other formats is that it allows two forms of the "don't repeat yourself" (DRY) principle to be applied: reuse by anchoring, and reuse by merge keys:

```
some_map: &my_map #the content of some_map can now be referred to!
  { the_answer: 42, the_beast: 666 }
list_of_map_copies: [*my_map, *my_map, *my_map] # multiple copies
merged:
  the_trinity: 3
  <<: *my_map # map contents are merged into this map
  the_beast: absent # one value of the merged map is redefined
# Contents of merged: { the_trinity: 3, the_answer: 42, the_beast: absent }
```

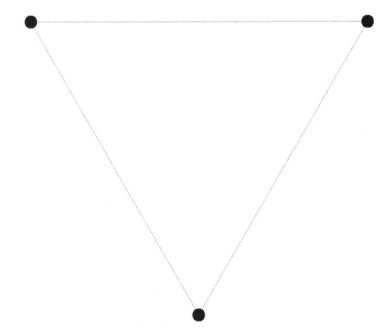

Fig. 3. Three devices in a bidimensional space.

3.2   Three Connected Devices

The Alchemist YAML specification must be a mapping containing at least the
incarnation key, expecting a string value. Node locations are expressed in the
deployments section while linking rules are specified in the **network-model**
section. Crucially, Alchemist allows context-sensitive loading of arbitrary Java
classes (or Java-compatible, thereby including Kotlin, Groovy, and Scala) implementing the required interfaces by specifying a map with a **type** key expecting an
associated string value and (optionally) a **parameters** key expecting a sequence.
As a first example, we write a specification displacing three nodes in a Euclidean
bi-dimensional space, specifying a connection rule that makes all of them connected.

```
incarnation: sapere # The incarnation is always mandatory
network-model:
  type: ConnectWithinDistance # class name, must implement LinkingRule
  parameters: [2] # Comm. radius (argument of the class' constructor)
deployments:
  - type: Point # Loads a class with this name implementing Deployment
    parameters: [0, 0] # Coordinates
  - { type: Point, parameters: [0.5, 0.85] }
  - { type: Point, parameters: [-0.5, 0.85] }
```

The simulator, as depicted in Fig. 3 shows three connected devices occupying the
specified positions. This simulation is not of great use, though: since there are no
reactions, the simulation concludes as soon as it is started, with the simulation
time going instantly to infinity.

3.3 A Grid of Devices Playing Dodgeball

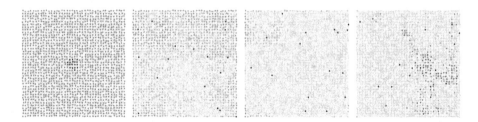

Fig. 4. Four subsequent snapshots of the simulation of the "dodgeball" example. Devices with a ball are depicted in black. All other devices' color hue depends on the hit count, shifting from red (zero hits) towards blue. (Color figure online)

We now showcase a more significant example, by deploying a grid of devices and making them play dodgeball. The program to be injected is rather simple: some nodes node will begin the simulation with a `ball`, and their goal will be to throw it to a random neighbor; whichever node gets hit takes a point, updates its score, and throws the ball again. This program is easy to write in a network of programmable tuple spaces, hence we write the following specification using the SAPERE incarnation.

```
incarnation: sapere
network-model: { type: ConnectWithinDistance, parameters: [0.5] }
deployments:
  type: Grid
  parameters: [-5, -5, 5, 5, 0.25, 0.25, 0.1, 0.1] # A perturbed grid
  contents:
    - molecule: "{hit, 0}" # Everywhere, no one has been hit
    - in: { type: Rectangle, parameters: [-0.5, -0.5, 1, 1] } # In this area...
      molecule: ball # ...every node has a ball
  programs:
    - time-distribution: 1 # Rate of program evaluation
      # 'program' strings get interpreted by the incarnation
      program: "{ball} {hit, N} --> {hit, N + 1} {launching}" # Hit taken
    - program: "{launching} --> +{ball}" # Throw the ball to a neighbor ASAP
```

This short specification covers several features at once and deserves an explanation. For every entry in the **deployments** section, **contents** and **programs** can be specified describing respectively the initial content of nodes and their behavior. Every entry under **contents** contains a **molecule**, the corresponding **concentration**, and optionally one or more **shapes** defining where these contents should be inserted (no shape means "in every node"). Molecule and concentration descriptors must be interpreted by the selected incarnation; more in general, whenever there is no explicitly specified implementation of the concept to be used specified via **type/parameters** key, the provided data is sent to the incarnation. This is also true for **time-distribution** and **program** entries found in elements of the **programs** section. Snapshots for the running example are provided in Fig. 4.

3.4   A Gradient on a Grid of Devices

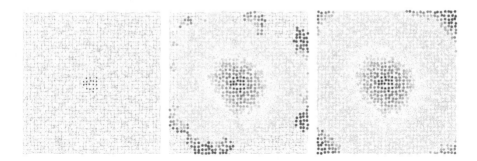

Fig. 5. Three subsequent snapshots of the simulation of the "gradient" example. Source devices have a central black dot. Devices' color hue depends on the gradient value, shifting from red (low) towards blue (high). (Color figure online)

Preparing more interesting computations is then a matter of writing more interesting specifications. In the following snippet, we implement a very simple specification of a gradient, a pattern that is considered to be the basis of many other patterns [8,9,29]. The specification is very similar to the previous one, and does not introduce any new concept:

```
incarnation: sapere
network-model: { type: ConnectWithinDistance, parameters: [0.5] }
deployments:
  type: Grid
  parameters: [-5, -5, 5, 5, 0.25, 0.25, 0.1, 0.1]
  contents:
    in: { type: Rectangle, parameters: [-0.5, -0.5, 1, 1] }
    molecule: source # Here is the source of the gradient
  programs:
    - time-distribution: 0.1 # Exponential with lambda=0.1
      # If there is a source, then the gradient is zero.
      program: "{source} --> {source} {gradient, 0}"
    - time-distribution: 1 # Exponential distribution with lambda=1
      # Send all neighbors your gradient value plus one
      program: "{gradient, N} --> {gradient, N} *{gradient, N+1}"
      # In case of multiple gradients, take the shortest
    - program: "{gradient, N}{gradient, def: N2>=N} --> {gradient, N}"
    - time-distribution: 0.1
      program: "{gradient, N} --> {gradient, N + 1}" # Aging process
    - program: "{gradient, def: N > 30} -->" # Death process
```

Snapshots of the execution can be found in Fig. 5.

3.5   Arbitrary Network Graphs

We now introduce more elaborate deployments. Right now, we experimented with points and grid, but the simulator offers much more flexibility. Besides deploying on points and grid, the simulator features:

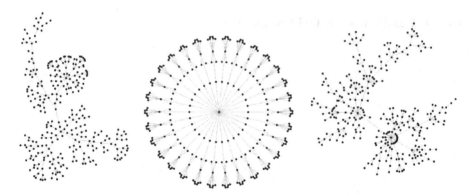

Fig. 6. A single environment with three advanced deployments. From left to right: a Lobster graph, a banana tree, and a scale-free network with preferential attachment.

- uniform random deployments within circles, eclipses, and polygons;
- deployments on (possibly perturbed) regular shapes (e.g., arcs);
- deployments in arbitrary positions;
- deployments relative to the current deployment (e.g., for adding nodes probabilistically close to others); and
- deployments on generated arbitrary graphs, via GraphStream [23].

To showcase some of the possibilities, we generate a deployment composed of three separate graphs: a Lobster graph [17], a Banana tree [28], and a scale-free network built with preferential attachment [12], using the snippet below.

```
incarnation: sapere
network-model: { type: ConnectWithinDistance, parameters: [0.5] }
deployments:
# parameters are node count, horizontal offset, vertical offset, zoom, graph type
  - { type: GraphStreamDeployment, parameters: [300, -30, 0, 0.8, Lobster, [5, 15]] }
  - { type: GraphStreamDeployment, parameters: [300, 0, 0, 2, BananaTree, 10] }
  - { type: GraphStreamDeployment, parameters: [300, 30, 0, PreferentialAttachment] }
```

The resulting environment is depicted in Fig. 6.

3.6   Node Mobility and Indoor Environments

All the previous examples run on a static network of devices in an endless bi-dimensional space. However, many interesting scenarios the simulator targets require mobility and a richer environment. In the following example, we show a group of mobile devices estimating the distance from a point of interest (the altar) while moving within a church, whose planimetry has been taken from an existing building. For the sake of simplicity, the movement here is modeled as a Lévy Walk [32], selected as it is a reasonable approximation of human walking [24]. Since self-stabilizing gradient on a mobile mesh network requires some tweaks to work appropriately [1], we switched to the Protelis incarnation and used the protelis-lang library [9] to implement the desired behavior in few lines of code.

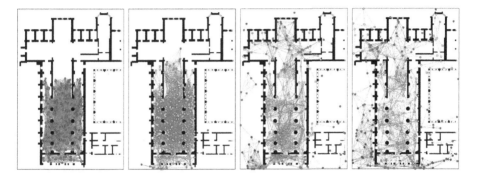

Fig. 7. Four snapshots of the simulation of mobile devices in a church. Devices progressively explore the location, while measuring the distance from a point of interest via gradient (red nodes are closer to the point of interest; purple ones are farther). (Color figure online)

```
incarnation: protelis
environment: { type: ImageEnvironment, parameters: [chiaravalle.png, 0.1] }
network-model: { type: ObstaclesBreakConnection, parameters: [50] }
deployments:
  type: Rectangle
  parameters: [300, 62, 15, 95, 200]
  programs:
    - time-distribution: 1
      program: >
        import protelis:coord:spreading
        let vector = self.getCoordinates() - [110, 325]
        distanceTo(hypot(vector.get(0), vector.get(1)) < 50)
    - program: send # Actual network message delivery
    - { type: Event, time-distribution: 1, actions: { type: LevyWalk, parameters: [1.4] } }
```

Comparing the code of this example with those in the previous sections highlights how the flexibility introduced by the incarnation mechanisms allows for programming scenarios with entirely different paradigms without changing the simulator. Besides the change of incarnation (and, hence, in the language used to program nodes), the most relevant change is the selection of a custom class for the environment, which loads an image turning pixels of the selected color into physical obstacles. Simulation snapshots are provided in Fig. 7.

3.7   Real-World Maps and GPS Traces

Finally, one relevant feature of Alchemist as a simulator for modern coordinated systems is the ability to exploit real-world geospatial data. The simulator can load data from OpenStreetMap exports, navigate devices towards a destination along streets by relying on GraphHopper[8] or by using GPS traces in GPX format, or even using the navigation system to interpolate sparse GPS traces, thus preventing nodes from taking impossible paths. Streets available for navigation

---

[8] https://www.graphhopper.com/.

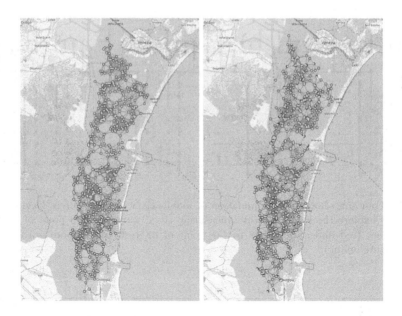

Fig. 8. 500 buoys deployed on the Venice lagoon.

can be selected based on the role of the node, which can be, for instance, bike, car, foot, wheelchair, hiking. For the sake of simplicity, we here present a simple scenario where water buoys are deployed in the Venice lagoon.

```
incarnation: sapere
environment: { type: OSMEnvironment }
network-model: { type: ConnectWithinDistance, parameters: [1000] }
_venice_lagoon: &lagoon
  [[45.20381, 12.25044], [45.22074, 12.26417], ..., [45.20381, 12.25044]]
deployments:
  type: Polygon
  parameters: [500, *lagoon]
  programs:
    time-distribution: 10
    type: Event
    actions: { type: BrownianMove, parameters: [0.0005] }
```

The complete sequence of coordinates is available as part of the Alchemist distribution[9] (all the examples presented in this work became part of the regression test suite of the simulator). Snapshots of the simulator are provided in Fig. 8.

4   In-Depth Analysis of Simulated Scenarios

Setting up a simulated environment is only the first step towards a scientific analysis. Usually, the system goes through a phase of debug and refinement and

---

[9] https://bit.ly/3cCfdnj.

is finally evaluated by analyzing its behavior by considering the metrics of choice under varying conditions.

Debugging a simulation requires the ability to reproduce the same behavior multiple times: an unexpected behavior requiring investigation may happen far into the simulation, or in corner conditions encountered by chance. Some simulators found in the literature, such as EdgeCloudSim [26], offer no possibility to exert such control. Alchemist was instead carefully crafted to guarantee reproducibility. Randomness is controlled by setting the random generator seeds separately for the deployments and the simulation execution, allowing for running different simulations on the same random deployment. Seeds are set at the top level of the simulation specification, as in the following snippet: `seeds: { simulation: 0, scenario: 0 }`. By default, Alchemist uses the Mersenne Twister pseudo-random generator, which guarantees high performance and very high dimensionality [13].

Alchemist provides first-class support for executing multiple simulations with varying conditions. Variables can be listed in the `variables` section of the simulation descriptor. Every variable has a default value and a way to generate other values. When a batch execution is requested, the cartesian product of all possible values for the selected variables is produced, the default values are used for non-selected variables, and then for each entry, a simulation is prepared and then executed (execution can be and usually is performed in parallel). Linear, logarithmic, and arbitrary variables are provided with the distribution, but custom generators can be easily implemented. Moreover, to favor reusability and apply the DRY principle, the simulator allows defining variables whose values possibly depend on values of other variables. Their values can be expressed in any JSR223[10]-compatible language (thereby including Scala, Kotlin, JavaScript, Ruby, Python, and Groovy), using Groovy as default. The variable definition mechanism is a powerful tool for creating rich simulations: values can be reused throughout the simulation specification, and can be computed based on other values, allowing for very advanced mechanisms such as environment sensitivity (e.g., react to the values of arbitrary environment variables), and dynamic simulation updates (e.g., by downloading components from a server).

Finally, the simulator provides tools for exporting data automatically. An `export` section on the simulation file instructs which data is considered interesting, and should be thus exported with the selected sampling frequency. Data can be exported separately for each node, or can be aggregated on the fly using any univariate statistic function (e.g., mean, sum, product, percentile, median...). The treatment of missing or non-finite values can be specified as well. Results are exported in comma-separated values files, easily importable in a variety of data analysis tools.

The following snippet showcases the aforementioned features by enriching the example presented in Sect. 3.6 with:

1. variables for the pedestrian walking speed, pedestrian count, and random seed;

---

[10] https://www.jcp.org/en/jsr/detail?id=223.

2. constants to ease the configuration of the simulation;
3. a Kotlin resource search expressed as a variable;
4. controlled reproducibility by controlling random seeds;
5. export of generated data (time and several statistics on the gradient).

```
variables:
  zoom: &zoom
    formula: 0.1 # Must be a valid Groovy snippet
  image_name: { formula: "'chiaravalle.png'" }
  image_path: &image_path
    language: kotlin # Pick whatever JSR223 language you like and add it to the classpath
    formula: > # The following is pure Kotlin code. other variables can be referenced!
      import java.io.File
      File("../..").walkTopDown().find { image_name in it.name }?.absolutePath ?: image_name
  # Linear free variable
  walking_speed: &walk-speed { default: 1.4, min: 1, max: 2, step: 0.1 }
  seed: &seed { default: 0, min: 0, max: 99, step: 1 } # 100 samples
  scenario_seed: &scenario_seed { formula: (seed + 31) * seed } # Variable-dependent
  people_count: &people_count
    type: GeometricVariable # A variable scanning a space with geometric segmentation
    parameters: [300, 50, 500, 9] # default 300, minimum 50, maximum 100, 9 samples
  seeds: { simulation: *seed, scenario: *scenario_seed} # Controlled reproducibility
export: # One entry per column
  - time
  - molecule: "default_module:default_program"
    aggregators: [mean, max, min, variance, median] # From Apache's UnivariateStatistic
    value-filter: onlyfinite # discards NaN and Infinity
environment: { type: ImageEnvironment, parameters: [*image_path, *zoom] }
... # See the previous example for missing code
deployments:
  type: Rectangle
  parameters: [*people_count, 62, 15, 95, 200]
  programs:
    ... # See the previous example for missing code
    - {type: Event,time-distribution: 1,actions: {type: LevyWalk,parameters: [*walk-speed]}}
```

Its execution in normal mode picks the default values of every variable, producing a CSV file that includes detail on the variables values, information on the time at which the simulation began, and descriptors for the meaning of each data column. Execution in batch mode with a selection of free variables generates instead one file for each of the possible variables combination. The following is an excerpt of the file content:

```
######################################################################
# Alchemist log file - simulation started at: 2021-03-30T14:11+0000 #
######################################################################
# walking_speed = 1.4, seed = 0.0, people_count = 300.0
#
# The columns have the following meaning:
# time default_module:default_program[Mean] default_module:default_program[Max] default_m...
0.0 NaN NaN NaN NaN NaN
100.0011337332612 158.7760995571516 259.2936556081146 0.0 1973.392001590659 154.960773862537
200.0011337332612 191.2437429491354 387.346209438406 0.0 3633.63195819356 191.956119047278
```

5   Concluding Remarks

The role of simulation in the development of cutting-edge, coordinated, and situated systems is paramount: it provides a way to exercise complex setups and corner situations from a single device, as well as ways to perform analysis to investigate the behavior of novel approaches and algorithms.

In this tutorial paper, we illustrated one simulation tool leveraged in several works in the literature: the Alchemist simulator. We first described its meta-model and explained the concept of "incarnation", opening the door to the simulation of a large variety of scenarios. Then, we dived into a sequence of increasingly complex examples, showcasing several of the many possibilities offered by Alchemist, among which: support for simulations in indoor environments, real-world maps, complex network graphs, and execution of aggregate programs [3]. Finally, we discussed how this tool can be leveraged for debugging the evolution of a complex networked system (by enforcing reproducibility), as well as for generating data to be fed to data analysis tools.

Acknowledgements. This work has been supported by the MIUR PRIN Project N. 2017KRC7KT "Fluidware".

References

1. Audrito, G., Damiani, F., Viroli, M.: Optimal single-path information propagation in gradient-based algorithms. Sci. Comput. Program. **166**, 146–166 (2018). https://doi.org/10.1016/j.scico.2018.06.002
2. Audrito, G., Pianini, D., Damiani, F., Viroli, M.: Aggregate centrality measures for IoT-based coordination. Sci. Comput. Program. **203**, 102584 (2021). https://doi.org/10.1016/j.scico.2020.102584
3. Beal, J., Pianini, D., Viroli, M.: Aggregate programming for the internet of things. IEEE Comput. **48**(9), 22–30 (2015). https://doi.org/10.1109/MC.2015.261
4. Casadei, R., Tsigkanos, C., Viroli, M., Dustdar, S.: Engineering resilient collaborative edge-enabled IoT. In: 2019 IEEE International Conference on Services Computing (SCC). IEEE (2019). https://doi.org/10.1109/scc.2019.00019
5. Casadei, R., Viroli, M., Audrito, G., Pianini, D., Damiani, F.: Engineering collective intelligence at the edge with aggregate processes. Eng. Appl. Artifi. Intelli. **97** (2021). https://doi.org/10.1016/j.engappai.2020.104081. http://www.sciencedirect.com/science/article/pii/S0952197620303389
6. David, V.: JSON: Main Principals. CreateSpace Independent Publishing Platform, North Charleston (2016)
7. Devreotes, P., Janetopoulos, C.: Eukaryotic chemotaxis: distinctions between directional sensing and polarization. J. Biol. Chem. **278**(23), 20445–20448 (2003). https://doi.org/10.1074/jbc.r300010200
8. Fernandez-Marquez, J.L., Serugendo, G.D.M., Montagna, S., Viroli, M., Arcos, J.L.: Description and composition of bio-inspired design patterns: a complete overview. Nat. Comput. **12**(1), 43–67 (2013). https://doi.org/10.1007/s11047-012-9324-y
9. Francia, M., Pianini, D., Beal, J., Viroli, M.: Towards a foundational API for resilient distributed systems design. In: 2nd IEEE International Workshops on Foundations and Applications of Self* Systems, FAS*W@SASO/ICCAC 2017, Tucson, AZ, USA, 18–22 September 2017, pp. 27–32 (2017). https://doi.org/10.1109/FAS-W.2017.116

10. Gelernter, D.: Generative communication in Linda. ACM Trans. Program. Lang. Syst. **7**(1), 80–112 (1985). https://doi.org/10.1145/2363.2433
11. Gibson, M.A., Bruck, J.: Efficient exact stochastic simulation of chemical systems with many species and many channels. J. Phys. Chem. A **104**(9), 1876–1889 (2000). https://doi.org/10.1021/jp993732q
12. Hidalgo, C.A., Barabási, A.: Scale-free networks. Scholarpedia **3**(1), 1716 (2008). https://doi.org/10.4249/scholarpedia.1716
13. Matsumoto, M., Nishimura, T.: Mersenne twister: a 623-dimensionally equidistributed uniform pseudo-random number generator. ACM Trans. Model. Comput. Simul. **8**(1), 3–30 (1998). https://doi.org/10.1145/272991.272995
14. Montagna, S., Pianini, D., Viroli, M.: Gradient-based self-organisation patterns of anticipative adaptation. In: Sixth IEEE International Conference on Self-Adaptive and Self-Organizing Systems, SASO 2012, Lyon, France, 10–14 September 2012, pp. 169–174 (2012). https://doi.org/10.1109/SASO.2012.25
15. Montagna, S., Pianini, D., Viroli, M.: A model for drosophila melanogaster development from a single cell to stripe pattern formation. In: Proceedings of the ACM Symposium on Applied Computing, SAC 2012, Riva, Trento, Italy, 26–30 March 2012, pp. 1406–1412 (2012). https://doi.org/10.1145/2245276.2231999. http://doi.acm.org/10.1145/2245276.2231999
16. Montagna, S., Viroli, M., Risoldi, M., Pianini, D., Di Marzo Serugendo, G.: Self-organising pervasive ecosystems: a crowd evacuation example. In: Troubitsyna, E.A. (ed.) SERENE 2011. LNCS, vol. 6968, pp. 115–129. Springer, Heidelberg (2011). https://doi.org/10.1007/978-3-642-24124-6_12
17. Morgan, D.: All lobsters with perfect matchings are graceful. Electron. Notes Discret. Math. **11**, 503–508 (2002). https://doi.org/10.1016/S1571-0653(04)00095-2
18. Pianini, D.: Danysk/discotec-2021-tutorial: 0.1.0 (2021). https://doi.org/10.5281/ZENODO.4701062. https://zenodo.org/record/4701062
19. Pianini, D., Casadei, R., Viroli, M., Natali, A.: Partitioned integration and coordination via the self-organising coordination regions pattern. Future Gener. Comput. Syste. **114**, 44–68 (2021). https://doi.org/10.1016/j.future.2020.07.032. http://www.sciencedirect.com/science/article/pii/S0167739X20304775
20. Pianini, D., Dobson, S., Viroli, M.: Self-stabilising target counting in wireless sensor networks using Euler integration. In: 11th IEEE International Conference on Self-Adaptive and Self-Organizing Systems, SASO 2017, Tucson, AZ, USA, 18–22 September 2017, pp. 11–20 (2017). https://doi.org/10.1109/SASO.2017.10
21. Pianini, D., Montagna, S., Viroli, M.: Chemical-oriented simulation of computational systems with ALCHEMIST. J. Simul. **7**(3), 202–215 (2013). https://doi.org/10.1057/jos.2012.27
22. Pianini, D., Viroli, M., Beal, J.: Protelis: practical aggregate programming. In: Proceedings of the 30th Annual ACM Symposium on Applied Computing, Salamanca, Spain, 13–17 April 2015, pp. 1846–1853 (2015). https://doi.org/10.1145/2695664.2695913. http://doi.acm.org/10.1145/2695664.2695913
23. Pigné, Y., Dutot, A., Guinand, F., Olivier, D.: Graphstream: a tool for bridging the gap between complex systems and dynamic graphs. CoRR abs/0803.2093 (2008). http://arxiv.org/abs/0803.2093
24. Rhee, I., Shin, M., Hong, S., Lee, K., Kim, S.J., Chong, S.: On the levy-walk nature of human mobility. IEEE/ACM Trans. Netw. **19**(3), 630–643 (2011). https://doi.org/10.1109/tnet.2011.2120618
25. Slepoy, A., Thompson, A.P., Plimpton, S.J.: A constant-time kinetic Monte Carlo algorithm for simulation of large biochemical reaction networks. J. Chem. Phys. **128**(20), 05B618 (2008). https://doi.org/10.1063/1.2919546

26. Sonmez, C., Ozgovde, A., Ersoy, C.: EdgeCloudSim: an environment for perfor-mance evaluation of edge computing systems. Trans. Emerg. Telecommun. Technol. **29**(11), e3493 (2018). https://doi.org/10.1002/ett.3493

27. Stevenson, G., Ye, J., Dobson, S., Pianini, D., Montagna, S., Viroli, M.: Combining self-organisation, context-awareness and semantic reasoning: the case of resource discovery in opportunistic networks. In: Proceedings of the 28th Annual ACM Symposium on Applied Computing, SAC 2013, Coimbra, Portugal, 18–22 March 2013, pp. 1369–1376 (2013). https://doi.org/10.1145/2480362.2480619. http://doi.acm.org/10.1145/2480362.2480619

28. Swaminathan, V., Jeyanthi, P.: Super edge-magic strength of fire crackers, banana trees and unicyclic graphs. Discret. Math. **306**(14), 1624–1636 (2006). https://doi.org/10.1016/j.disc.2005.06.038

29. Viroli, M., Audrito, G., Beal, J., Damiani, F., Pianini, D.: Engineering resilient col-lective adaptive systems by self-stabilisation. ACM Trans. Model. Comput. Simul. **28**(2), 1–28 (2018). https://doi.org/10.1145/3177774

30. Viroli, M., Bucchiarone, A., Pianini, D., Beal, J.: Combining self-organisation and autonomic computing in CASs with aggregate-MAPE. In: 2016 IEEE 1st Inter-national Workshops on Foundations and Applications of Self* Systems (FAS*W). IEEE (2016). https://doi.org/10.1109/fas-w.2016.49

31. Viroli, M., Casadei, R., Pianini, D.: Simulating large-scale aggregate mass with alchemist and scala. In: Proceedings of the 2016 Federated Conference on Com-puter Science and Information Systems, FedCSIS 2016, Gdańsk, Poland, 11–14 September 2016, pp. 1495–1504 (2016). https://doi.org/10.15439/2016F407

32. Zaburdaev, V., Denisov, S., Klafter, J.: Lévy walks. Rev. Mod. Phys. **87**(2), 483–530 (2015). https://doi.org/10.1103/revmodphys.87.483

33. Zambonelli, F., et al.: Developing pervasive multi-agent systems with nature-inspired coordination. Pervasive Mobile Comput. **17**, 236–252 (2015). https://doi.org/10.1016/j.pmcj.2014.12.002

Author Index

Printed in the United States
by Baker & Taylor Publisher Services